D1.10/7.

P9-CMF-720

To Cynthia

Christmas 2010.

1 at 80

W.B.CLARKE CO.
BOOKSELLERS & STATIONERS
— Co —
26 & 28 TREMONT ST. &
30 COURT SQ. BOSTON.

Ralph Waldo Emerson.

COMPLETE WORKS. *Centenary Edition.* 12 vols., crown 8vo. With Portraits, and copious notes by ED-WARD WALDO EMERSON. Price per volume, $1.75.
1. Nature, Addresses, and Lectures. 2. Essays: First Series. 3. Essays: Second Series. 4. Representative Men. 5. English Traits. 6. Conduct of Life. 7. Society and Solitude. 8. Letters and Social Aims. 9. Poems. 10. Lectures and Biographical Sketches. 11. Miscellanies. 12. Natural History of Intellect, and other Papers. With a General Index to Emerson's Collected Works.

Riverside Edition. With 2 Portraits. 12 vols., each, 12mo. gilt top, $1.75; the set, $21.00.

Little Classic Edition. 12 vols., in arrangement and contents identical with *Riverside Edition*, except that vol. 12 is without index. Each, 18mo, $1.25; the set, $15.00.

POEMS. *Household Edition.* With Portrait. 12mo, $1.50; full gilt, $2.00.

ESSAYS. First and Second Series. In Cambridge Classics. Crown 8vo, $1.00.

NATURE, LECTURES, AND ADDRESSES, together with **REPRESENTATIVE MEN.** In Cambridge Classics. Crown 8vo, $1.00.

PARNASSUS. A collection of Poetry edited by Mr. Emerson. Introductory Essay. *Household Edition.* 12mo, $1.50.
Holiday Edition. 8vo, $3.00.

EMERSON BIRTHDAY BOOK. With Portrait and Illustrations. 18mo, $1.00.

EMERSON CALENDAR BOOK. 32mo, parchment-paper, 25 cents.

CORRESPONDENCE OF CARLYLE AND EMERSON, 1834-1872. Edited by CHARLES ELIOT NORTON. 2 ols. crown 8vo, gilt top, $4.00.
Library Edition. 2 vols. 12mo, gilt top, $3.00.

CORRESPONDENCE OF JOHN STERLING AND EMERSON. Edited, with a sketch of Sterling's life, by ED-WARD WALDO EMERSON. 16mo, gilt top, $1.00.

LETTERS FROM RALPH WALDO EMERSON TO A FRIEND. 1838-1853. Edited by CHARLES ELIOT NORTON. 16mo, gilt top, $1.00.

THE CORRESPONDENCE BETWEEN EMERSON AND GRIMM. Edited by F. W. HOLLS. With Portraits. 16mo, $1.00, *net.* Postpaid, $1.05.

For various other editions of Emerson's works and Emerson Memoirs see catalogue.

HOUGHTON MIFFLIN COMPANY
BOSTON AND NEW YORK

JOURNALS

OF

RALPH WALDO EMERSON

1820–1872

VOL. III

W. D. STRATTON DEL.

Ezra Ripley

See His. of Cor. Lodge Sept. 21st. 1841.

JOURNALS

OF

RALPH WALDO EMERSON

WITH ANNOTATIONS

EDITED BY

EDWARD WALDO EMERSON

AND

WALDO EMERSON FORBES

1833–1835

BOSTON AND NEW YORK

HOUGHTON MIFFLIN COMPANY

The Riverside Press Cambridge

1910

COPYRIGHT, 1910, BY EDWARD WALDO EMERSON

ALL RIGHTS RESERVED

Published November 1910

CONTENTS

VOYAGE TO EUROPE
RETURN

JOURNAL XXIV
1833

(From Pocket Note-book)

CONTENTS

JOURNAL XXV
1834
(From Journal A)

CONTENTS

JOURNAL XXVI
1835
(From Journal B)

CONTENTS xiii

CONTENTS

ILLUSTRATIONS

JOURNAL

VOYAGE TO EUROPE.
CITIES AND MEN. RETURN

JOURNAL XXIV

1833

(From Pocket Note-books and Q)

AT SEA. *January 2, 1833.*

SAILED from Boston for Malta, December 25, 1832, in Brig Jasper, Captain Ellis, 236 tons, laden with logwood, mahogany, tobacco, sugar, coffee, beeswax, cheese, etc. A long storm from the second morn of our departure consigned all the five passengers to the irremedial chagrins of the stateroom, to wit, nausea, darkness, unrest, uncleanness, harpy appetite and harpy feeding, the ugly " sound of water in mine ears," anticipations of going to the bottom, and the treasures of the memory. I remembered up nearly the whole of *Lycidas*, clause by clause, here a verse and there a word, as Isis in the fable the broken body of Osiris.

Out occasionally crawled we from our several holes, but hope and fair weather would not ; so there was nothing for it but to wriggle again into the crooks of the transom. Then it seemed strange that the first man who came to sea did not turn round and go straight back again. Strange that because one of my neighbours had some trumpery logs and notions which would sell for a few cents more here than there, he should thrust forth this company of his poor countrymen to the tender mercies of the northwest wind.

We study the sailor, the man of his hands, man of all work; all eye, all finger, muscle, skill and endurance: a tailor, a carpenter, cooper, stevedore and clerk, and astronomer besides. He is a great saver, and a great quiddle, by the necessity of his situation.

The Captain believes in the superiority of the American to every other countryman. "You will see," he says, "when you get out here how they manage in Europe; they do everything by main strength and ignorance. Four truckmen and four stevedores at Long Wharf will load my brig quicker than a hundred men at any port in the Mediterranean." It seems the Sicilians have tried once or twice to bring their fruit to America in their own bottoms, and made the passage, he says, in one hundred and twenty days.

P. M.

A crop of meditations in the berth. Thought again of the sailor, and how superficial the differences. How shallow to make much of mere

coat and hat distinctions. You can't get away from
the radical, uniform, interior experiences which
peep out of the new faces, identical with those of
the old. New tongues repeat the old proverbs,
primeval truths. The thought occurred, full of
consolation, that if he would deal towards himself with severest truth, man must acknowledge
the Deity. So far from being a conventional idea,
built on reason of State, it is in strict soliloquy,
in absolute solitude when the soul makes itself
a hermit in the creation, that this thought naturally arises. This unavoidable acknowledgment
of God, this valid prayer, puts the soul in equilibrium. In this state the question whether your
boat shall float in safety or go to the bottom is
no more important than the flight of a snow-flake.

January 3.

I rose at sunrise, and under the lee of the
spencer-sheet had a solitary, thoughtful hour.
All right thought is devout.

> The clouds were touched
> And in their silent faces might be read
> Unutterable love.

They shone with light that shines on Europe,
Afric, and the Nile, and I opened my spirit's

ear to their most ancient hymn. What, they said to me, goest thou so far to seek — painted canvas, carved marble, renowned town? But fresh from us, new evermore, is the creative efflux from whence these works spring. You now feel in gazing at our fleecy arch of light the motions that express themselves in arts. You get no nearer to the principle in Europe. It animates man. It is the America of America. It spans the ocean like a hand-breadth. It smiles at Time and Space. Yet welcome, young man! The Universe is hospitable. The Great God, who is Love, hath made you aware of the forms and breeding of his wide house. We greet you well to the Place of History, as you please to style it, to the mighty Lilliput or ant-hill of your genealogy, if, instructed as you have been, you must still be the dupe of shows, and count it much, the three or four bubbles of foam that preceded your own on the Sea of Time. This strong-winged sea-gull and striped sheer-water that you have watched as they skimmed the waves under our vault, they are works of art better worth your enthusiasm, masterpieces of Eternal power, strictly eternal because now active, and ye need not go so far to seek what ye would not seek at all if it were not within you. Yet welcome and hail! So sang in

my ear the silver-grey mists, and the winds and
the sea said Amen.

Thursday, *January* 3.　N. lat. 37° 53.

Dr. Johnson rightly defends conversation
upon the weather. With more reason we at sea
beat that topic thin. We are pensioners of the
wind. The weathercock is the wisest man. All
our prosperity, enterprise, temper, come and go
with the fickle air. If the wind should forget to
blow, we must eat our masts. Sea-farmers must
make hay when the sun shines. The gale collects
plenty of work for the calm. Now are we all await-
ing a smoother sea to stand at our toilette. A
head wind makes grinning Esaus of us. Happy
that there is a time for all things under the moon,
so that no man need give a dinner-party in a brig's
cabin, nor shave himself by the gulf lightning.

Saturday evening, *January* 5.

I like the latitude of 37° better than my bitter
native 42°. We have sauntered all this calm day
at one or two knots the hour, and nobody on
board well pleased but I, and why should I be
pleased? I have nothing to record. I have read
little. I have done nothing. What then? Need
we be such barren scoundrels that the whole

beauty of heaven, the main, and man, cannot entertain us unless we too must needs hold a candle
and daub God's world with a smutch of our own
insignificance. Not I, for one. I will be pleased,
though I do not deserve it. I will act in all up
to my conceit of last week, when I exulted in the
power and art with which we rode tilting over
this January ocean, albeit, to speak truth, our individual valours lay very sick the while, lodged
each in the waistcoat pocket of the brave brig's
transom. So that each passenger's particular share
in the glory was much the same as the sutler's
or grocer's who turns his penny in the army of
Leonidas or Washington. The southing latitude
does not yet make early mornings. The steward's
lanthorn and trumpery matutinal preparations
are to me for the rosy ray, the silver cloud, or
chaunt of earliest bird. But days will come.

Poor book, this *Scelta di Goldoni*. He is puffed
in the Preface, and also by Sismondi, as the Re-
storer or Reformer of the Italian stage, etc., etc.
Not a just sentiment, or a well-contrived scene
in the book. His highest merit that of a good
phrase - book. Perrin might as well knit his
conversations into a dialogue and call it a
Drama.

Sunday, *January* 6.
Lat. 37° 23; long. 39° 59 W.

Last evening, fair wind and full moon suddenly lost in squall and rain. There are no at-
tractions in the "sailor's life." Its best things are
only alleviations. " A prison with the chance of
being drowned." It is even so, and yet they do
not run blind into unmeasured danger, as seems
to the landsman ; these chances are all counted
and weighed, and experience has begotten this
confidence in the proportioned strength of spars
and rigging to the ordinary forces of wind and
water, which, by being habitual, constitutes the
essence of a sailor's fearlessness. Suppose a student confined to a ship, I see not why he might
not trim his lamp to as good purpose as in college attic. Why should he be less efficient in his
vocation than the poor steward who ingloriously
deals ever in pork and beans, let the quadrant
or the chart or the monsoon say what they will.
The caboose is his Rome.

It occurred forcibly this morning, whether suggested by Goldoni, or Bigelow, or some falsetto
of my own, that the thing set down in words is
not affirmed. It must affirm itself, or no forms
of grammar and no verisimilitude can give it evi-

dence. This is a maxim which holds to the core of the world.

Storm, storm ; ah we ! the sea to us is but a lasting storm. We have had no fine weather to last an hour. Yet I must thank the sea and rough weather for a truckman's health and stomach, — how connected with celestial gifts !

The wind is the sole performer in these parts of nature, and the royal Æolus understands his work well, and to give him his due, shifts the scene and varies the accompaniment as featly and as often as the audience can desire. Certainly he rings his few chimes with wondrous skill of permutation. Sometimes we, his pets, are cross, and say 't is naught but salt and squalls, and sometimes we are ourselves and admit that it is divine Architecture.

> What is it to sail
> Upon the calm blue sea,
> To ride as a cloud
> Over the purple floor
> With golden mists for company ?
> And Day and Night are drest
> Ever in their jocund vest,
> And the water is warm to the hands,
> And far below you see motes of light
> By day, and streams of fire by night.

What is it to sail upon the stormy sea,
To drive with naked spars
Before the roaring gale,
Hemmed round with ragged clouds,
Foaming and hissing and thumping waves?
The reeking cabin is cold and wet,
The masts are strained, and the sail is torn,
The gale blows fiercer as the night sets in
Scarce can the seaman aloft master his struggling reef.
Even the stout captain in his coat of storms
Sighs as he glances astern at the white, white combs,
And the passenger sits unsocial
And puts his book aside
And leans upon his hand.
Yet is the difference less
Between this grey sea and that golden one
Than 'twixt the moods of the man that sails upon it
To-day and yesterday.

What is a passenger? He is a much-endur-
ing man who bends under the load of his leisure.
He fawns upon the captain, reveres the mate, but
his eye follows the steward; scans accurately, as
symptomatic, all the motions of that respectable
officer. The species is contemplative, given to
imitation, viciously inquisitive, immensely capable of sleep, large eaters, swift digesters, their
thoughts ever running on men and things ashore,

and their eye usually squinting over the bulwark to estimate the speed of the bubbles.

January 7.

W. long. 36° 11 ; N. lat. 37° 4.

Sailors are the best dressed of mankind. Convenience is studied from head to heel, and they have a change for every emergency. It seems to me they get more work out of the sailor than out of any other craftsman. His obedience is prompt as a soldier's, and willing as a child's, and reconciles me to some dim remembrances of authority I wondered at. Thin skins do not believe in thick. Jack never looks an inch beyond his orders. " Brace the yards," quoth the master; "Ay, ay, sir," answers Jack, and never looks over the side at the squall or the sea that cometh, as if it were no more to him than to the capstan.

But though I do not find much attraction in the seaman, yet I can discern that the naval hero is a hero. It takes all the thousand thousand European voyages that have been made to establish our faith in the practicability of this our hodiurnal voyage. But to be Columbus, to steer WEST steadily day after day, week after week, for the first time, and wholly alone in his opinion, shows a mind as solitary and self-subsistent as any that ever lived. I am learning the use of the quadrant. Another voyage would make an astronomer of me. How delicately come out these stars at sea! The constellations show smaller, and a ship, though with the disadvantage of motion, is a fine observatory. But I am ashamed of myself for a dull scholar. Every day I display a more astounding ignorance. The whole world is a millstone to me. The experiment of the philosopher is but a separation to bring within his optics the comprehension of a fact which is done masterly and in harmony in God's laboratory of the world.

Wednesday, *January* 9. W. long. 28° 58.

Still we sail well, and feed full, and hope tomorrow to make St. Mary's, the southernmost of the Azores. When the abbey grew rich the fat monk cut up all his quills for toothpicks. So do we.

Thursday eve at 9 o'clock passed St. Mary's, a dim, black hummock of land. Our dead reckoning agreed with its longitude in the bearings to a mile.

January 13.

We have but fourteen degrees of longitude to make to reach the rock of Gibraltar, but the fickle wind may make those fourteen longer measure than all we have meted. A gale, day before yesterday; yesterday a heavy sea, and a cold head-wind to-day. Yet still we hope and drift along. In the ocean the vessel gains a large commission on every mile sailed, even with a wind dead ahead. In a narrow sea much less. A sea voyage at the best is yet such a bundle of perils and inconveniences that no person as much a lover of the present moment as I am would be swift to pay that price for any commodity which anything else would buy. Yet if our horses are somewhat wild, and the road uneven and lonely and without inns, yet experience shows us that the coward eye magnifies the dangers.

Sunday. W. long. 17° 2.

Let us insist on having our say. We but half express ourselves, but ever draw diagonals between our own thought and the supposed thought of our companion, and so fail to satisfy either. Now God made the model and meant we should live out our idea. It may be safely trusted as proportionate and of good issues, so that it be faithfully expressed, but God will not have his work made manifest by cowards. And so it takes a divine man to exhibit anything divine, Socrates, Alfred, Columbus, Wordsworth, or any other brave preferrer of the still voice within to the roar of the populace — a thing very easy to speak and very hard to do for twenty-four hours. The rest are men potentially, not actually, now only pupas or tadpoles, — say rather quarries of souls, heroes that shall be, seeds of gods.

Sunday, *January* 13.

In the wonderful store of the memory carry we power and peace. It is the monument of how high antiquity. The sides of the pyramids cannot contain the story of half so much time, nor be inscribed with anything like the magic of its method. Its method is myriad-fold. Its order comprehends a thousand lines, right, left, oblique, curved, and waving. Every point lives, and is centre or extreme in turn. As the lightning shineth out of one part of heaven even unto the other part, so one thought in this firmament flashes its light over all the sphere.

A man looks upon himself as a mere circumstance and not as the solid, adamant, mundane ground-plan of a universal man. He thinks his internals are evanescent opal shades, and won't bear criticism and description. Let him turn the telescope on them. Let him compare them with durable things. He will find they outshine the

sun, and will grind to powder the iron and the
stone of outward permanence.

January 14. W. long. 14° 14.

Well, blithe traveller, what cheer? What have
the sea and the stars and the moaning winds and
the discontented thoughts sung in your atten-
tive ears? Peeps up old Europe yet out of his
eastern main hospitably, ho? Nay, the slumber-
ous old giant cannot bestir himself in these his
chair days to loom up for the pastime of his up-
start grandchildren, as now they come, shoal after
shoal, to salute their old progenitor, the old Adam
of all. Sleep on, old sire, there is muscle and nerve
and enterprise enow in us, your poor spawn, who
have sucked the air and ripened in the sunshine
of the cold west, to steer our ships to your very
ports and thrust our inquisitive, American eyes
into your towns and towers and keeping-rooms.
Here we come, and mean to be welcome. So be
good now, clever old gentleman.

I comfort the mate by assuring him that the
sea life is excellent preparation for life ashore.
No man well knows how many fingers he has
got, nor what are the faculties of a knife and a
needle, or the capabilities of a pine board, until
he has seen the expedients and the ambidexter-

ous invincibility of Jack Tar. Then he may buy
an orchard, or retreat to his paternal acres, with
a stock of thrifty science that will make him
independent of all the village carpenters, masons,
and wheelwrights, and add withal an enchanting
beauty to the waving of his yellow corn and
sweetness to his shagbarks in his chimney corner.
No squally *Twelve o'clock! Call the Watch!*
shall break his dreams.

Tuesday, *January* 15.
W. long. 13° 27.

Calm, clear, warm, idle day; holiday to the
senses, rest to the sailor, vexation to the captain, dubiously borne by the passenger.

Yesterday, or day before, saw three sail, one
Englishman. To-day, one French brig, and sa-
luted them both by exchanging the sight of our
colours. John Bull, they say, is very sulky at
sea, or assuredly sometimes very rude. But how
comes my speculative pencil down to so near
a level with the horizon of life, which commonly
proses above?

I learn in the sunshine to get an altitude and
the latitude, but am a dull scholar as ever in
real figures. Seldom, I suppose, was a more in-
apt learner of arithmetic, astronomy, geography,

political economy, than I am, as I daily find to my cost. It were to brag much if I should there end the catalogue of my defects. My memory of history—put me to the pinch of a precise question—is as bad; my comprehension of a question in technical metaphysics very slow, and in all arts practick, in driving a bargain, or hiding emotion, or carrying myself in company as a man for an hour, I have no skill. What under the sun canst thou do then, pale face? Truly not much, but I can hope. "In a good hope," said Bias, "the wise differ from the unwise." I am content to belong to the great *all*, and look on and see what better men can do, and by my admiration realize a property in their worth. I did not put me here; yet God forbid I should therefore decline the responsibility into which I am born. Space and Time and venerable Nature and beautiful stars and all the various fellow beings, I greet ye well, and will not despond, but even out of my acre God shall yet rear himself some tardy fruit. If not, still is it not sublime unprofitably to pray and praise?

Wednesday, *January* 16.

I rose betimes and saw every fold of the banner of the morning unrolled from starlight to full day. We are as poor as we are rich. We brag of our memory, but in the lonely night-watch it will not always befriend us, but leaves the scholar's brain as barren as the steward's. But that I sat in the confessional last night, I should parade my rags again. The good Captain rejoices much in my ignorance. He confounded me the other day about the book in the Bible where God was not mentioned, and last night upon St. Paul's shipwreck. Yet I comforted myself at midnight with *Lycidas*. What marble beauty in that classic pastoral. I should like well to see an analysis of the pleasure it gives. That were criticism for the gods.

The inconvenience of living in a cabin is that people become all eye. 'T is a great part of well-being to ignorize a good deal of your fellow man's history and not count his warts nor expect the hour when he shall wash his teeth.

January 17.

Lat. 36° 29 N.; long. 9° 48 W.

Another day as beautiful as ever shines on the monotonous sea, but a wind so soft will not fill our sails, and we lie like a log, so near our haven too. Ἀτρυγήτη θάλασσα; the sea is a blank, and all the minstrelsy of nature rings but a few changes

on the instrument. The more it should send us
to the inner music; but that is a capricious shell
which sometimes vibrates wildly with multitu-
dinous impulses, and sometimes is mute as wood.
The inner shell is like its marine archetype, which
murmurs only where there is already noise.

Friday, *January* 18.
Lat. 36° 36 N.; long. 8° 20 W.

Well, thou navigating muse of mine; 't is now
the hour of Chinese inspiration, the post-tea-cup-
time, the epical creative moment to all thinking
heads of the modern world; and what print have
the ethereal footsteps of Night and Morn left
upon your tablets? Another day, profusion of
the divine munificence, yet taken and spent by
us as by the oysters. The boar feeds under the
tree, and never looks up to see who shakes down
the mast, and I glide in leisure and safety and
health and fulness over this liquid Sahara, and the
Invisible Leader, so venerable, is seldom wor-
shipped and much a stranger in the bosom of
his child. We feel sometimes as if the sweet and
awful melodies we have once heard would never
return ; as if we [were deaf?] and fear we shall
not again aspire to the glory of a moral life, of
a will as punctual as the little needle in the bin-

nacle over my head. The sea tosses on the horns
of its waves the framework of habits so slight and
epicurean as mine, and I make the voyage one
long holiday, which, like all holidays, is dull.

Saturday, *January* 19.

Mem. No trust to be put in a seaman's eye.
He can see land wherever he wishes to see it, and
always has a cloud, and " the stuff " ready to
cover up a mistake. No word suits the sea but
I hope. Every sign fails.

STRAITS OF GIBRALTAR,
January 20.

Last evening they saw land from the masthead,
and this morn broke over the bold and picturesque mountains of Africa behind Cape Spartel
and Tangiers. On the left was Cape Trafalgar
and Spain. The passengers greeted each other
and mused, each in his own way, on this animating vision. But now, as Tarifa light opened upon
us, we have encountered an adverse current, a
thing unknown in the books, or to the sailors in
these waters, where they say the current always
sets from the ocean into the Mediterranean.
Meantime all the other craft, great and small,
are flying by us and we seem anchored in the
middle of the stream. What is this to me beyond

my fellow-feeling for the master? Shall not I be content to look at the near coast of Andalusia and Morocco? I have seen this morn the smokes of Moorish fishers or mountaineers on one side and of Spanish on the other. We could not quite open Tangier Bay enow to see that Mauretanian town, but the watch towers and the cultivated enclosures and the farm-houses of the Spaniard are very discernible. Not many weeks ago I should scarce have been convinced that I should so soon look on these objects, yet what is their poetry, or what is it not? Is not a hut in America a point that concentrates as much life and sentiment as a hut in Europe or on the ragged side of Mount Atlas? Ah! it is all in the anointed eye. Yet will not I refine overmuch on the love of the remote and the renowned, nor affirm them both to be only a mixture of colors upon the retina of the eye, nor say of a man, He is mammiferous, and of beauty, It is but gelatine and oxygen.

January 21.

A squall with copious rain helped us out of our straits, and last evening I saw the lights of the barracks at Gibraltar on one side and at Ceuta on the other. The summit of the hill at Gibraltar is 1500 feet high.

seem, on all trivial emergencies, to be oppressed with an universal ignorance. If I rightly consider that for this point of time which we call a Life, *tout commence*, I shall rejoice in the omen of a boundless future and not be chagrined. Oh heavens ! no. It is, however, a substantial satisfaction to benefit your companions with your knowledge, — a pleasure denied me. " Time," said friend Carlyle, " brings roses "; a capital *mot*, putting a little rouge on the old skeleton's cheek.

February 10.

Perhaps it is a pernicious mistake, yet, rightly seen, I believe it is sound philosophy, that wherever we go, whatever we do, self is the sole subject we study and learn. Montaigne said, himself was all he knew. Myself is much more than I know, and yet I know nothing else. The chemist experiments upon his new salt by trying its affinity to all the various substances he can command, arbitrarily selected, and thereby discloses the most wonderful properties in his subject. And I bring myself to sea, to Malta, to Italy, to find new affinities between me and my fellow men, to observe narrowly the affections, weaknesses, surprises, hopes, doubts, which new sides of the panorama shall call forth in me. Mean, sneakingly however, that all the curiosity manifested was on our part. Our cousins of Asia and Europe did not pay us the compliment of a second glance.

In quarantine, our acquaintance has been confined chiefly to the Maltese boatmen, a great multitude of poor, swarthy, good-natured people, who speak their own tongue, not much differing from the Arabic, and most of them know very few words of Italian and less of English.

(From Q)

HARBOR OF MALTA, MARSA MUSCETTE, *February* 3.

Here in the precincts of St. John, the isle of old fame under the high battlements, once of the Knights and now of England, I spend my Sunday, which shines with but little Sabbath light. "*Tout commence*," as Père Bossuet says. It is hardly truer of me at this point of time, when I am setting foot on the Old World and learning two languages, than it is of every day of mine, so rude and unready am I sent into this world. Glad, very glad, to find the company of a person quite the reverse of myself in all these particulars in which I fail most, who has all his knowledge, and it is much and various, at his sudden command. I

fully to the religious impression of holy texts
and fine paintings and this soothfast faith, though
of women and children. How beautiful to have
the church always open, so that every tired way-
faring man may come in and be soothed by all
that art can suggest of a better world when he
is weary with this. I hope they will carve and
paint and inscribe the walls of our churches in
New England before this century, which will
probably see many grand granite piles erected
there, is closed. To be sure there is plenty of
superstition. Everywhere indulgence is offered,
and on one convent on our way home I read
this inscription over the gate, "*Indulgentia ple-
naria, quotidiana, perpetua, pro vivis et defunc-
tis.*" This is almost too frank, may it please
your holiness.

February 17.

Visited St. John's again and attended mass.
The bishop, a venerable old man, was present,
but did not officiate. This noble temple was
built by the Grand Master La Cassiera, and
chiefly adorned with painting by Preti, who lies
buried here. (*Vide* Abela.) Mrs. Davy told me
it was built about 1560. The lordly heads of
the Grand Masters still command the eye in
marble or on canvas around the walls, and their

marble and mosaic and pictures and gilding; the
walls are eloquent with texts and the floor covered with epitaphs. The Verger led me down
into a dim vault full of solemn sculpture and
showed me the tomb of L'Isle Adam, the Grand
Master of the Knights of St. John, to whom
Charles V gave the island of Malta when he and
his knights had been driven by the Turks from
Rhodes. Next to him rests the body of La
Valette, who so bravely defended the island
against the Sultan.

But I shall have more to say about this
fine temple when I have paid another visit.
Everywhere as I went, the wretched beggars
would steal up beside me, with, " *Grazia, Signore,
sono miserabile. Uno grano per carità.*" " Look
hard at a Maltese," said my friend, Mr. H.,[1]
" and he instinctively holds out his hand." I
went to the churches of St. Popilius and St.
Thomas. The first is no other than " Publius,
the chief man of the island," in Acts xxviii, and
much honour hath he in Malta, at least on the
walls of his church.

In all these churches there were many worshippers continually coming in, saying their
prayers, and going their way. I yielded me joy-

[1] A Mr. S. P. Holbrook.

notched cross surmounts or underlies every
ornament. The music of the organ and chaunting friars very impressive, especially when we
left the kneeling congregation in the nave, and
heard it at a distance, as we examined the pictures in a side oratory. I went into several
churches, which were all well attended. How
could anybody who had been in a Catholic
church devise such a deformity as a pew?

Went at 11 o'clock to Mr. Temple's plain
chapel on the third storey of his dwelling-house,
and heard with greedy ears the English Bible
read, and Watts's psalms sung, and a good sermon. A small congregation of English; one
Armenian, who is translating the Bible into his
tongue. Mr. Temple and Mr. Halleck conduct
the missionary press here and print in modern
Greek, in Italian, in Armenian, and Turkish.

The Maltese is Arabic with a mixture of Italian.
They have translated Adams's *Arithmetic* and
Peter Parley's Geography (Πέτρου Ὁμιλήτου) and
the best tracts into Greek. The names look odd
enough. Ἡ δύναμις τῆς ἀληθείας, and Ἡ θυγ-
άτηρ τοῦ γαλακτοπόλου, are droll masks for
Scott's *Force of Truth* and *The Dairyman's Daughter*. I brought away Scougal's *Life of God in the
Soul of Man*, in Italian.

The missionary press for the Mediterranean is established here for the sake of the protection of this government. There is only protection, no countenance. It was a stipulation of the Maltese in their capitulation to the English in —— that the scriptures should not be printed in the Maltese (?). [*sic*]

February 20.

I went to the terrace on the top of Mr. Temple's house. All the roofs are flat, and afford this valuable accommodation. I saw many persons walking on the tops. Last Friday, Mr. Temple said he saw Mt. Etna very distinctly from hence, and it is very frequently seen. It is one hundred and fifty miles distant. He is sure the atmosphere is much more transparent than with us; that Venus and Jupiter give more light.

Mr. Temple rents his lofty house for one hundred and forty dollars, containing his Chapel and Press. It rented once for 1000 scudi = $400. Noble houses everywhere, thanks to the beautiful material for building which constitutes the soil of the island. The Maltese stone is very soft and easily wrought, and when well selected, the house will last a thousand years. The architecture is in fine taste, the apartments twenty or thirty feet high, — floors, walls, stairs, all of this cold, clean, sightly stone; the balconies supported with sculptured work, and the openings adorned with vases. Instead of paper, the walls and ceilings are covered with ordinary frescoes, wherein Æsop and the Old Testament furnish the subjects. Visited the Armoury in the Palace, and saw the arms of the old knights, of every form and size, much the same show, I suppose, as is in the Tower of London. The hall might be two hundred feet long.

The library of the knights contains 40,000 volumes, and a venerable Ptolemaic bookstall it is. I sat down and read in Abela's old folios, *Melita Illustrata.*

Through the politeness of Mr. Eynaud, the American consul, I received a card of invitation from Sir Frederick Ponsonby, the governor, to attend a fancy dress ball at the Palace. A very gay and novel scene, but hardly equal to the place and expectation. As the consul did not appear very early, my friends and I presented each other to Sir Frederick, who conversed a few moments very pleasantly. We thought he resembled George IV. A few beautiful faces in the dancing crowd; and a beautiful face is worth going far to see. That which is finest in beauty is *moral*. The most piquant attraction of a long-descended

maiden is the imputation of an immaculate innocence, a sort of wild virtue (if I may so term it),
wild and fragrant as the violets. And the imagination is surprised and gratified with the strong contrast, meeting the Divinity amidst flowers and
trifles.

> The days pass over me
> And I am still the same;
> The aroma of my life is gone
> Like the flower with which it came.[1]

Called upon Mrs. Davy, a very agreeable
woman. Dr. Davy (brother to Sir Humphry)
is given to chemical pursuits. Much younger
than I expected, and of simple manners. I was
sorry I could not accept of their invitation to
dine, as they were well named, well educated,
well mannered, and well acquainted with Malta.

Visited the workshop of Sigismundo Dimeck,
a sculptor in Maltese stone: beautiful work. If
I had a great house in America, I would send
to the Signor for a pair of vases which I saw,
four feet high, two feet diameter, richly carved
with ornaments *à la Raffaelle*; price, eight dol-

1 These lines are found in Journal Ψ (1831), but in a
book in which Mr. Emerson copied his verses he gives the
date as 1833, so it is here introduced.

lars apiece. Another pair of the same size and as good to my eye, though with less costly ornament, price, five dollars. Venetian oil is put in them to make them hold water. A *Bocale* one foot high and beautiful, seventy-five cents. *Vaso Etrusco,* one dollar.

Convicts in chains sweep the streets in Malta. The Maltese milkman drives his goats through the street, and milks you a pint at your door. Asses and mules *passim.*

February 21.

At 8 o'clock P. M. we embarked for Syracuse in a Sicilian brigantine, *Il Santissimo Ecce Homo,* and a most ridiculous scene our ship's company offered, they to us and we to them. The little brig was manned with fourteen men, who were all on a perfect level with each other. The steersman sat down at the helm, and when they brought him his supper, the captain affectionately took his post whilst he ate. The boy was employed in sitting down by the steersman and watching the hour-glass so that he might turn it when it ran out. But the whole interest of master and men was concentrated on us, his five passengers. We had hired for thirty dollars the whole cabin, so they put all their heads into the scuttle and companion-way to behold all that we did, the which seemed to amuse them mightily. When anything was to be done to sails or spars, they did it who had a mind to it, and the captain got such obedience as he could. In the morning the mate brought up his gazetteer to find Boston, the account of which he read aloud, and all the crew gathered round him whilst he read. They laughed heartily at the captain and passed jokes upon him, and when the little boy did something amiss everybody gave him a knock. A cask of blood-red wine was on tap, from which everybody drank when it pleased him, in a quart measure. Their food was a boiled fish called *purpo* (which looks like an eel and tastes like lobster), with bread and green onions eaten raw. Their little vessel sailed fast, and in sixteen hours we saw the ancient city of Syracuse. Abundance of fuss and vexation did the Sanità and the Dogana give us before we were suffered to land our baggage, but our captain and mate helped us all they could, and our money opened all the gates at last.

SICILY

Syracuse, *February* 23.

Shall I count it, like the Berber at Rome, the greatest wonder of all to find myself here? I

have this day drank the waters of the fountain
Arethusa and washed my hands in it. I ate the
very fragrant Hyblæan honey with my breakfast. I have been into the old Temple of Minerva, praised for its beauty by Cicero, and now
preserved and concealed by having its pillars
half buried in the walls of the cathedral. A
modern façade conceals the front, but the severe
beauty of a Parthenon peeps from the sides in
projecting flutes and triglyphs. It was seven in
the morning, and I found the priests saying
mass in the oratories of the church. The American consul called upon our party in the forenoon, and we rode with him into the country.
We stopped at a crumbled arch, reputed as the
spot where Cicero found the globe and cylinder, the tomb of Archimedes. Did I hold my
breath for awe? Then went we to the catacombs,
old enough, nothing else, mere excavations in
the living rock for cemeteries, but the air was
soft and the trees in bloom, and the fields covered with beautiful wild flowers to me unknown,
and amidst ruins of ruins Nature still was fair.
Close by, we found the aqueduct, which once
supplied the magnificent city of Hiero, now
turning a small grist-mill. Then we went to
Dionysius' Ear; a huge excavation into the

hard rock which I am not going to describe. Poor people were making twine in it, and my ear was caught on approaching it by the loud noise made by their petty wheels in the vault. A little beyond the entrance the floor was covered with a pool of water. We found a twine-maker who very readily took us, one after another, on his shoulders into the recess 250 feet, and planted us on dry land at the bottom of the cave. We shouted and shouted and the cave bellowed and bellowed; the twine-maker tore a bit of paper in the middle of the cave, and very loud it sounded; then they fired a pistol at the entrance and we had our fill of thunder.

I inquired for the tyrant's chamber in the wall, the focus of sound where he was wont to hear the whispers of his prisoners, — but in this unvisited country it is inaccessible. High up the rock, seventy or eighty feet, they pointed to a little inlet to which once there was a stair, but not now. If we had time and spirit would we not go up thither in baskets, as sundry English have done? I affirm not. A little way off, along the same quarry of rock, we found another great excavation in which they were making saltpetre. It was the place from which the great pillars of

the Temple of Minerva, it is said, were taken.
Then we visited the Theatre, or rather the rows
of stone benches which are all of it that remains.
From this spot we looked down upon the city
and its noble harbour, and a beautiful, sad sight
it was. The town stands now wholly within the
little peninsula, the ancient Ortygia, (not a third
of the size of the peninsula of Boston, I judge)
and the three great suburbs, or parts, Neapoli,
Tycha and Acradina, have almost no house or
church where they stood. And Syracuse is very
old and shabby, with narrow streets and few
people and many, many beggars. Once 800,000
people dwelt together in this town. Its walls were,
according to historical measurements, twenty-
two English miles in circuit. Of its two ports, the
northern was called the Marmoricus, because
surrounded with marble edifices. The southern
is five miles round, and is the best harbour in
the Mediterranean Sea.

In the old time every Sicilian carried honey
and wheat and flowers out of the port, and threw
them into the sea as soon as he lost sight of the
statue of Minerva aloft on her temple. Once
Dion, once Timoleon, once Archimedes dwelt
here, and Cicero dutifully visited their graves.

I lodge in the Strada Amalfitana.

In a Caffè in our street, they have had the good taste to paint the walls in very tolerable frescoes, with Archimedes drawing the famous galley by means of a windlass, and a sign over our Locanda contains this sentence of Cicero's 4th oration *in Verrem*, " *Urbem Syracusas elegerat.*"

Was it grand or mournful that I should hear mass in this Temple of Minerva this morn? Though in different forms, is it not venerable that the same walls should be devoted to divine worship for more than 2500 years? Is it not good witness to the ineradicableness of the religious principle? With the strange practice that in these regions everywhere confounds pagan and Christian antiquity, and half preserves both, they call this cathedral the church of " Our Lady of the Pillar."

Abundance of examples here of great things turned to vile uses. The fountain Arethusa, to be sure, gives name to the street, *Via Aretusa*, in which it is found ; but an obscure dark nook it is, and we walked up and down and looked in this and that courtyard in vain for some time. Then we asked a soldier on guard where it was. He only knew that " *Questa è la batteria,*" nothing more. At last an old woman guided us to the spot, and I grieve, I abhor to tell, the fountain was bubbling up its world-renowned waters within four black walls, serving as one great washing-tub to fifty or sixty women, who were polluting it with the filthy clothes of the city.

It is remarkable now, as of old, for its quantity of water springing up out of the earth at once, as large as a river. Its waters are sweet and pure and of the colour of Lake George.

All day from the balcony, Mount Etna is in sight, covered with snow. From the parlour window I look down on the broad marshes where the Carthaginian army, that came to rescue Syracuse from the Romans, perished.

They say in this country you have but to scratch the soil and you shall find medals, cameos, statues, temples.

February 24.

Visited the Latomie of the gardens of the Capuchins, a strange place. It is a large and beautiful garden, full of oranges and lemons and pomegranates, in a deep pit, say 120 feet below the surrounding grounds. All this is a vast excavation in the solid rock, and we first came upon it from above and peeped down the precipice into this fragrant cellar far below us. "*Opus est ingens magnificum regum ac tyrannorum. Totum ex saxo in mirandam altitudinem depresso,*" etc. CICERO. All this excavation is manifestly the work of art,—Cyclopean all. After circumambulating the brink above, we went to the Convent and got admission to the garden below. A handsome and courteous monk conducted us, and showed us one huge arch wherein he said the Athenian prisoners recited the verses of Euripides for their ransom; wild and grand effect. All Syracuse must have been built out of this enormous quarry, traces of works on a vast scale in oldest time.

Went into the Convent, and the Fathers set before us bread, olives, and wine. Our conductor then showed us the dormitories (over each of which was a Latin inscription from the Bible or the Fathers), the Chapel, etc., of the House. There is no better spot in the neighborhood of Syracuse than the one they have chosen. The air, the view, the long gallery of the chambers, the peace of the place, quite took me, and I told the *Padre* that I would stay there always if he would give me a chamber. He said, "I should have his," which he opened, a little neat room with a few books, *Theologia Thomæ ex Charmes,* and some others. My friend's whip-cords hung by the bedside.

There are only twenty-two or twenty-three persons in this fine old house. We saw but four or five. I am half resolved to spend a week or fortnight there. They will give me board, I am informed, on easy terms. How good and pleasant to stop and recollect myself in this worn-out nook of the human race, to turn over its history and my own.

But, ah me!

Hence we went to the Campo Santo where several Americans have been buried; and thence to other Latomie, the gardens of the Marquis di Casal. Similar to those we had left, but the rich soil is now filled with flowers in wildest profusion of scent and colour. The bergamot lemon, the orange, the citron, we plucked and ate; and lavender and rosemary and roses and hyacinths and jasmine and thyme, which were running wild all over the grounds, we filled our hands and hats with.

Here we found the Marchesino, or son of the Marchese, who was very polite to us, and Mr. Baker, the English consul, and his family, whom we greeted warmly for the love of the father-land and language. Well pleased, we came back to the Locanda, where we received the American consul, Signor Nicosia, and his friend Signor Giuseppe Ricciardi to dine.

February 25.

Still, melancholy old metropolis! under the moon, last eve, how wan and grey it looked. Took a boat this morning and crossed the Porto Maggiore and sailed up the mouth of the river Anapus; full of canes and bulrushes and snails, and a very little, narrow, mean puddle to be famed in song. We did not go up so far as the fountain Cyane, but disembarked about three miles lower, where the stream was an oar's length wide. It was a pretty fable of Pluto's metamorphosis of Cyane, and if we had more time should have stamped on the very ground where "gloomy Dis" stamped, and the rather that our "plan" afterwards showed us this was the spot of the Athenian encampment. No wonder Proserpine gathered flowers; they grow everywhere of prettiest forms and liveliest colours now in February, and I stopped ever and anon to pick them. On the banks of the Anapus grows the papyrus, the immortal plant. It is a sightly clean, green triangular stem, 20 feet high, surmounted by a bunch of threads which the people call *parroca* (periwig). We cut down a good many, and then crossed the fields to the columns of the Temple of Olympian Jove.

Here stand the broken shafts, the sole remains of the temple which Gelo enriched with the spoils of the Carthaginians 2500 years ago. The site is a commanding one, facing the centre of the mouth of the Great Harbor. Seven of these fluted columns were standing in the last century, but earthquakes are added to Time here in the work of destruction.

We crossed the bridge of the Anapus and went home by way of the catacombs. We sat down on the benches of the Theatre, which was entire in the days of Nero. We asked a goatherd who smoked his pipe on the same bench what they were for? " *Per il mulino, mulino ;* " we could not easily get him by our questions beyond the mill ; at last he said, " *antichità.*" On the lowest circuit of benches we read the inscriptions ΒΑΣΙΛΙΣΣΑΣ ΦΙΛΙΣΤΙΔΟΣ and ΒΑΣΙΛΙΣΣΑΣ ΝΕΡΗΙΔΟΣ. There are medals with the first inscription, supposed to denote the daughter of Philistas, wife of the elder Dionysius.

In the afternoon, I went to the Museum and saw the Venus Kallipyge, dug up here in 1810, a headless beauty.

February 27.

At dinner, a *Frate dei Padri Capuccini* was announced, who brought olives and lemons in his hand, and would accompany us to the Latomie of the church of St. John. Thither we went, and descended into subterranean caverns cut regularly in the living rock. Two Fathers and two boys attended with torches. On each side of the main passages were catacombs, some larger, some less. Occasionally the ceiling was vaulted up to admit light and air. I asked how far these long passages extended; the friar said, he knew not how far, but the air was bad, and no one went further than we. Cicero visited them before us.

Then went to the church, very old, small and poor, but by stone stairs descended into one far older, which they say is St. John's church, and coeval with the planting of Christianity in Sicily. The bold carving of the granite all around made me think it of Greek age and afterward converted to this use.

Signor Ricciardi, a friend of the consul Nicolini's, was very civil to us and spoke good English. At parting he gave each of us a handful of sugar plums.

CATANIA, *March* 1.

Fine strange ride and walk yesterday coming
by mules from Syracuse hither, 42 miles, thirteen hours. Our party (three gentlemen, two
ladies) were accommodated with seven beasts, —
two for the *lettiga* containing the ladies, two for
the baggage, one for each saddle. The morning
road led us by catacombs without number. What
are they but evidences of an immense ancient population that every rock should be cut into sep-
ulchres. The road, a mere mule-path through
very stony soil, was yet not so rough but that
I preferred walking to riding, and for an hour
or two kept up easily with the caravan. Fine
air, clear sun. Mount Ætna right before us,
green fields, laborers ploughing in them, many
flowers, all the houses of stone. Passed the trophy
of Marcellus, a pile of broken masonry, and yet
it answers its purpose as well as Marcellus could
have hoped. Did he think that Mr. Emerson
would be reminded of his existence and victory
this fine spring day 2047 years to come?

Saw the town of Melilli. Dined from our own
knapsack at the strangest tavern; hills of olive
trees all around, an oil-mill or press adjoining,
and a dozen big Morgiana jars thereby; what
seemed the remains of some most ancient church

or temple, with the stumps of pillars still standing, in the rear, and the hostelry itself a most
filthy house, the common dwelling of men, women, beasts and vermin. "*Siamo pronti, Signore,*"
then said the muleteer, which he of our party to
whom it was said, misapprehending to be a call
for brandy, we waited yet a little. The afternoon
ride was pleasanter much,—flowers abounding,
the road smooth, and Ætna glorious to behold
with his cap of smoke, and the mountainettes
like warts all over his huge sides. Then wound
the road down by the seaside, and for many
miles we traversed a beach like that of Lynn
paved with pretty shells. We crossed the Simæ-
thus in a ferry, and going a little inland, we
tramped through miles of prickly pears gigantic,
but, though Catania had been in sight much of
the time since twelve o'clock, nothing could be
ruder than this mule-path from Syracuse to a
city of 70,000 souls. Had I opened my eyes
from sleep, here, almost under the shadows
of the town, I might have thought myself near
Timbuctoo. Yet has nature done all it could
for this drowsy nation. I suppose the bay of
Naples cannot be so beautiful as the spacious
bay, round the shore of which we straggled and
stumbled with tinkling mules, and sighing and

shouting drivers. *Tzar, tzar, gia, hm,* and many
an odd, nondescript, despairing sound they utter
to that deliberate animal. As the day went down
the mules began to tire, and one slipt into the
mud, and was with difficulty got out. Another
fell down with the *lettiga.* The sun set, the moon
rose, and still we did not reach the town, so
near at noon, till eight o'clock.

Town of lava of earthquakes; the mountain
is at once a monument and a warning. Houses
are built, streets paved with lava; it is polished
in the altars of the churches. Huge black rocks
of it line the shore, and the white surf breaks
over them. A great town full of fine old buildings; long regular streets thronged with people,
a striking contrast to the sad solitude of Syracuse. Cathedral church of St. Agatha. What ex-
hilaration does the mere height of these prodigious churches produce! We feel so little and
so elated upon the floor. All the interior and
exterior of this edifice is costly, and the cost
of ages. The ancient Roman amphitheatre was
robbed for the columns and bas-reliefs of its
porch and much of its walls. Its niches and altars
shine with many colored marbles, and round
the whole ample square whereon the church
stands runs a large marble fence.

But what is even this church to that of the Benedictines? Indeed, my holy Fathers, your vows of poverty and humility have cost you little. Signor Ricciardi of Syracuse gave me a letter to Padre Anselmo Adorno, the *Cellerájo* of this monastery, and this morn I waited upon his reverence in his cell, and the kings of France and England, I think, do not live in a better house. The Padre with great courtesy showed us the church and its paintings, and its organ, here reputed the finest in Europe. It imitates sackbut, harp, psaltery and all kinds of music. The monk Donatus who built it, begged that he might be buried under it, and there he lies. To my ignorance, however, the organ neither appeared very large nor very richly toned. But the church shall be St. Peter's to me till I behold a fairer shrine. Have the men of America never entered these European churches, that they build such mean edifices at home? Contini was the architect, but Father Anselm only knew that it was more than a hundred years old. But oh the marbles! and oh, the pictures, and oh the noble proportions of the pile! A less interesting exhibition was the Treasury of the Convent, some silver richly wrought, seats and stools embroidered and gilt, and a wardrobe, — drawers full of copes and things of cloth-of-gold and silver. Then the long lofty cloisters, galleries of chambers, then gardens, too artificially laid out. About 50 monks are laid up in clover and magnificence here. They give bread twice in a week, one roll to every comer. I saw hundreds of women and children in the yard, each receiving her loaf and passing on into a court, that none should come twice to the basket.

Visited the Museum of the Prince of Biscari, one of the best collections of the remains of ancient art. Bronzes, marbles, mosaics, coins, utensils dug up all over Sicily, of Greek and Roman manufacture, are disposed with taste and science. A head of Scipio took my fancy, and some more heads. The Prince of Biscari is a venerable name here. He was the Roscoe, the Petrarch of the town. Everywhere his beneficent hand is shown in restoring the old and saving the new.

I have been under the cathedral into the ancient baths; and into the subterranean ruins of the ancient theatre ; and now I will leave this primeval city, said to have been built by the *Siculi* 80 years before the destruction of Troy ! and engage with the *Vetturo* for a visit to Messina.

I have been to the Opera, and thought three

taris, the price of a ticket, rather too much for the whistle. It is doubtless a vice to turn one's eyes inward too much, but I am my own comedy and tragedy. Did ye ever hear of a magnet who thought he had lost his virtue because he had fallen into a heap of shavings? Our manners are sometimes so mean, our blunders and improprieties so many and mulish, that it becomes a comfort to think that people are too much occupied with themselves to remember even their neighbor's defects very long.

MESSINA, *March.*

From Catania my ride to this city was charming. The distance is but 60 miles, but that is two days' journey here. Mount Etna was the grand spectacle of the first day, and a fine sight it is. This monarch of mountains, they say, supports a population of 115,000 souls, and is 180 miles in circuit. And its ample sides are belted with villages and towers up almost to the snow. As the wind blew fresh, I *smelt* the snowbanks. Village of Giarre; old country; Catholic all over, scarce a house or a fence but hath a shrine or cross or inscription. *"Basta a chi non ha. Basta a chi morra."* Another, *"Viva la Divina Providenza,"* and a thousand more. It is a poor philosophy that dislikes these sermons in stones. But what green fields, and trees in bloom, and thick villages the turns of the road showed ; and my Sicilian companions would break out, " *O che bella veduta !* " These companions were four, the priest of the church of St. Iago in Messina, named Itellario, his two nephews Lorenzo and Gaetano, and Francesco Nicolozi, a tailor.

I name them all because they were very kind to me ; they speedily found I was a stranger and took great pleasure in hearing my bad Italian and in giving me the names of things and places. They brought their vivers with them, and at Giardini, where we spent the night, they made me dine with them and paid all reckonings in the morning. It was amusing enough, first, to see how a Sicilian dines. Then their intercourse with me was all a comedy (their pronunciation and dialect are very different from Tuscan). When I could not understand, they would raise their voices, and then all say something, and then the worthy priest after a consultation among them inquired if I could understand Latin, and I declaring that I could, he essayed to communicate in that tongue, but his Sicilian accent made his Latin equally unintelligible to me. All the household collected gradually around us. At last I hit upon the sense of what they would say, and much acclamation and mutual congratulation there was. Coachey came in too, and he told them I was a *sacerdote*, a *prete* in my own country, a fact he had picked up in Catania. This was wonders more. Then at every sentence which I forged and uttered was profound silence, followed by acclamations, " *che bravo signore!* " so modulated as only Italians can.

The little dark Locanda was on the beach of Cape [Taormina or Schiso?] and the roar of the sea lulled me to sleep. Next morning I awoke right early and found myself in the most picturesque of places. High overhead was Taormina, so high and steep that it seemed inaccessible, and if men could get there, not safe to live on the edge of a rock. Presently we set forth, and every step of the road showed new beauty and strangeness. The ruins of the amphitheatre at Taormina, in very good preservation, I saw, and much I doubt if the world contains more picturesque country in the same extent than in the thirty miles betwixt Giardini and Messina.

PALERMO, *March* 7.

Yesterday at noon I left Messina in the steamboat and passed betwixt Scylla and Charybdis, which have long lost their terrors, probably fabulous at first. Then saw I Stromboli, and the Lipari Islands, and smoke ascending from the crater of the first, and as night grew darker, a faint light of fire. Three very pleasant Englishmen recently from Naples and about to travel in Greece were on board. All the English I have yet seen, I have found courteous, contrary to report. Palermo is a fine sight from the sea. Bold, mountainous coast like all the north and east of Sicily. 160,000 inhabitants. Arrived on shore at 9 o'clock and passed the usual gauntlet of petty extortions. My lessons cost me much. Visited the consul.

I have visited the cathedral, built in 1158. A rich and stately church with some fine bas-reliefs. Saw the tombs of four sovereigns. The first was Roger, the first king of Sicily, 1154; Emperor Henry VI, 1197; Constantia, 1198; Frederic II, 1250.

At the Viceroy's palace, I saw nothing but a small chapel which they vaunted much. I went to the Capuchin Convent. That pleased me better. I like these Capuchins, who are the most esteemed of the Catholic Clergy. Their profession is beggary, but they distribute large alms to the poor. You approach their houses through a regiment of beggars. The Fathers were at dinner, so I took a turn in their sober garden. Then came a monk, and led me down into their cemetery. A strange spectacle enough, — long aisles, the walls of which on either side are filled with niches, and in every niche the standing skeleton of a dead Capuchin; the skull and the hands appearing, the rest of the anatomy wrapped in cerements. Hundreds and hundreds of these grinning mortalities were ranged along the walls, here an abbot, there a general of the convent; every one had his label with his name, when in the body, hanging at his breast. One was near 300 years old. On some the beard remained, on some the hair. I asked the monk how many there were? He said, since 300 years half a million; and he himself would stand there with his brothers in his turn.

My cicerone conducted me next to the Spedale dei Pazzi. I did not know where I was going, or should not have visited it. I could not help them and have seen enough of their sad malady without coming to Sicily. Then to the pleasant gardens of the Prince di Butera. At the *tavola rotonda* of the Giacheri perhaps eight persons dined. I believe no one but I spoke English. So I sat mute. The same gentlemen spoke alternately French, Spanish and Italian. A traveller should speak all the four, and his pocket should be a well-spring of *taris* and *bajocchi*.

Noble Flora or public garden; parterres and fountains and statues; and the Marina fine, far better than the good one of Messina.

Mr. Gardner tells me there are 400 churches and convents in Palermo. I have visited several beautiful ones. Art was born in Europe and will not cross the ocean, I fear. In the university, a good collection of casts and pictures; one Rubens, one Vandyke, one Domenichino; and many things from Pompeii, and Sicilian excavations.

Mr. Gardner, the American consul, lives in a fine house. Mrs. Gardner has a rich collection of shells and fossils. She tells me, all her society is English; none native. If you ask a Sicilian to your house, he will bring twenty more. They will always accept your invitations, but never ask you in return to visit them, but at their box at the opera. Their pride is in an equipage to ride on the Marina. Even shoemakers and hairdressers will go hungry to keep a carriage.

No learned or intelligent men, or next to none. Abate Ferrara is. The daughters are sent to a convent for their education, and learn to make preserves and needlework. The English here, and now some Sicilians, send their sons to Switzerland to excellent schools.

The steamboat must stay another day, and I must use philosophy. So I have been to the Monte Reale on foot and I suppose the world has not many more beautiful landscapes than the plain and the port of Palermo as seen therefrom. Olive and orange and lemon groves wide around. After visiting St. Simon's church and the Benedictine Convent, I followed my vivacious little guide Raimondo to his house and he set before me wine and olives and oranges and bread.

At the *tavola rotonda* with eight persons we had five languages. At the opera in the evening I had a thought or two that must wait a more convenient page. I do not know whether I can recommend my *domestique de place*, Michele Beleo, to the patronage of my friends, but I promised to remember his name. And now for Naples.

AT SEA IN THE STEAMBOAT RE FERDINANDO.
March 11.

I tried last night in my berth to recall what had occurred at the opera. Ποίημα; what is really good is ever a new creation. I could not help pitying the performers in their fillets and shields and togas, and saw their strained and unsuccessful exertions and thought on their long toilette and personal mortification at making such a figure. There they are, the same poor Johns and Antonios they were this morning, for all their gilt and pasteboard. But the moment the prima donna utters one tone, or makes a gesture of natural passion, it puts life into the dead scene. I pity them no more. It is not a ghost of departed things, not an old Greece and Rome, but a Greece and Rome of this moment. It is living merit which takes ground with all other merit of whatever kind, — with beauty, nobility, genius and power. O trust to nature, whosoever thou art, even though a strutting tragedy-prince. Trust your simple self and you shall stand before genuine princes. The play was tedious, and so are the criticisms.

Two pleasant young Englishmen, who had just ascended Etna, on board the boat. One named Barclay, the other Hussey, fond of geology. Kind, domestic manners are more elegant than too civil ones. "This is the most capital place of all," was better than twenty Sirs and scrupulosities.

NAPLES

Vedi Napoli e poi muori

NAPLES, *March* 12.

And what if it is Naples, it is only the same world of cake and ale, of men and truth and folly. I won't be imposed upon by a name. It is so easy, almost so inevitable, to be overawed by names, that on entering this bay it is hard to keep one's judgment upright, and be pleased only after your own way. Baiæ and Misenum and Vesuvius, Procida and Posilipo and Villa Reale sound so big that we are ready to surrender at discretion and not stickle for our private opinion against what seems the human race. Who cares? Here's for the plain old Adam, the simple, genuine self against the whole world. Need is, that you assert yourself, or you will find yourself overborne by the most paltry things. A young man is dazzled by the stately arrangements of the hotel, and jostled out of his course of thought and study of men by such trumpery considerations. The immense regard paid to clean shoes and a smooth hat impedes him, and the staring of a few dozens of idlers in the street hinders him from looking about him with his own eyes; and the attention which he came so far to give to foreign wonders is concentrated instead on these contemptible particulars. Therefore it behoves the traveller to insist first of all upon his simple human rights of seeing and of judging here in Italy, as he would in his own farm or sitting-room at home.

NAPLES, *March* 13.

Howbeit, Naples is a fine city, though it rains very fast to-day, — a beautiful city beyond dispute, but merely from its wonderful situation and its *Chiaja*, and not from the magnificence of streets or public buildings. I have not yet found St. Martin's, but have straggled into several churches nowise remarkable.

When I was at home and felt vaunty, I pestered the good folks with insisting on discarding every motive but the highest. I said you need never act for example's sake; never give pledges, etc. But I think now that we need all the advantages we can get, that our virtue wants all the crutches; that we must avail ourselves of our strength, and weakness, and want of appetite, and press of affairs, and of calculation, and of fear, as well as of the just and sublime considerations of the love of God and of self-respect. Not that any others will bear comparison with these, but be-

cause the temptations are so manifold and so
subtle and assail archangels as well as coarser clay,
that it will not do to spare any strength.

The remembrance of the affectionate, anxious
expectation with which others are intent upon
your contest with temptation is a wonderful pro-
vocative of virtue. So is it when in a vast city
of corrupt men you ask, who are the elegant and
great men, to reflect that in all and by all you
may be making yourself the elegant, the great,
the good man, day by day.

AT NAPLES

We are what we are made; each following Day
Is the Creator of our human mould
Not less than was the first; the all-wise God
Gilds a few points in every several life;
And as each flower upon the fresh hillside,
And every coloured petal of each flower,
Is sketched and dyed each with a new design,
Its spot of purple and its streak of brown,
So each man's life shall have its proper light,
And a few joys, a few peculiar charms,
For him round in the melancholy hours
And reconcile him to the common days.

Not many men see beauty in the fogs
Of close, low pinewoods in a river town;

Yet unto me not morn's magnificence,
Nor the red rainbow of a summer eve,
Nor Rome, nor joyful Paris, nor the halls
Of rich men blazing hospitable light,
Nor wit, nor eloquence, — no, nor even the song
Of any woman that is now alive, —
Hath such a soul, such divine influence,
Such resurrection of the happy past,
As is to me when I behold the morn
Ope in such low, moist roadside, and beneath
Peep the blue violets out of the black loam;
Pathetic, silent poets that sing to me
Thine elegy, sweet singer, sainted wife! [1]

March 14.

I climbed up this morning to St. Martin's sumptuous church and saw the fine bold paintings of Spagnoletto, excepting the dead Christ, for that chapel was shut, and the keeper gone to the city. But what pomp of marble and sculpture and painting! A Nativity by Guido. I staid long alone. There is a famed view of the city from the adjoining monastery and what a noise came up from its 400,000!

[1] In the Journal, a few lines were defective, and they are here printed as Mr. Emerson later copied them into his Verse book, and as given in the Appendix to the later editions of the *Poems*.

March 15.

A nation of little men, I fear. No original art remains. I have been to the Academia and seen the works of Raffaelle, Titian, Guido, Correggio. A good many artists were making indifferent copies of the best. I hear nothing of living painters, but perhaps there are. A rich collection of marble and bronze and frescoes, etc., from Herculaneum, Pompeii, and the Baths of Caracalla. Many fine statues, Cicero, Aristides, Seneca; and Dianas, Apollos, etc., without end. Nothing is more striking than the contrast of the purity, the severity expressed in these fine old heads, with the frivolity and sensuality of the mob that exhibits and the mob that gazes at them. These are the countenances of the first-born, the face of man in the morning of the world, and they surprise you with a moral admonition as they speak of nothing around you, but remind you of the fragrant thoughts and the purest resolutions of your youth.

March 16.

Last night, stayed at home at my black lodging in the Croce di Malta and read Goethe. This morn sallied out alone, and traversed, I believe for the seventh time, that superb mile of the Villa

Reale; then to the tomb of Virgil. But here the effect of every antiquity is spoiled by the contrast of ridiculous or pitiful circumstances. The boy who guided me was assailed by men, women and children with all manner of opprobrium. A gang of boys and girls followed me, crying, "*Signore, C'è un mariolo!*" [1] Yea, the venerable silence of the poet's sepulchre must be disturbed with the altercation of these Lilliputians. The tomb is well enough for so great a name, but its rich ashes are long ago scattered. It has an aperture which looks down into the entrance of the Grotto of Posilipo. Then descending, I passed through this Cyclopean excavation to the bright and beautiful country of vineyards and olive groves beyond with the fine ridges of Camaldoli.

Presently I met a company of muleteers who set up a shout "*ladre*" and "*mariolo*" when they saw my cicerone; so I hasted to get rid of my suspicious companion, and engaged another to conduct me to the Grotto del Cane. Through lanes of plenty he led me to the beautiful Lake of Agnano and the Grotto where they expose a dog to the sulphurous vapor, and the animal in a short time loses all signs of life, but is restored by being brought out. They offered the

1 "He's a cheat!"

poor dog for the experiment if I would pay six
carlines; I told them I would not; so the dog
was saved his fainting. A pleasant place is this
little lake.

Thence I followed my guide for two or three
miles to the Solfatura of Pozzuoli and saw these
volcanic springs of ever-boiling sulphur. The soil
was hot under my feet and the mountain smoked
above at different openings. We always look at
volcanoes with great respect. Thence to Pozzuoli and the well-preserved remains of the Coliseum or amphitheatre. Here, underground, I
could have a lively recollection of that great
nation for whose amusement these fabrics were
reared, but above ground in Pozzuoli, it is impossible to connect the little dirty suburb full of
beggars, and beggar-boatmen, and beggar-coach-
eys with the most ancient city which the Cu-
mæans founded, the old Dicæarchia, and, long
after, the Puteoli of Cicero, his "little Rome,"
as he affectionately called this garden of palaces.
Alas! no! here by the Temple of Serapis, one
stout fellow tried to pick my pocket of my torn
handkerchief, and here, too, my guide worried
me with demanding three or four times as much
as his due, and a swarm of boys settled on me
with "antiquities" to sell, old coins and frag-

ments of brass and copper, and beggars, as usual a regiment. Ah, sirs of Naples! you pay a high price for your delicious country and famed neighborhood in this swarming, faithless, robber population that surrounds and fills your city to-day. I was very glad to see no more antiquities, but to get home as fast as I could. I dined with Mr. Rogers, and found some pleasant gentlemen at his hospitable house.

One must be thoroughly reinforced with the spirit of antiquity to preserve his enthusiasm through all the annoyances that await the visitor of these ruins. Long ago when I dreamed at home of these things, I thought I should come suddenly in the midst of an open country upon broken columns and fallen friezes, and their solitude would be solemn and eloquent. Instead of this, they are carefully fenced round like orchards, and the moment the unhappy traveller approaches one of them this vermin of ciceroni and padroni fasten upon him; a class of people whose looks and manners are more like those of MacGuffog and the Duke of Alsatia than the vain and flippant character I had imagined as the exhibitor *con amore*. What with these truculent fellows, and the boys, and the beggars and the coachmen, all sentiment is killed in the bud, and most men clap both hands on their pockets and run.

March 17.

This morning under the kind guidance of Mr. Durante I have visited six or seven churches, the finest in the city. They are truly splendid and compare with the best I have seen. The Cathedral is a suite of churches, and there the blood of St. Januarius is annually liquefied. Its wealth must be immense. They showed me thirty busts of saints, large as life, composed of solid silver, and lamps, and angels, and candelabra, many more. Huge gates of brass richly carved admitted us to this chapel. It was thronged with worshippers; so was the nave of the Cathedral.

Then the private chapel of the family of the Severini, in the Strada St. Severino, contains the famous veiled statues, which are wonders in their way.

Then Santa Clara, Santo Geronimo, St. Laurentio, Gesù Nuovo, St. Gaetano; all which I trust I shall find again, for they were superb structures and of their ornaments was there no end. Such churches can only be finished in ages. They were all well attended this Sabbath morn. Who can imagine the effect of a true and worthy form of worship in these godly piles ! It would ravish us. I do not mean the common Protestant service, but what it should be if all were actual worshippers. It would have something of this Catholic ceremony too, and yet not show a priest trotting hither and thither, and buzzing now on this side then on that.

These mighty dwelling-houses rise to five and six tall stories, and every floor is occupied by a different family. Opposite my window at the Crocelle, on the fourth storey, a family lived with poultry cackling around them all day, 40 feet from the ground; and to-day I observe a turkey in the chamber across the street, stepping about the second storey. A goat comes up stairs every day to be milked. But the woes of this great city are many and conspicuous. Goethe says, he shall never again be wholly unhappy, for he has seen Naples; if he had said *happy*, there would have been equal reason. You cannot go five yards in any direction without seeing saddest objects and hearing the most piteous wailings. Instead of the gayest of cities, you seem to walk in the wards of a hospital. Even Charity herself is glad to take a walk in the Villa Reale, and extricate herself from beggars for half an hour. Whilst you eat your dinner at a *trat-*

toria, a beggar stands at the window, watching every mouthful.

March 19.

It rains almost every day in showers, to the great discomfiture of all the inhabitants of the town where people live out of doors. The streets are full of tables and stands of all sorts of small tradesmen. When the shower comes, the merchant takes out his pocket-handkerchiefs and covers up his table-full of goods. Then rises the cry of "*La carozza! la carozza!*" from the thousands of hackney coachmen that infest every street and square.

It takes one "grand tour" to learn how to travel.

March 20.

And to-day to the Lake Avernus, to the Lucrine Lake, to Baiæ, the Arco Felice or gate of Cuma; and at Baiæ to the Temple of Venus, the Temple of Mercury and many, many nameless ruins. A day of ruins. The soil of Baiæ is crumbled marble and brick. Dig anywhere, and they come to chambers and arches and ruins. What a subterranean taste these Roman builders had. On each side I saw structures peeping out of the ground that must have been originally built into the side of the hill. Here and there could be traced for some distance in the hillside the remains of a floor composed of small pieces of white marble. I broke some out. It is a most impressive spot. Before you is this ever beautiful bay, and Capri (always more like a picture than a real island), and Vesuvius with his smoke; and about you are the great remains of this pleasure-ground of the Roman Senators, their magnificent Nahant, not only broken by time but by earthquakes, and covered even with new soil by the volcanic action which has raised Monte Nuovo, a large hill within a fourth of a mile from this spot. Then, to what base uses turned! the Temple of Venus, which is almost all standing, and even some delicate bas-reliefs remain upon the ceiling, is now a cooper's shop, and asses bray in it. They turn the chambers of the Roman ladies into little stables for the goats, and all Baiæ and Pozzuoli swarm with the gang of ciceroni and beggars. I saw the lake of Avernus, a beautiful little sheet of water, but what gave it its evil classic name, it is not easy to see. Nor did the Acherontian marsh at all suggest the images of the sheeted dead and the Judges of Hell. As to the Lucrine Lake, it is not above three times the size of Frog Pond, nor quite three times as pretty.

March 21.

Well, I have been to Herculaneum and Pompeii. Herculaneum is nothing but a specimen of the mode of destruction, a monument of the terrors of the volcano. . . .

March 23.

Judge of your natural character by what you do in your dreams. If you yield to temptation there, I am afraid you will, awake. If you are a coward then, I jalouse of your courage by day.

Sunday.

Attended service in the English Chapel. Rev. Mr. B. read the prayers very well, and the liturgy sounded well and kindly in my ear. But nothing could be more insipid, inane than the sermon. It was a counterpart of the "Noodle's Oration," or the "Song by a Person of Quality." I thought how always we are beginning to live, and how perfectly practicable at all times is the sublime part of life, the high hours, for which all the rest are given.

March 25.

I left Naples in Angresani's coach with my townsmen Messrs. Grant and Warren, and two English people. We dined at Molo di Gaeta;

and I think I have seen nothing since I stood
on the Monte Reale at Palermo, which was
richer than the view from this pleasant Locanda.
Strange costumes upon the road at Fondi. But
we rode all night and passed in safety the Pon-
tine marshes, molested neither by malaria nor
by robbers. As we drew nigh to the imperial
city, the stately ruins of the aqueducts began
to appear, then the tomb of Cecilia Metella,
and we entered the city by the Gate of St. John.

ROME
ROME, *March* 27.

It is even so; my poor feet are sore with
walking all this day amongst the ruins of Rome.

> Alone in Rome! why Rome is lonely too;
> Besides you need not be alone, the soul
> Shall have society of its own rank,—
> Be great, be true, and all the Scipios,
> The Catos, the wise patriots of Rome,
> Shall flock to you and tarry by your side
> And comfort you with their high company.
> Virtue alone is sweet society;
> It keeps the key to all heroic hearts,
> And opens you a welcome in them all.
> You must be like them, if you desire them,
> Scorn trifles, and embrace a better aim
> Than wine, or sleep or praise;

Hunt knowledge as the lover woos a maid,
And ever in the strife of your own thoughts
Obey the nobler impulse. That is Rome.
That shall command a Senate to your side;
For there is no might in the universe
That can contend with love. It reigns forever.
Wait then, sad friend, wait in majestic peace
The hour of heaven. Generously trust
Thy fortune's web to the beneficent hand
That until now has put his world in fee
For thee. He watches for thee still. His love
Broods over thee; and as God lives in heaven,
However long thou walkest solitary,
The hour of heaven shall come, the man appear.[1]

March 28.

We came hither Tuesday, a little after noon,
but that day I saw nothing but a passing view
of the Coliseum as we entered the city, and afterwards the yellow Tiber. Yesterday morn at
nine I set forth with a young Englishman, Mr.
Kingston, and crossed the Tiber and visited St.
Peter's. Another time I will say what I think
about this temple. From St. Peter's to the
Chambers of Raffaele and saw the pictures of

1 As in the case of the lines written at Naples, the better
form of these verses, as copied in the Verse book, is here given.
They are printed in the Appendix to the *Poems*.

the great master. It was a poor way of using so
great a genius to set him to paint the walls of
rooms that have no beauty and, as far as I see,
no purpose. Then we threaded our way through
narrow streets to the Temple of Vesta, and the
house of Rienzi, "last of Romans," then to the
FORUM and the Coliseum. Here we spent some
hours in identifying ruins and fixing in mind
the great points of the old topography.

March 29.

I went to the Capitoline hill, then to its Museum and saw the Dying Gladiator, the Antin-
ous, the Venus,— to the gallery, then to the
Tarpeian Rock, then to the vast and splendid
museum of the Vatican, a wilderness of marble.
After traversing many a shining chamber and
gallery I came to the Apollo and soon after
to the Laocoön. 'T is false to say that the casts
give no idea of the originals. I found I knew
these fine statues already by heart and had admired the casts long since much more than I
ever can the originals.

Here too was the Torso Hercules, as familiar
to the eyes as some old revolutionary cripple.
On we went from chamber to chamber, through
galleries of statues and vases and sarcophagi and

bas-reliefs and busts and candelabra — through all forms of beauty and richest materials — till the eye was dazzled and glutted with this triumph of the arts. Go and see it, whoever you are. It is the wealth of the civilized world. It is a contribution from all ages and nations of what is most rich and rare. He who has not seen it does not know what beautiful stones there are in the planet, and much less what exquisite art has accomplished on their hard sides for Greek and Roman luxury.

In one apartment there were three statues of Canova, the Perseus, and two fighting gladiators. Then lions and horses and fauns and cupids and cars; then the sitting philosophers, and such Scipios and Cæsars! It is vain to refuse to admire; you must in spite of yourself. It is magnificent.

Even all this unrivalled show could not satisfy us. We knew there was more. Much will have more. We knew that the first picture in the world was in the same house, and we left all this pomp to go and see the Transfiguration by Raphael. A calm, benignant beauty shines over all this picture and goes directly to the heart. It seems almost to call you by name. How the father of the poor mad boy looks at the Apostles! and the sister! And the sweet and sublime face of Jesus above is beyond praise, and ranks the artist with the noble poets and heroes of his species, — the first born of the earth. I had thought in my young days that this picture and one or two more were to surprise me with a blaze of beauty, that I was to be delighted by I know not what bright combination of colours and forms, but this familiar, simple, home-speaking countenance I did not expect.

March 30.

I have seen St. John Lateran's and the Pantheon, and the Baptistery of Constantine, and the sad remnants of the palaces of the Cæsars, and many many ruins more. Glad I was amidst all these old stumps of the past ages to see Lewis Stackpole, as fresh and beautiful as a young palm tree in the desert. Rome is very pleasant to me, as Naples was not, if only from one circumstance, that here I have pleasant companions to eat my bread with, and there I had none.

This morning went with young Warren and Grant [1] to Thorwaldsen's studio and saw his fine

1 Probably James Sullivan Warren, a friend of Dr. Holmes, and in Europe all the time; he is mentioned more than once in Morse's *Life and Letters of Holmes*. Grant may have been Patrick Grant, who graduated the year before Dr. Holmes at Harvard; he is pleasantly mentioned by Emerson a few pages later.

statue of Byron. 'T is good as a history. I saw
three or four rooms of stone things, but nothing
else to look at. Then to the Barberini Palace and
saw the Beatrice Cenci of Guido and the Fornarina of Raffaelle.

Thence to the Borghese Palace and saw Raffaelle's portrait of Cæsar Borgia and many fine
things, but nothing that pleased me more than
a Madonna by Andrea del Sarto. Whoso loves
a beautiful face, look at this.

Then to the Colonna Palace, a proud old mansion of this ancient family, — the finest suite of
apartments I have ever seen, and hung around
with master pictures, and many of them portraits
of the heroes and the beauties of their own line.
Two fine portraits of Luther and Calvin by Titian, and the martyrdom of St. Sebastian by
Guido. But I liked the whole show, — the hall
itself, better than any part of it. William Pratt
very kindly acted the part of cicerone and introduced me to his relatives.

Then I found under the Capitoline hill the famous Mamertine Prison, the scene of the death
of Cethegus and Lentulus, and of the captivity of
St. Peter and St. Paul, and the reputed dungeon
of the " Roman daughter."

This P. M. I went to the palace of Cardinal

Wield, where Bishop England delivered a discourse, in explanation of the ceremonies of the Catholic Church to-morrow (Palm Sunday), to the English and American residents. I was led in the evening, so easy is it to be led, to a violin concert. I was glad, however, to learn the power of a fiddle. It wailed like a bugle, and reminded me of much better things and much happier hours.

Sunday, *March* 31.

I have been to the Sistine Chapel to see the Pope bless the palms, and hear his choir chaunt the Passion. The Cardinals came in, one after another, each wearing a purple robe, an ermine cape, and a small red cap to cover the tonsure. A priest attended each one, to adjust the robes of their eminences. As each cardinal entered the chapel, the rest rose. One or two were fine persons. Then came the Pope in scarlet robes and bishop's mitre. After he was seated, the cardinals went in turn to the throne and kneeled and kissed his hand. After this ceremony the attendants divested the cardinals of their robes and put on them a gorgeous cope of cloth-of-gold. When this was arranged, a sort of ornamental baton made of the dried palm leaf was brought to his Holiness and blessed, and each of the cardinals went again to the throne and received one of these from the hands of the Pope. They were supplied from a large pile at the side of the papal chair. After the cardinals, came other dignitaries, bishops, deans, canons,— I know them not, but there was much etiquette, some kissing the hand only, and some the foot also of the Pope. Some received olive branches. Lastly several officers performed the same ceremony.

When this long procession of respect was over, and all the robed multitude had received their festal palms and olives, his Holiness was attended to a chair of state, and, being seated, was lifted up by his bearers, and, preceded by the long official array and by his chaunting choir, he rode out of the chapel.

It was hard to recognize in this ceremony the gentle Son of Man who sat upon an ass amidst the rejoicings of his fickle countrymen. Whether from age or from custom, I know not, but the Pope's eyes were shut or nearly shut as he rode. After a few minutes he reëntered the chapel in like state, and soon after retired and left the sacred college of cardinals to hear the Passion chaunted by themselves. The chapel is that whose walls Michel Angelo adorned with his Last Judgment. But to-day I have not seen the picture well.

All this pomp is conventional. It is imposing to those who know the customs of courts, and of what wealth and of what rank these particular forms are the symbols. But to the eye of an Indian I am afraid it would be ridiculous. There is no true majesty in all this millinery and imbecility. Why not devise ceremonies that shall be in as good and manly taste as their churches and pictures and music?

I counted twenty-one cardinals present. Music at St. Peter's in the afternoon, and better still at Chiesa Nuova in the evening. Those mutilated wretches sing so well it is painful to hear them.

Monday.

To-day at the Grotto of Egeria, whence came the laws of Rome; then to the tomb of Cecilia Metella, "the wealthiest Roman's wife." A mighty tomb; the wall is thirty feet thick. Then to the tomb of Scipio, then to the Spada Palace, and saw the statue of Pompey, at whose base great Cæsar fell, then to the Palace Farnesina, to see Raffaelle's Frescoes. Here Raffaelle painted whilst Michel Angelo locked himself up in the Sistine Chapel. Then to the Vatican. And at night to an American soirée.

Tuesday, *April* 2.

What is more pathetic than the studio of a young artist? Not rags and disease in the street move you to sadness like the lonely chamber littered round with sketches and canvas and colour-bags. There is something so gay in the art itself that these rough and poor commencements contrast more painfully with it. Here another enthusiast feeds himself with hope, and rejoices in dreams, and smarts with mortifications. The melancholy artist told me that, if the end of painting was to please the eye, he would throw away his pallet. And yet how many of them not only fail to reach the soul with their conceptions, but fail to please the eye.

These beggarly Italians! If you accept any hospitality at an Italian house a servant calls upon you the next day and receives a fee, and in this manner, the expense of your entertainment is defrayed. In like manner, if you are presented to the Pope, it costs you five dollars.

Plain good manners and sensible people — how refreshing they are! A bashful man is cramped among the fine people who have polished manners but dull brains; but he is relieved and recreated by a better influence and regains his natural shape and air and powers.

To-day I have seen the fine church of Santa Maria Maggiore, the third best in Rome. Then the Doria Palace. There was Nicholas Machiavel by Titian and landscapes of Claude Lorraine.

Wednesday, *April* 3.

The famous *Miserere* was sung this afternoon in the Sistine Chapel. The saying at Rome is, that it cannot be imitated, not only by any other choir, but in any other chapel in the world. The Emperor of Austria sent Mozart to Rome on purpose to have it sung at Vienna with like effect, but it failed.

Surely it is sweet music, and sounds more like the Eolian harp than anything else. The pathetic lessons of the day relate the treachery of Judas and apply select passages from the prophets and psalms to the circumstances of Jesus. Then whilst the choir chaunt the words "*Traditor autem dedit eis signum, dicens, Quem osculatus fuero, ipse est, tenete eum,*" all the candles in the chapel are extinguished but one. During the repetition of this verse, the last candle is taken down and hidden under the altar. Then out of the silence and the darkness rises this most plaintive and melodious strain (the whole congregation kneeling), "*Miserere mei, Deus*," etc. The sight and the sound are very touching.

Everything here is in good taste. The choir are concealed by the high fence which rises above their heads. We were in Michel Angelo's chapel which is full of noblest scriptural forms and faces.

Thursday.

These forms strike me more than I expected, and yet how do they fall short of what they should be. To-day I saw the Pope wash the feet of thirteen pilgrims, one from each nation of Christendom. One was from Kentucky. After the ceremony, he served them at dinner; this I did not see. But Gregory XVI is a learned and able man; he was a monk and is reputed of pure life. Why should he not leave one moment this formal service of fifty generations and speak out of his own heart — the Father of the Church to his children, — though it were but a single sentence or a single word? One earnest word or act to this sympathetic audience would overcome them. It would take all hearts by storm.

To-night I heard the *Miserere* sung in St. Peter's and with less effect than yesterday. But what a temple! When night was settling down upon it and a long religious procession moved through a part of the church, I got an idea of its immensity such as I had not before. You walk about on its ample, marble pavement as you would on a common, so free are you of your neighbors; and throngs of people are lost upon it. And what beautiful lights and shades on its mighty gilded arches and vaults and far windows and brave columns, and its rich-clad priests that look as if they were the pictures come down from the walls and walking.

Thence we came out (I was walking with two painters, Cranch and Alexander) under the moon and saw the planet shine upon the finest fountain in the world, and upon all the stone saints on the piazza and the great church itself. This was a spectacle which only Rome can boast, — how faery beautiful! An Arabian Night's tale.

Good Friday.

The Mystery of the *Tre Ore* is said and shewn in all the churches, in some with scenic representations. I have seen nothing affecting, though it is sometimes, I am told, very much so. Many religious processions in the streets, muffled in black with staves surmounted with death's-heads.

This night I saw with Cranch the great Coliseum by moonlight. It is full of dread.

Saturday.

I did not go to the baptism of the Jew to-day. Usually it is a weary farce. 'T is said they buy the Jews, at 150 scudes the head, to be sprinkled. This man was respectable. This P. M. I heard the Greek mass. The chaunts are in Armenian.

Sunday.

This morning the Pope said mass in St. Peter's. Rich dresses, great throngs, lines of troops, but not much to be said for the service. It is Easter, and the curtains are withdrawn from the pictures and statues to my great joy, and the Pope wears his triple crown instead of a mitre.

At twelve o'clock the benediction was given. A canopy was hung over the great window that is above the principal door of St. Peter's, and there sat the Pope. The troops were all under arms and in uniform in the piazza below, and all Rome and much of England and Germany and France and America was gathered there also. The great bell of the church tolled, drums beat, and trumpets sounded over the vast congregation.

Presently, at a signal, there was silence, and a book was brought to the Pope, out of which he read a moment and then rose and spread out his hands and blessed the people. All knelt as one man. He repeated his action (for no words could be heard), stretching his arms gracefully to the north and south and east and west, pronouncing a benediction on the whole world. It was a sublime spectacle. Then sounded drums and trumpets, then rose the people, and everyone went his way.

This evening I have seen the illumination of the church. When it was dark, I took the well-known way and on reaching the Bridge of St. Angelo found the church already hung with lights from turret to foundation. But this was only partial. At the moment when the bell in the tower tolled 8 o'clock, out flashed innumerable torches in the air and the whole edifice blazed with fires which cast the first lamps into shade and lit up every face in the multitude of the piazza as with daylight. But it is very melancholy to see an illumination in this declining church and impoverished country.

I love St. Peter's church. It grieves me to think that after a few days I shall see it no more. It has a peculiar smell from the quantity of

incense burned in it. The music that is heard in it
is always good and the eye is always charmed. It
is an ornament of the earth. It is not grand, it is
so rich and pleasing; it should rather be called
the sublime of the beautiful.

Tuesday.

To-day I went with Cranch and Wall to the
Palazzo Chigi, a good gallery; there is the Laura
of Paul Veronese; to the Farnese, a fine palace
where are Annibal Caracci's frescoes, but saw no
pictures beside. Then we crossed the Tiber in
a boat to the Corsini Palace, whose noble gardens
ascend the side of *Mons Janiculum*; pleasant walk
and far prospect of the Apennines and of Mount
Soracte. Then to the Sciarra Palace, whose gallery is one of the best in Rome. Quick eye had
Cranch to detect a Titian everywhere. He admires him as an *original* painter. Here was
Guido's Magdalen; Leonardo da Vinci's Mod-
esty and Vanity; Titian's Mistress; Raffaelle's
Portrait of himself; and fine pictures by Garofalo.

All the Americans are gone, and I who lately
knew them not, now feel quite alone, my countrymen and countrywomen have been so civil and
social. Miss Bridgen is a most intelligent and
excellent lady, and young Grant has made me
much a debtor by his courtesy.

April 10.

Walked alone in the spacious grounds and fine groves of the Villa Borghese, whilst the birds sang to me. I thought it would be good to spend an hour there by myself every day. Ποίημα πρά-ξεως.

[*April*] 11.

How have all nations and ages contributed to the magnificence of the Vatican! If we could only know the history of each marble there, when and by whom, and for whom it was carved; of what luxurious villa it formed an ornament, it would open to us the story of the whole world. Each has figured in splendid scenes and served the pleasure of the lords of mankind. Then again, most gladly would I know the place of all these works in the history of art; how this vase and that statue were designed, what the sculptor and what his patron thought of them, and the marks of the eras of progress and decline. But now they amaze me and beget a vague curiosity which they cannot satisfy, nor can any living man.

I went up to the top of St. Peter's and climbed into the copper ball. It is necessary to go up into the dome in order to estimate the prodigious dimensions of the edifice. It takes one's breath away, to look down into the church from the

Giro within the cupola, and at first the temptation is terrible to throw yourself down, though the walk is wide and the railing is high. With some pauses and some conversation I succeeded in getting round the dizzy promenade; but, like many things in Rome, it is a quite unimaginable spot. The view from the exterior of the cupola, of the Campagna di Roma is delicious, from the Apennines on one side to the Sea on the other, and Tiber flowing through his marble wilderness below.

April 13.

Rome fashions my dreams. All night I wander amidst statues and fountains, and last night was introduced to Lord Byron![1] It is a graceful termination to so much glory that Rome, now in her fallen state, should be the metropolis of the arts. Art is here a greater interest than anywhere else. The Caffès are filled with English, French and German artists, both sculptors and painters. The number of *mosaicistas* and print-shops is surprising. Rinaldi has just finished a mosaic picture of Pæstum, which is valued at a thousand louis d'or.

I am indebted to my new-found countryman[2]

1 Meaning, first rightly appreciated *Childe Harold.*
2 John Cranch, the portrait-painter.

for some most pleasant hours, a grateful relief to sights of ruins. I do not yet fall in with that class of English I had hoped to see, those best educated gentlemen, namely, who are not bred with a view to any profession, nor even to politics, but only to maintain the old honours of their houses. In such a class one would hope to find chivalry and learning and sense; but I am not so fortunate as to meet them, but of dandies an abundance. A gentleman, I suppose, is as rare as a genius. Those who usurp the name are often masses of selfishness and littleness.

Sunday, *April* 14.

Attended divine service at the English Chapel. To preach well you must speak the truth. It is vain to say what has been said every Sunday for a hundred years, if it is not true.

April 15.

Few pictures please me more than the Vision of St. Romoaldo by Andrea Sacchi in the Vatican. What a majestic form is the last Carmelite in the train who ascends the steps! One is greater for knowing that such forms can be. What a cant of the head has this same figure! Look at him.

I shall, I think, remember few sculptures better when I get back into my chimney corner than the beautiful head of the Justice who sits with Prudence on the monument of Paulus III, on the left of the Tribuna in St. Peter's. It was designed by Michel Angelo, executed by William de la Porta; but where in the universe is the archetype from which the artist drew this sweetness and grace? There is a heaven.

I have been to see the library of the Vatican. I think they told me the hall was a quarter of a mile long. Afterwards, the Elgin marble-casts. What heads and forms!

In Rome all is ruinous. In the garden before my window the flowerpots stand upon blocks made of the capitals of old columns, turned upside down. Everywhere you may see in the walls and the foundations of houses fragments of carved and fluted stone now cemented in with rough stones, but once the ornament of the Luculli or Scauri, or even of Vesta or Jove.

April 17.

I have been to the church of St. Onofrio to see the tomb of Tasso. Then, in the convent, the courteous fathers showed us his bust in wax. He died in the convent, and this head was taken at the time from the corpse. A noble head it is, full of independence and genius. It resembles strongly the prints I have seen of his head, but is better, I should think, than any. I shall always like him the better for having seen this face. I have never yet learned to feel any strong interest in a poet so imitative, but since God marked him, I will attend to him.

In the convent was also a beautiful Madonna by Leonardo da Vinci.

I neglected on the 15th to record my visit to the church Aracœli, once the Temple of Jupiter Capitolinus; a dim-lighted, spacious and lofty temple worthy of its name and fame and location. Here, if I rightly remember, Gibbon says, he conceived the design of writing his History. Its Scala might be called the Giants' Staircase, and on some of the steps were half-effaced inscriptions. What a memorandum is each step to the historical eye that can see the priest of Jove, ages back, climbing the same hill, burning incense on the same spot.

What pleasant fountains all over Rome, in every villa, garden, and piazza. An eye for beauty is nature's gift to this people; they delight in bright colours and in all ornaments. As we sat in the Caffè we agreed that it was decorated and furnished with a beauty and good taste which could not be rivalled in America.

No man should travel until he has learned the language of the country he visits. Otherwise he voluntarily makes himself a great baby, — so helpless and so ridiculous.

[In Italy, the little airs of the street-singers took Mr. Emerson's fancy. He used to recall this verse of the inebriate's pathetic explanation and appeal to his wife : —

> " Son caduto quì per terra,
>   Sol del vin la causa fu, —
>   La sua virtù
>   E la mia rovina.
>   Cara Bettina,
>   Ajutami tu !"]

In Rome at the best *trattoria* you may get a good dinner for 15 *bajocchi*. Thus to-day and yesterday I have dined at the Lepri on this fash-ion : " Macaroni a la Napolitana," 3 ; " Mon-gana con spinnagio," 5 ; " crema in piátta," 5 ; and two rolls of bread to eat with it, 2 ;= 15 cents for a good dinner in the best house. Add one or two for waiter. My breakfast at the most

expensive caffè in Rome costs 16 cents. Coffee
in the evening 5, and my chamber at the Gran
Bretagna 50 cents.

*La pianta uomo nasce più robusta in Italia che
in qualunque altra terra, — e quegli stessi atroci
delitti che vi si commettono, ne sono una prova.*[1]

HOTEL DI GRAN BRETAGNA, PIAZZA DI SPAGNA.
ROME, *April* 20.

Yesterday I went with Cranch and Smith and
Wall[2] to Tivoli. I cannot describe the beauty of
the Cascade, nor the terror of the Grotto, nor the
charm of the iris that arched the torrent. The
Temple of Vesta is one of the most beautiful of
ruins and in a chosen place. The whole circuit
of about four miles which we made with the cicerone showed everywhere a glorious landscape.
All was bright with a warm sun. The ground
was sprinkled with gay flowers, and among

---

1 "The plant, Man, in Italy springs up stronger than in any
other land whatsoever, and the atrocious crimes there done are
a proof." — ALFIERI.

2 Mr. Wall, a young artist of New Bedford, Mass., in
whom Mr. Emerson found a pleasant acquaintance and travelling companion. His copy of the Three Fates in the Pitti
Palace, then attributed to Michael Angelo, always hung over
the fireplace in Mr. Emerson's study.

others that pink thing with a spicy smell we used
to call "Rabbit's ears." [1] Then there was the
great aloe with its formidable, fleshy spine growing about, and (which is a rare sight) one of
these plants was in bloom. We found the remains of the villa of Catullus, then the reputed
site of the house of Horace, and hard by, the
arched ruins of the Villa of Quintus Varus. Here
too, they say, Mæcenas lived; and no wonder that
poet and patron should have come to this fair
specular mount, escaping from the dust of the
Capital. The Campagna lies far and wide below,
like a sea. Then we went to the Villa d' Este,
whose beauty in my eyes outshone the beauty
of the cascade. Such trees, such walls, such
fountains, such grottoes, such adornments, the
long, long house, — all its empty halls painted
in fresco; the piazza with its vast prospect, the
silver river, the sun that shone, and the air that
blew, — I would fain keep them in my memory
the fairest image of Italy. The Villa belongs to
the Duke of Modena, who never saw it, and it
is occupied only by a *custode*.

I have paid a last visit to the Capitoline
Museum and Gallery. One visit is not enough,
no, nor two, to learn the lesson. The Dying

1 Cyclamen (?).

Gladiator is a most expressive statue, but it will always be indebted to the muse of Byron for fixing upon it forever his pathetic thought. Indeed Italy is Byron's debtor, and I think no one knows how fine a poet he is who has not seen the subjects of his verse, and so learned to appreciate the justness of his thought and at the same time their great superiority to other men's. I know well the great defects of *Childe Harold.*

In the Gallery I coveted nothing so much as Michel Angelo's portrait by himself.

ROME, *April* 21.

I went this morn to the Church of Trinità de' Monte to see some nuns take the veil. Can any ceremony be more pathetic than to see youth, beauty, rank, thus self-devoted to mistaken duty. I went this afternoon to see Michel Angelo's statue of Moses, at the church of San Pietro in Vinculo, and it is grand. It seems he sought to embody the Law in a man. Directly under the statue, at the side where the whole face is seen, the expression is terrible. I could wish away those emblematic horns. "*Alzati, parla!*" said the enthusiastic sculptor.

FROM A LETTER TO MISS EMERSON

Rome, *April* 22.

"Here is matter for all feeling," said Byron, and yet how evanescent and superficial is most of that emotion which art and magnificence can awaken. It yields in me to the interest the most ordinary companion inspires. I never get used to men. They always awaken expectations in me which they always disappoint, and I am a poor asteroid in the great system, subject to disturbances in my orbit, not only from all the planets, but from all their moons. The wise man, the true friend, the finished character, we seek everywhere, and only find in fragments. Yet I cannot persuade myself that all the beautiful souls are fled out of the planet, or that always I shall be excluded from good company and yoked with green, dull, pitiful persons. After being cabined up by sea and by land, since I left home, with various little people, — all better to be sure and much wiser than me, but still such persons as did not help me, — how refreshing was it to fall in with two or three sensible persons with whom I could eat my bread and take my walk and feel myself a free man once more of God's universe. Still these last were not instructors, and I want in-

structors. God's greatest gift is a Teacher, and
when will he send me one full of truth and of
boundless benevolence and of heroic sentiments?
I can describe the man. I know the idea well,
but where is its real blood-warm counterpart?
I know whilst I write thus that the creature is
never to dawn upon me like a sunburst. I know
too well how slowly we edge along sideways to
everything good and brilliant in life, and how
casually and unobservedly we make all our most
valued acquaintances. And yet I saw Ellen at
once in all her beauty, and she never disappointed
me, but in her death. And why may not the
Master whom the soul anticipates, so appear?
Our stern experience replies with the tongue of all
its days: Son of Man! it saith, all giving and receiving is reciprocal; you entertain angels unawares, but they cannot impart more or higher
things than you are in a state to receive, but every
step of your progress affects the intercourse you
hold with all others; elevates its tone, deepens its
meaning, sanctifies its spirit, and when time and
suffering and self-denial shall have transfigured
and glorified this spotted self, you shall find your
fellows also transformed, and their faces shall
shine with the light of wisdom and the beauty
of holiness. You who cling with both hands to

the literal word and to venerable traditions will, no doubt, find in my complaints a confession and a self-accusation. You will perhaps say I do not receive whom Heaven gives. But you must not say any such thing. For I am, you see, speaking truly as to my Maker. Jesus, who has done so much to raise and sweeten human life, and who prized sincerity more than sacrifice, cannot be to me what he was to John. My mother, my brothers, my companions, must be much more to me in all respects of friendship than he can be.

> "How small, of all that human hearts endure,
>   The part that laws or kings can cause or cure:
>   Still to ourselves in every place consigned,
>   Our own felicity we make or find."

In Rome it is not the diameter nor the circumference of the columns, it is not the dimensions nor the materials of the temples, which constitute their chief charm. It is the name of Cicero; it is the remembrance of a wise and good man; it is the remembrance of Scipio and Cato and Regulus; the influence of human character, the heroes who struggled, the patriots who fell, the wise men who thought, — the men who contended worthily in their lifetime in the same trials

which God in this city and this year is placing
before each of us. Why are you dazzled with
the name of Cæsar? A part as important, a soul
as great, a name as dear to God as his or any
other's is your own.

It will take you long to learn another tongue
so as to make yourself fully understood by those
who speak it, but your actions are easy of translation. They understand what you do. Temperance is good English and good French and good
Italian. Your courage, your kindness, your honesty, are as plain to a Turk as his own alphabet.
In Boston they have an eye for improvement, a
thing which does not exist in Asia nor in Africa.

And so I left, on the twenty-third of April,
the city built on seven hills, the Palatine, the
Capitoline, Cœlian, Aventine, Quirinal, Viminal,
and Esquiline.

April 26.

Passignano. Here sit I this cold eve by the
fire in the Locanda of this little town on the
margin of the lake of Thrasimene, and remember Hannibal and Rome. Pleases me well the
clear pleasant air which savors more of New
England than of Italy. To-day we came from

Spoleto to Perugia on the top of how high a
hill with mighty walls and towers far within the
gates of the town. Old cathedral, and all around
architectural ornaments of the Middle Ages. But
were I a proprietor in Perugia, I would sell all
and go and live upon the plain. How prepos-
terous too it is to live in Trevi, where the
streets must make with the horizon an angle
of 45 degrees. Yet here in Umbria every height
shows a wide prospect of well-cultivated country.

April 27.

Passed a peaceful night close by the dreadful
field of Hannibal and Flaminius. This morning
we crossed the Sanguinetto and left the pontifi-
cal state. We passed by Cortona, the venerable
Etruscan town, then by Arezzo, the birthplace
of Petrarch, and stopped at night at Levane.

Next morn (April 28) through the beautiful
Val d' Arno we came to Figline, to Incisa, and
in the afternoon to fair Florence.

[April 29.]

And how do you like Florence? Why, well.
It is pleasant to see how affectionately all the
artists who have resided here a little while speak

of getting home to Florence. And I found at once that we live here with much more comfort than in Rome or Naples. Good streets, industrious population, spacious, well-furnished lodgings, elegant and cheap caffès. The Cathedral and the Campanile, the splendid galleries and no beggars, make this city the favorite of strangers.

How like an archangel's tent is this great Cathedral of many-coloured marble set down in the midst of the city, and by its side its wondrous Campanile! I took a hasty glance at the gates of the Baptistery which Angelo said ought to be the gates of Paradise, " *digne chiudere il Paradiso,*" and then at his own David, and hasted to the Tribune and to the Pitti Palace. I saw the statue that enchants the world. And truly the Venus deserves to be visited from far. It is not adequately represented by the plaster casts, as the Apollo and the Laocoön are. I must go again and see this statue. Then I went round this cabinet and gallery and galleries till I was well-nigh " dazzled and drunk with beauty." I think no man has an idea of the powers of painting until he has come hither. Why should painters study at Rome? Here, here.

I have been this day to Santa Croce, which is to Florence what Westminster Abbey is to

England. I passed with consideration the tomb of Nicholas Machiavelli, but stopped long before that of Galileus Galileo, for I love and honor that man, except in the recantation, with my whole heart. But when I came to Michael Angelo Buonaroti my flesh crept as I read the inscription. I had strange emotions. I suppose because Italy is so full of his fame. I have lately continually heard of his name and works and opinions; I see his face in every shop window, and now I stood over his dust.

Then I came to the empty tomb of Dante, who lies buried at Ravenna. Then to that of Alfieri.

PIAZZA SANTA MARIA NOVELLA, NO. 4599.

May 1.

Of my journey from Rome to this city I cannot give a good account. I came in a *vettura* with Messrs. Wall, Walsh, and Mayer, Mr. O'Flanagan, an Irish priest, and Signor Dracopoli, a Greek returning to New Smyrna after an absence of ten years for his education in Rome. The journey occupied five days and a half. The first night was spent at Città Castellana. The second day we arrived a little after noon at Terni, and visited the great cascade of Velino. Nature never disappoints us. Her grand and beautiful things always satisfy the eye, and this does. Still I think the grotto under the cascade at Tivoli better deserves the name of "the hill of waters," — has more of the terrible in it than anything I saw here.

"Won't you go to America with me, little fellow?" — "*Non signore.*" — "In America all the little boys are taught to read and write."— "*In Terni, anzi,*" he replied.

Great abundance of the spicy, red flowers which they call *capuccini.* Terni was the birthplace of Tacitus. The next morning we came to Spoleto, where Hannibal received a repulse after his victory at Thrasimene, and we were shown the Porta di Fuga, named from that event. Here too was a prodigious aqueduct 300 feet high. From Spoleto to Foligno, where we passed the night. All the streets of this town have been shaken by earthquakes; the houses lean, and are kept from falling by timbers which cross the street from house to house. Between Foligno and Vene we saw the "Temple of small and delicate proportion" dedicated to Clitumnus. Strange dreams at Foligno.

Next morn from Foligno to Assisi through fertile fields, and up the mountain to Perugia.

Perugia has outgrown its walls, which are far within the town. It commands a wide prospect of cultivated territory. The difference of cultivation is very great between the fat Umbria and the lean Sabina. On we came to the little hamlet of Passignano on the margin of the lake of Thrasimene.

May 2.

I revisited the Tribune this morning to see the Venus and the Fornarina and the rest of that attractive company. I reserve my admiration as much as I can; I make a continual effort not to be pleased except by that which ought to please *me*, and I walked coolly round and round the marble lady ; but when I planted myself at the iron gate which leads into the chamber of Dutch paintings, and looked at the statue, I saw and felt that mankind have had good reason for their preference of this excellent work, and I gladly gave one testimony more to the surpassing genius of the artist.

To-day I had a singular pleasure. Mr. Ritchie's kindness procured me the privilege of seeing the apartments occupied by Lord Byron when he was in Florence. They are part of the palace of the Duke of San Clementi, who is Mr. R.'s neighbor. The rooms were very very richly

furnished and hung with tapestry. There were
five in a range, and the last opening into a large
dining-hall. Below was a large hall which Byron
fitted up as a theatre. The palace is in the Via
San Sebastiano.

How bare and poor are these Florentine
churches after the sumptuous temples of Naples
and Rome! Ah! ah! for St. Peter's, which I can
never more behold. Close by my door is the
church of Santa Maria Novella which Michel
Angelo called his *bride*, — my eye has not yet
learned why; it still looks naked and unfinished
to me. The church of St. John's in Malta, he
might well have distinguished by such a name.

Evening. Beautiful days, beautiful nights. It
is to-day one of the hundred *festas* of this holiday people; so was yesterday, so is to-morrow.
The charming Cascina and the banks of the Arno
are thronged, but moonshine or sunshine are
indispensable to a *festa;* as they say in France,
"There will be no revolution to-day, for it
rains."

(From Q)

FLORENCE, Tuesday, *May* 7.

" Ah! l' aurora della vita
    E l' aurora del dolor."

May 8.

To-day I heard, by Charles's letter, of the death of Ellen's mother. Fast, fast the bonds dissolve that I was so glad to wear. She has been a most kind and exemplary mother, and how painfully disappointed! Happy now. And oh, what events and thoughts in which I should have deepest sympathy does this thin partition of flesh entirely hide! Does the heart in that world forget the heart that did beat with it in this? Do jealousies, do fears, does the observation of faults, intervene? Dearest friends, I would be loved by all of you: dearest friend! we shall meet again.

(From Note-book)

Florence, *May* 9.

I rode out this evening with Mr. Miles in the beautiful Cascina. Its walks and groves extend from the Prato Gate of the city out for miles along the right bank of the Arno. It is full of sweet singing birds, the robin and the nightingale, and of quails, partridges and rabbits kept for game by the Grand Duke.

I saw Jerome Buonaparte on horseback. He resembles the pictures of his brother Napoleon, though utterly devoid of his energy of expression. His brother Louis also lives in Florence.

The Emperor of Austria is responsible for the good behaviour of the family.

I went last night to a theatre and heard a whole opera very respectably performed, with all scenic pomp and music and numbers, and paid one paul, 10 cents, for my seat. A seat in the pit costs 2 crazies.

I have visited the palace and gallery of the Principe Corsini, where are Carlo Dolcis and Salvator Rosas in plenty; the original sketch by Michel Angelo of his Last Judgment; a fine portrait by Rembrandt of himself, and some other good pictures in many fine rooms. The Prince himself is gone to Naples as proxy for the Grand Duke, to marry the sister of the King.

All night the street echoes with the songs of this musical people. They have fine voices and repeat the airs of the operas. But the *boys!*

May 10.

Visited Professor Amici and saw his optical instruments. He is reputed the maker of the best microscopes in Europe. He has also made a telescope for Herschel in London. He has a microscope whose magnifying power is 6000 diameters, or 36,000,000 superficies. To instruments of this enormous power he applies the camera lucida and then draws the outline of the object with pencil. His experiments upon polarized light are beautiful. The price of his best instruments is 800 francs. He has just made one for Dr. Jarvis for $45.

Speak out, my boy, speak plain, *non capisco.* " *Ed io anche non intendo lei,*" said the beggar.

May 11.

Last night I went to the Pergola, and to my eyes, unused to theatres, it was a glorious show. The prima donna, Signora Delsere, is a noble Greek beauty, full of dignity, and energy of action, and when she sung the despair of Agnes, she was all voice. She had moreover so striking a resemblance to a valued friend in America that I longed to know who and what Signora Delsere was, much more than the issue of the play. But nobody knew. The whole scenery and the dresses of the performers were in admirable taste, everything good but the strutting of the actors. Is it penal for an actor to *walk?* Before the play was done, my eyes were so dazzled with the splendor of light and colors that I was obliged to rest them and look at my shoes for half an hour, that I might keep them for the last act.

For my seat in the pit, where the ladies sit also, I paid three pauls, 30 cents.

I ought not to forget the ballet between the acts. Goethe laughs at those who force every work of art into the narrow circle of their own prejudices and cannot admire a picture as a picture, and a tune as a tune. So I was willing to look at this as a ballet, and to see that it was admirable, but I could not help feeling the while that it were better for mankind if there were no such dancers. I have since learned God's decision on the same, in the fact that all the *ballerine* are nearly idiotic.

(From Q)

May 11.

How little is expressed or can be ! In the least action what an infinity is *understood* ! I heard *La Straniera* performed last night. Moreover cannot a lesson of wisdom and glory be got even from the hapless prima donna of an Italian opera? At least one is informed of the extent of female powers and warned not to be too easily satisfied with the accomplishments of vulgar pretty women.

I have heard that the old king George was so impatient of his state that he delighted to dress himself plainly and escape in a morning from

Windsor to the market, or the lanes, and mix in
a crowd. Well, I have seen a man, the lord of quite
another sort of principality, forced to pay the same
price for all his knowledge and to unking himself and take knocks from such "*parmaceti*"
gentlemen in order to have a peep at men.

(From Note-book)

May 12.

I dined to-day with Mr. Askew at his villa,
seven miles out of Florence, and all the road was
through a garden. We rode on our return through
a *shower* of flies, all the way.

I gladly hear much good of the Order of Mis-
ericordia. I see these philanthropists now with
quite new feeling, when they carry by the dead
with their hasty chaunt. This order is composed
of men of all professions and ages and ranks, who,
for a penance, or for love, enter into it for a longer
or shorter period. They devote themselves to all
works of mercy, especially to the care of the sick.
They watch and tend them, but never speak, and
their faces are never seen, being always covered
with a silken hood. They are not known to each
other. Cardinals and Princes sometimes take the
dress of this order for a time. The last Grand
Duke was once a member. Miss Anna Bridgen

tells me that she saw in Rome a coachman driving
a splendid coach with chasseurs attendant, who
attempted to pass directly through a funeral procession, when one of the Misericordes ran forward and laid a powerful arm upon the rein of
the horse and lifted his veil to the coachman,
who instantly drew up his horses and waited with
the utmost respect for the train to pass.

They have taken down the old marble bench
on which Dante used to sit and look at the beautiful Campanella [*sic*], and set it into the pavement with the inscription, " *Sasso di Dante.*"
Well he might sit and admire that charming tower,
which is a sort of poem in architecture. One might
dream of such a thing, but it seems strange that
it should have been executed in lasting stone.
Giotto built it, that old Gothic painter.

May 15.

To-day I dined with Mr. Landor at his villa
at San Domenica di Fiesole. He lives in a beautiful spot in a fine house full of pictures and with
a family most engaging : he has a wife and four
children. He said good and pleasant things, and
preferred Washington to all modern great men.
He is very decided, as I might have expected, in
all his opinions, and very much a connoisseur,

in paintings. He was not very well to-day, and I go to breakfast with him next Friday. Mr. Hare was present, the author of *Guesses at Truth*, and Mr. Worsley.[1] . . .

May 16.

This day is the festival of the Ascension, which is a great annual holiday of the Florentines, and pours them all out under the trees and along the lawns of the beautiful Cascina. There they keep a sort of rural Saturnalia. The Grand Duke came up towards evening and took a turn round the square in his coach and bowed gracefully to the bowing multitude. His little children were with him in the coach.

In the evening, the grounds were light as day with countless lamps hung in the trees, and in the centre of all an obelisk of flambeaux. Then played the band, and all the people danced. I believe this rude ball was continued all night. I left them in full activity about ten o'clock.

1 The rest of the account of this visit to Landor, and most of that of May 17, are here omitted because printed in the first chapter of *English Traits*. In the notes to the Centenary Edition of that volume some of Landor's spicy but good-tempered comments on Mr. Emerson's account of his views are given, which Mr. Landor published in " An Open Letter " to him soon after the publication of *English Traits*.

May 18.

Visited Mr. Landor again yesterday. He lives in the Villa Ghirardesca.

Mr. Landor has a fine cabinet of pictures, and as Greenough remarked, he, in common with all collectors, imagines that his are the only masterpieces. — "*Ne sutor*," etc. And I remembered the story of Voltaire and Congreve. Mr. Hare told me that Mr. Landor has not more than twelve books in his library.[1]

(From Q)

I told Landor I thought it an argument of weak understanding in Lord Chesterfield, his slippery morality. It is inexcusable in any man who pretends to greatness to confound moral distinctions. True genius, whatever faults of action it may have, never does. Shakspeare never does, though a loose liver. But such fry as Beaumont and Fletcher, and Massinger, do continually. And Chesterfield did. Well for him if he had often thought and spoken as when he said, "I judge by every man's truth of his degree of understanding."

I think it was of Socrates that Landor dared

[1] I. e., at a time. He gave away his books (see *English Traits*).

to say,—so far can a humorsome man indulge a whim,—"He was a vulgar sophist and he [Landor] could not forgive vulgarity in anybody; if he saw it in a wise man, he regretted it the more."

(From Note-book)

Noon. I went to the Museum of Natural History, and to the representation in wax of the Plague of Florence, and saw how man is made, and how he is destroyed. This museum contains an accurate copy in wax from nature of every organ and process in the human frame, and is beautiful and terrible. For in life Nature never intends that these things should be uncovered.

I have looked into Santa Croce this afternoon, and if I spoke ill of it before, I will unsay it all. It is a grand building, and its windows of stained glass charm me. It is lined and floored with tombs, and there are two or three richly finished chapels. In one is a fine painting of the Last Supper by Vasari. While we were walking up and down the church, the organ was played, and I have never heard a more pleasing one. I saw the bust of Michel Angelo and his eight wrinkles.

When I walk up the piazza of Santa Croce I

feel as if it were not a Florentine, no, nor an European church, but a church built by and for the human race. I feel equally at home within its walls as the Grand Duke, so *hospitably* sound to me the names of its mighty dead. Buonaroti and Galileo lived for us all; as Don Ferranto says of Aristotle, " *Non è nè antico nè moderno ; è il filosofo senza più.*"

I met the fair Erminia to-day. These meetings always cost me a crazie, and it is fit that she should not be slighted in the journal. Erminia is a flower-girl who comes to the caffè every morning, and if you will not buy her flowers she gives them to you and with such a superb air. She has a fine expression of face and never lets her customers pass her in the street without a greeting. Every coach too in Florence that ventures to stop near the Piazza di Trinità is a tributary of Erminia's. I defy them to escape from her nosegays. She has a rich pearl necklace, worth I know not how much, which she wears on *festas*. Mr. Wall wishes to paint her portrait, but she says she is not handsome enough, " *E brutto il mio ritratto.*"

Went again to the opera to see a piece called *Ivanhoe.* What a miserable abuse, to put a woman of dignity and talent into man's clothes to play the part of Wilfrid. The Signora Delsere who delighted me so much the other night was strutting about ineffectually with sword and helmet. They had spoiled a fine woman to make a bad knight. I came home disgusted.

The Italians use the superlative too much. Mr. Landor calls them the nation of *issimi*. A man, to tell me that this was the same thing I had before, said, "*È l' istessissima cosa*"; and at the *trattoria*, when I asked if the cream was good, the waiter answered, "*Stupendo.*" They use three negatives; it is good Italian to say, "*Non dite nulla a nessuno.*"

May 19.

Hot weather steadily for three weeks past, and Florence is a degree of latitude farther north than Boston. Six or seven blazing hours every day, when, as the Florentines say, "there's nobody but dogs and Englishmen in the streets." Then the pleasant evening walk from 6 to 7 or 8 o'clock upon the Cascina, or the banks of the little sylvan Mugnone, or in the Boboli gardens. And wherever I go, I am surrounded by beautiful objects: the fine old towers of the city; the elegant curve of the Ponte Trinità; the rich purple line of the Apennines, broken by the bolder summit of the marble mountains of Carrara. And all, all is Italian; not a house, not a shed, not a field, that the eye can for a moment imagine to be American.

Miss Anna Bridgen said very wittily, that so inveterate were her Dutch instincts, that she sees almost no work of art in Italy, but she wants to give it a good scrubbing; the Duomo, the Campanella, [*sic*] and the statues.

May 21.

Rose early this morning and went to the Bello Sguardo out of the Roman gate. It was a fine picture, this Tuscan morning, and all the towers of Florence rose richly out of the smoky light on the broad green plain. I passed the Michelozzi villa, where Guicciardini wrote his history. Returning, I saw the famous fresco painting on the wall within the city, directly opposite the Roman gate, the work of Giovanni da San Giovanni; executed, they say, to show the skill of Tuscan art. A story is told that, some Roman painter having been sent for to execute a public work in Florence, the Florentine artists painted this wall that he might see it on his entrance into the city. When he came and saw this painting, he inquired whose work it was; and being informed it was done by Florentines, he returned immediately to Rome, saying that they had no occasion for foreign artists.

(From Q)

I like the sayers of No better than the sayers of Yes.

On bravely through the sunshine or the showers
Time hath his work to do and we have ours.

"Il tempo il suo mestiere, ed io il mio."

(From Note-book)

I have finished the *Promessi Sposi*, and I rejoice that a man exists in Italy who can write such a book. I hear from day to day such hideous anecdotes of the depravity of manners, that it is an unexpected delight to meet this elevated and eloquent moralist. Renzo, and Lucia, Fra Cristoforo, and Federigo Borromeo, — all are excellent, and, which is the highest praise, all excite the reader to virtue.

May 25.

It is the *festa* of San Zenobio, once bishop of Florence, and at the churches the priests bless the roses and other flowers which the people bring them, and they are then esteemed good for the cure of headache and are laid by for that purpose. Last night in the Duomo I saw a priest carrying a silver bust of San Zenobio, which he put upon the head of each person in turn who came up to the barrier. This ceremony also protects him from the headache for a year. But, asked I of my landlady, do you believe that the bust or the roses do really cure the headache of any person? "*Secondo alla fede di ciascuno*," she replied.

It is my *festa* also.[1]

(From Q)

Is not Santa Croce a grand church? Nobody knows how grand who only sees it once. Its tombs! Its tombs! And then the mighty windows of stained glass which a man sees at noon and thinks he knows what they are worth, and comes back after sunset and finds to his delight (I did) a wholly novel and far more beautiful effect. They should be seen just about the hour of candle-light. We came out to Europe to learn what man can,—what is the uttermost which social man has yet done. And perhaps the most satisfactory and most valuable impressions are those which come to each individual casually and in moments when he is not on the hunt for wonders. To make any sincere good use, I mean

1 His birthday.

what I say, of what he sees, he needs to put a double and treble guard upon the independency of his judgment. The veriest Luther might well suspect his opinion upon the Venus or the Apollo.

(From Note-book)

I wrote to G. A. S.[1] yesterday, what I have found true, that it is necessary for the traveller, in order to see what is worth seeing, and especially *who* is worth seeing in each city, to go into society a little. Now no man can have society upon his own terms. If he seek it, he must serve it too. He immediately and inevitably contracts debts to it which he must pay, at a great expense, often, of inclination, and of time, and of duty.

"*Comanda niente, Signore?*" *Niente.* "*Felice notte, Signore.*" *Felice notte.* Such is the dialogue which passes every evening betwixt Giga and me when the worthy woman lights my lamp, and leaves me to Goethe and Sismondi, to pleasant study hours and to sound sleep.

I have been to the *Academia delle Belle Arti*, and there saw an unfinished work of Michel Angelo's. His opinion was asked concerning a

1 George A. Sampson of Boston, a near friend who died not long after.

block of marble, whether it were large enough to make a statue of? "Yes," he said, "a colossus." And the inquirers doubting, he went to work, and cutting a little here and a little there, rudely sketched a figure of gigantic dimensions and left it so, a sort of sculptor's puzzle.

Tuesday morn, *May* 28.

Sad I leave Florence, the pleasant city. I have not even seen it all, and between negligence and mishap have failed to see the library. The system of *mezzaria* or *metayer* is universal in the agriculture of Tuscany. The introduction of the potato into general use, and the culture of Saracenic grain has done much to alleviate the distress of the peasantry. Labor is dog-cheap. The hat manufacturer is almost peculiar. Mr. Miles tells me that it takes one woman one week to make a hat, and he usually orders a thousand hats in a week. The taxation seems very irregular and sometimes enormous; every ox that enters the gates of Florence pays eleven *francesconi* at the gate.

May 28.

Left Florence. Stopped at the Pratolino, five miles out of the city, to see the colossal statue of Father Apennine by John of Bologna.

It is grand if only from its size. They call it 60 feet high, meaning probably that in a standing posture it would be so high. I got up into his neck and head and looked out of his ear. Fine mountain scenery to the frontier of the Roman state. At last on reaching a new height we saw the Adriatic Sea. We slept at Lacca, the first village on the Roman territory, 36 miles from Florence.

May 29.

At 4 A. M. we set forward, and passing through a picturesque country, arrived at Bologna (25 miles) at 10 ½ o'clock. Here we visited the celebrated statue of Neptune by John of Bologna (good enough, but why so famous?), the gallery of the Academy and of the Palazzo Lambacari, both rich in Guidos, Caraccis, Guercinos; the museum and library founded by Marsilius, 100,000 volumes; the Cathedral, the Church of San Domenico where is Guido's fresco, Paradise, and where lie the bones of Guido, of the two Caraccis, and also of St. Dominick.

Here too are two leaning towers, one deviating nine feet from the perpendicular, and a good story is told of their building. All the streets are lined with porticoes so that the inhabitants walk always under cover, which, in the

rain, and under this dangerous sun, is a great
public convenience. From the gate of the city
a portico three miles in length, formed of 650
arcades, leads to the church of the Madonna
della Guardia. In the piazza were planted some
pieces of artillery which have stood there since
the *soi-disant* revolution, two years ago. There
are here 75,000 souls.

May 30.

From Bologna to Ferrara, 32 miles; nearly
all the way the road was paved, and lined with
trees. Arrived at Ferrara at 4 P. M. Visited Tasso's prison, a real dungeon. There I saw Byron's
name cut with his penknife in the wall. The
guide said his father accompanied him, and that
Byron stayed an hour and a half in the prison and
there wrote. We visited the Cathedral, — fine
old Gothic exterior built in 1100; then the Library, where is Ariosto's tomb, his inkstand,
medals and chair. I sat in his chair. They were
shown by an old man who entered into the spirit
of his profession as the showman. Thence to the
Campo Santo, passing through the Jews' Quarter,
of whom there are 2800, who are shut up every
night, as in Rome, like dogs. At the Campo
Santo two monuments by Canova. What a
desolate town! The streets appeared like State

Street on Sunday, and the grass grew. There are 24,000 inhabitants. Under the Dukes there were 70,000. It is the native place of Garofalo, Guercino, Canova. A prolegate of the Pope administers the government.

May 31.

From Ferrara to Rovigo across the Po in a ferry. The stream was wide and strong, about as wide as the Connecticut at Hartford. The road all day was lined with poplars on each side. Fine, bold taste displayed in all their architecture. Every church is a new and pleasing plan. Every chimney is built on an ornamental design. At night we reached Monselice, after crossing the Adige. Saw our honest countryman the Indian corn growing well.

Monselice is the most picturesque town I have seen in Italy. It has an old ruin of a castle upon the hill, and thence commands a beautiful and extraordinary view. It lies in the wide plain, a dead level, whereon Ferrara, Bologna, Rovigo, Este, Padua stand, and even Venice we could dimly see on the horizon, rising with her tiara of proud towers. What a walk and what a ride, delightful picture! To Venice 38 miles.

June 1.

This morn we stopped half a mile this side

of the village of Battaglia on the road to Padua, sent the *Vettura* on to the market-place, and walked over to Arqua to see the tomb of Petrarch, and the house where he spent his latter days. Both are striking and venerable objects. The house is vacant and clean; its windows look out upon mountains. His portrait and his interviews with Laura are painted in fresco on the walls. They show his chair and the chamber where he died. Good, good place. It does honor to his head and heart. There grow the pomegranate and fig and olive.

At noon at Padua. Three rich churches; as usual in Italy, unlike all others, — the Duomo, and San Antonio and San Justin. Visited the grand Hall, the ancient Sala di Giustizia, 300 feet long, 100 wide, 100 high, without other support than the walls. Stewartson,[1] Wall and I then went for our breakfast to the most beautiful caffè in Europe. Nothing can exceed the taste and splendor of this room. Visited the University, 1600 students, 62 professors. Heard the professor Caldania lecture upon anatomy with a subject; the form of the Lecture room was an in-

[1] Probably young Dr. Stewartson of Philadelphia, mentioned with high regard in Dr. Holmes's letters from Paris in the year 1833. See Morse's *Life of Holmes*.

verted cone. Saw the Museum. The quadrangle
of the University is a venerable place, covered
with armorial bearings.

VENICE

From Padua to Venice, 20 miles: crossed the
Brenta and passed a profusion of fine villas, all the
grounds full of statues, not quite as thick as they
could stand. Far the most splendid of all was
the Villa Imperiale, built by Palladio. Arrived
at Mestre, the place of embarcation for Venice,
5 miles off. Here we took a boat and sailed for
the famous city. It looked for some time like
nothing but New York. We entered the Grand
Canal and passed under the Rialto, and presently
stepped out of the boat into the front entry of
the Gran Bretagna. The front entry of the Gran
Bretagna opens also upon a little bridge which
connects by a narrow alley with the Piazza of
St. Mark, so out we went under the full moon
to see the same. It was all glorious to behold.
In moonlight this Arabesque square is all en-
chantment, so rich and strange and visionary.

(From Q)

VENICE, *June* 2.

The ancient metropolis of the merchants. In
coming into it, it seemed a great oddity but not

at all attractive. Under the full moon, later in the evening, St. Mark's Piazza showed like a world's wonder, but still I pity the people, who are not beavers, and yet are compelled to live here.

But what matter where and how, as long as all of us are estranged from truth and love, from Him who is truth and love. Sometimes I would hide myself in the dens of the hills, in the thickets of an obscure country town. I am so vexed and chagrined with myself, — with my weakness, with my guilt. Then I have no skill to live with men, that is, with such men as the world is made of; and such as I delight in I seldom find. It seems to me, no boy makes so many blunders or says such awkward, contrary, disagreeable speeches as I do. In the attempt to oblige a person I wound and disgust him. I pity the hapless folks that have to do with me. But would it not be cowardly to flee out of society and live in the woods? I comfort myself with a reference to the great and eternal revolution which, under God, bears the good of us all, — thine and mine, and that of each by the instrumentality of the other, on the wings of these dull hours and months and years.

I collect nothing that can be touched or tasted

or smelled, neither cameo, painting nor medallion; nothing in my trunk but old clothes; but I value much the growing picture which the ages have painted and which I reverently survey. It is wonderful how much we see in five months, in how short a time we learn what it has taken so many ages to teach.

(From Note-book)

Again I have been to St. Mark's and seen his horses and his winged lion, the Bridge of Sighs, the Doge's Palace, the Piazza, the canals. We took a gondola, three of us (that is, one too many for the perfect enjoyment of that cunning vehicle) and proceeded to the churches and the Academy. There is Titian's picture of the Assumption of the Madonna, so glorified by the painters. The young men whom I converse with prefer it to Raphael. There also is another of Titian's, the Presentation of the Virgin, yet a child, to the High Priest; a very large picture, and I thought I might call it the *handsomest* picture I have seen, but certainly not the best. It lacks the expression of Raffaelle. It will not do to compare anything, in my opinion, with his Transfiguration. A great man will find a great subject, or which is the same thing, make any subject great, and what tenderness and holiness beams from the face of the Christ in that work, — what emotion. I have never yet seen the face copied in all the *soi-disant* copies of that picture.

In the Academy is a cast of the Hercules of Canova. The original is in the Torlonia Palace at Rome. It is a tremendous action. Here too are casts of his best works. The chair in which he has seated Mme. Buonaparte is the same beautiful form I admired in the Caffè at Padua. Grand pictures here of Paul Veronese, Tintoretto and Titian.

These churches of Venice surpass all the churches in Florence in splendor. The Chiesa dei Carmeliti has eight chapels, built at the expense of eight families, and they are superb. The Chiesa dei Gesuiti is a most costly imitation in marble of tapestry hangings throughout the interior. Hiram and Solomon could not beat it.

In the Chiesa della Salute is a monument to Canova, built from Canova's design of a tomb for Titian. Canova's design, however, if that little model I saw in the Academy be it, is more impressive than this gorgeous marble execution of the same in the Salute. These churches are all rich with monuments, on many of which is figured the horned bonnet worn by the Doges of

Venice. From these we came to the Ducal Palace up the Giant Staircase.

At the side of the door we were shown the "Lion's Mouth," a hole in the wall into which anciently were thrown the anonymous accusations of any citizen for the eye of the Council of State. Thence we were conducted to the Library, then to the Hall, a grand chamber whose whole walls and ceiling are adorned by the best pictures of great size by Paul Veronese and his son, and Tintoretto, and Palma Vecchio, and Palma Giovane, and Bonifacio. All the paintings are historical. This hall and the adjoining chambers contain in this splendid way a chronicle of the Republic. The portraits of one hundred and sixteen doges hang round on high, among which is the black board where should be the head of Marino Faliero. On the ceiling, most of the pieces are allegorical (which is as bad in painting as it is in poetry), and at one extremity of the Hall a Paradise by Tintoretto, a picture of amazing size. From this hall to the Audience Chamber where the Doge and his Council received foreign ambassadors, then to the Council Chamber of the Three Hundred, with its rostrum and other realities. After seeing these noble apartments we were conducted to the prisons below and all the hideous economy and arrangement of them explained. I saw the little blackened chamber from whose walls Lord Byron had those sad inscriptions copied, and passed the dreaded door opening on the Bridge of Sighs down to the third noisome story of the subterranean dungeon. It is a sickening place, and 't is enough to make one dance and sing that this horrid tyranny is broken in pieces. To be sure the Austrians are here, but their rule is merciful to that whose story is written here in stone and iron and mire. The policy of the Venetian government kept even the existence of their state prison a secret, and on the approach of the French in 1796, they hastily built up the secret passages. The French acted with good sense in opening these damnable holes to the day and exposing them to the public, in order to make their own invasion popular.

After leaving the Ducal Palace we climbed the stairs of the Campanile to the lookout, an essential part of the traveller's duty at Venice, for, as in the city you are always in a gutter, it needs to get up into this tower to have any sight of its shape and extent. The day was not very clear, but the view was noble.

The Campanile itself is [a] beautiful tower,

but it cannot compare with Giotto's wonder at Florence, the poem in stone. I should attempt to describe St. Mark's Piazza, the glory of Venice, and without which the city would not be worth visiting, but that the common prints of it are so good. There stand the painted masts whereon the Republic hung her banners. As it is the only piece of ground in the city where a thousand men could find elbow-room, its daily importance can easily be conceived.

We took a long sail across the harbor to the immense arsenal, a place of all manner of naval works, three miles in circuit. The Bucentaur is gone, but there they show a model of it, and upon it all the places of state, and the garrulous showman tells all the story of the annual marriage of the Adriatic.

Here too is an armory where they show without a blush the golden keys of Venice that were made in 1797 to be presented to Napoleon. Worse things are various inventions for torture and a nameless thing for an incredible, indecent cruelty ascribed to Francesco da Carrara.

I am speedily satisfied with Venice. It is a great oddity, a city for beavers, but, to my thought, a most disagreeable residence. You feel always in prison, and solitary. Two persons may

live months in adjoining streets and never meet,
for you go about in gondolas, and all the gondolas are precisely alike, and the persons within
commonly concealed; then there are no news-
rooms; except St. Mark's Piazza, no place of
public resort. It is as if you were always at sea.
And though, for a short time, it is very luxurious to lie on the eider-down cushions of your
gondola and read or talk or smoke, drawing to,
now the cloth-lined shutter, now the Venetian
blind, now the glass window, as you please, yet
there is always a slight smell of bilgewater about
the thing, and houses in the water remind one
of a freshet and of desolation, anything but
comfort. I soon had enough of it. . . .

I ought not to forget that I went to the
Manfrini Palace and saw its famous gallery of
paintings, and Giorgione's picture.

And so we left the ocean-Rome.

Tuesday, *June* 4.

With our trusty *Vetturino* who brought us
from Florence, we left Mestre this morn for
Padua, and then for Vicenza, where we pass the
night. This is the city of Palladio and embel-
lished with his architecture. The Campo Marzio
is a beautiful public walk. Went thence to the

Duomo and the Basilica. Many fine palaces in this town.

June 5.

To Verona 30 miles. The chief object of interest is the amphitheatre built in Trajan's time, a smaller coliseum, but in excellent preservation and still used as a theatre. A play was getting up in the arena when we came away. Then to what is called Juliet's tomb, a very apocryphal sepulchre; then to the Duomo to see an Assumption of the Madonna, by Titian; to San Giorgio to see pictures of Paul Veronese. This is his own town, and of Maffei also. Saw the Roman bridge built by Vitruvius over the Adige.

There are 12,000 soldiers now in this town. A large part of them are employed in rebuilding the ancient walls. The population from 50,000 to 60,000. This place suffered much in the French invasion in 17—. And I saw many walls honeycombed with musket-shot.

We do not make many miles in a day, but our journey has many alleviations, and we are very companionable travellers, and some of our Tuscan conversations with the vetturino ludicrous enough. "Vetturino!" shouted my friend Stewartson from within the coach; "Vetturino! Perchè non arrangiate questo window?" Then

we find a hospitable caffè every evening where
we find an ice, and the oriental narcotic, and
Wall and Stewartson their cigar.

June 6.

To-day from Verona to Brescia, 40 miles.
From Verona in the morning to Lago di Guarda,
and crossed the smooth sliding Mincio and spent
our three hours of nooning at Defenzano. 'Tis
Corpus Christi day, and for a week past wherever we have been we have seen preparations
for celebrating this *festa* with what pomp each
city could. A splendid procession is everywhere
made under awnings, and in many places I believe over carpets laid along the streets. Even
in this little village every house has hung out
its quilts and damask and brocade, and the walls
are lined. At the altar in the church, officiate
little girls dressed out in white and gold with
wings for angels.

We passed to-day many beautiful villas, and,
what was new and pleasant, we saw no beggars.
The women in this country universally wear in
their hair silver pins with heads as large as eggs;
they remind one of an electrical machine. All
the way they were stripping the mulberry trees
of leaves for the food of the silkworms which
are in every house. I went into a house and

begged to see the animals; the padrona led me upstairs and showed me the creatures in every age and state. She had given up the whole of the *primo piano*, or what we call the second storey, to them.

Then to Brescia. All the Italian towns are different and all picturesque. The well-paved Brescia, the Church of the Madonna dei Miracoli, — how daintily it is carved without to the very nerves of the strawberry and vine leaf! Italy is the country of beauty, but I think specially in the northern part. Everything is ornamented. A peasant wears a scarlet cloak. If he has no other ornament, he ties on a red garter or knee-band. They wear flowers in the hat or the buttonhole. A very shabby boy will have the eye of a peacock's feather in his hat. In general the great-coats and jackets of the common people are embroidered, and the other day I saw a cripple leaning on a crutch very finely carved. Every fountain, every pump, every post is sculptured, and not the commonest tavern room but its ceiling is painted. Red is a favorite color, and on a rainy morning at Messina the streets blazed with red umbrellas.

In Brescia they have lately made some excavations of their antiquities, and laid open the floor and shafts of the pillars of a Roman temple of Hercules. They have found a fine bronze Victory there. At a fountain in the piazza was a statue of Canova's. I thought a clever mason might make as good a one.

In Brescia 4000 soldiers. Porticoes in all these towns in North of Italy.

The roads seem the best and costliest I have ever seen, but there are no bad roads in Italy. Buonaparte, with whatever intent, was a great benefactor to this whole peninsula from Naples northward.

I notice that the new buildings erected or erecting are in as bold and as beautiful a style as old ones. Every church, every villa is original; and what gates they can make to a villa or a palace !

June 7.

To-day crossed the Mela. In all this Lombard region they write on a signpost the name of each town thus :—

COMUNE DI OSPEDALETTO
CAPO LUOGO DEL SECONDO DISTRETTO
PROVINCIA DI BRESCIA,

and a similar threefold inscription in every village. We begin to see goitres on both men and

women. The Vettura stopped at noon at Calcio.
Wall and I have walked on towards Triviglio,
and now, whilst he sketches, I sit upon an arch
that crosses a brook and listen to a bird's song;
't is surely the nightingale.

June 8.

This morn at 10 o'clock entered Milan by a
broad and splendid street. Saw the top of the
cathedral from far upon the road, and got a nearer
view of its glories before arriving at the hotel.

June 9.

This cathedral is the only church in Italy that
can pretend to compare with St. Peter's. It is a
most impressive and glorious place, without and
within. And its exterior altogether as remarkable
and deserving minute attention as its interior.
It was begun by Andrea Commodia in 1386 and
is not yet finished, though always being built.
When completed, it will have 7000 statues, great
and small, upon the outside; there are now
5000. It is all built, to the minutest part, of
white marble, and, as the showman asserted,
would have cost a mountain of gold, but that
the founder had left to it a quarry of marble.
Forty-two artists are perpetually employed upon
it. The walk upon the top of the church is

delightful from the novelty and richness of the scene. Neighbored by this army of marble saints and martyrs, with scores of exquisitely sculptured pinnacles rising and flowering all around you, the noble city of Milan beneath, and all the Alps in the horizon,—it is one of the grandest views on earth. Then, inside the church, the grand Gothic perspective of the aisles, the colour of the light which all enters through stained glass, the richness and magnitude of all the objects,—truly it is good to be there.

An immense surface in this cathedral is glass window. Thus behind the great altar are three huge windows only separated by sashes, each of which is wide by twelve panes (each pane one foot) and high by twelve panes (each pane two feet), and over all a great arch in which the glass is of irregular shape. These huge windows contain the whole history of mankind from Adam and Eve down, each pane being a separate picture.

Underneath the church is the sumptuous tomb of St. Charles Borromeo, whose history is the glory of Milan and has furnished Manzoni with a hero in *I Promessi Sposi*.

The kindness of the Conte del Verme has shown me and my friends all the curiosities of

Milan. In his coach we have made the circuit of the city and, as travellers say, "killed it thoroughly." We visited not less than eight churches beside the cathedral, some of them very rich. At one they showed me tapestry between two and three centuries old, which was as delicately pictured as if done by a camel's-hair pencil. We went to the Ospitale Grande, which is the most considerable institution of the sort in Europe. A magnificent charity. There are 2500 beds and almost all are full. Its aid is gratuitous. Everybody is received who applies, and we walked through corridor after corridor of beds whereon lay the sick of all manner of diseases. Great and good and sad, this hospital is a little city in itself.

A very different spectacle was the Palazzo di Brera which has a rich gallery of paintings, a great public Library, and an astronomical observatory, which were all shown us. Then we visited the Triumphal Arch, l' Arco del Sempione, designed and begun by Napoleon as the termination of the road of the Simplon from Paris to Milan. Its finishing [is] by the Austrian Government, of course with some variation in the bas-reliefs. Then to the Ambrosian Library and Museum, where I saw Petrarch's

copy of Virgil, all written by himself; and to
the Ospitale dei Frati, — *Fate bene fratelli*, — and
to the castle, and to the Arena, and to a *collegio*
and to a Registry office, etc., etc.

My friend the count speaks with no good
will of the Austrian Government, so jealous, so
rapacious, which holds Italy down by the pointed
cannon. There are 96,000 or 97,000 Austrian
troops in Lombardy. When he solicited a passport to go to the United States of America, it
was 16 months before it was granted him.

I visited the church of San Domenico to see
the famous fresco painting of the Last Supper by
Leonardo da Vinci. It is sadly spoiled by time
and damp. The face of Christ is still very remarkable.

Milan is a well-built town with broad streets
and a little railroad of stone for the wheels to
run upon in the middle of the street. It looks
too modern to be so conspicuous in European
history as it has been, for Lombardy was the
theatre of every war.

There is an advantage which these old cities
have over our new ones that forcibly strikes an
American, namely, that the poorest inhabitants
live in good houses. In process of time a city is
filled with palaces, the rich ever deserting old

ones for new, until beggars come to live in what were costly and well-accommodated dwellings. Thus all the trattorias, even of little pretension, have their carved work and fresco painting, as this of the Marino where I dine with my companions.

(From Q)

MILAN, *June* 10.

Architecture — shall I speak what I think? — seems to me ever an imitation. Accustomed to look at our American churches as imitative, I cannot get it out of my head that these which I now see are only more splendid and successful imitations also. I am perplexed with my inveterate littleness; I must and will see the things in detail and analyse all, every noble sentiment to the contrary notwithstanding. It seems to me nothing is truly great, nothing impresses us, nothing overawes, nothing crowds upon us, and kills calculation. We always call in the effect of imagination, coax the imagination to hide this and enlarge that, and even St. Peter's, nor this frost-work cathedral at Milan, with its 5000 marble people all over its towers, can charm down the little Imp.

It is in the soul that architecture exists, and

Santa Croce and this Duomo are poor far-behind imitations. I would rather know the metaphysics of architecture, as of shells and flowers, than anything else in the matter. But one act of benevolence is better than a cathedral, so do your duty, yours. Architecture, said the lady [1] is frozen music. And Iarno says in *Wilhelm* that he who does the best in each one thing he does, does all, for he sees the connexion between all good things.

(From Note-book)

Tuesday, June 11.

Left Milan in the diligence, with Wall and Stewartson and the Misses Bridgen. Before sunset we arrived on the beautiful banks of the Lago Maggiore, and crossed the Adda, which is there an arm of the lake, at Sesto Calendo, and stopped at Arona to dine. Though we passed directly below the famous colossal statue of San Carlo Borromeo, after leaving Arona, it was so dark that I could not see it, which I regretted much. We rode all night and reached Domo d' Ossola next morn to breakfast [in] the town at the foot of the Alps. The *maître d'hôtel* here spoke English, and we were much cheated, two facts which are said to be concomitant. The

<hr>

1 Madame de Staël.

whole of the day, 12 June, was spent in crossing
the mountain by the celebrated road of the Simplon, cut and built by Buonaparte. Let it be a
glory to his name, him the great Hand of our
age. Truly it is a stupendous work, passing
through every variation of ragged mountain
scenery, now through the earth or solid rock in
the form of a tunnel, now in successive easy in-
clined planes called galleries climbing the sides
of a precipice, now crossing some rift in the
mountain on a firm bridge, and so working its
way up from the hot plain of Lombardy to cold
waterfalls and huge snowbanks, and up and up-
ward to the bleak hamlet of Sempione which
almost crowns the top. Here we see our own
breath, and are very glad to get into the house
and avoid the cold air. Over a wild mountain
cascade and within a gallery cut through the
rock Buonaparte has had the honesty to write,
" *Italo Aere. Nap. Imp. MDCCCV.*" Céard was
his principal engineer.

And these, I thought, are the mountains
of freedom. This queer ridge of matter is of
such proved moral efficiency. Let their Spartan
hymn ascend. I saw a good many of the Swiss
peasantry on the hillsides: how different from
the Italians on one side, or the French on

the other, but exactly resembling the faces and dresses of their countrymen who emigrate to the United States. It is marvellous to see their houses on such narrow lodgments, half way up a mural precipice, as was said of Cortona, "like a picture hanging on a wall." What can they do with their children?

We dined at Sempione and soon began the descent of the mountain; the wheel of the diligence is chained and shod with a heavy log of green wood; yet the descent at some points looks perilous enough. The mountain views are very fine. No extensive prospect is commanded in the ascent or from the top, but we see many noble summits of the chain as we come down toward Briga.

We arrived safely at Briga at the foot of the mountain after sunset. We have left the Italian speech behind us, and though in Switzerland, all is French. After supper we set forward again, and unluckily, having taken my place outside by day, I was compelled to ride the whole cold night *sub Jove frigido*, and was very thankful to one of my fair friends within, who loaned me a *shawl* for the occasion. At dawn we reached Sion, and in the forenoon Martigny. We had taken our places for Martigny, intending to visit

Mont Blanc from thence. But the sky was overcast and it rained a little, and we were afraid of a storm, so we relinquished our purpose, or at least postponed it for consideration at Geneva.

June 13.

On we came, passing the fine cascade of Pissevache, and stopped an hour at St. Maurice. Thence in more convenient vehicles through a country of grandest scenery passing through Clarens and along the banks of Lake Leman, by the castle of Chillon, then through Vevay, and we reached Lausanne before nightfall.

The repose and refreshment of a good hotel were very welcome to us after riding two nights; but the next morning (14th) was fine, and Mr. Wall and I walked out to the public promenade, a high and ornamented grove which overlooks the lake and commands the view of a great amphitheatre of mountains.

We are getting toward France. In the café where we breakfasted we found a printed circular inviting those whom it concerned to a rifle-match, to the intent, as the paper stated, " of increasing their skill in that valuable accomplishment, and of drawing more closely the bonds of that regard with which we are," etc.

After breakfast I inquired my way to Gibbon's house and was easily admitted to the garden. The summer-house is removed, but the floor of it is still there, where the History was written and finished. I stood upon it and looked forth upon the noble landscape of which he speaks so proudly. I plucked a leaf of the lime tree he planted, and of the acacia, — successors of those under which he walked. I have seen however many landscapes as pleasant and more striking.

At 10 o'clock we took the steamboat for Geneva and sailed up Lake Leman. The passage was very long, seven hours, for the wind was ahead, and the engine not very powerful. We touched at Coppet. The lake is most beautiful near Geneva. It was not clear enough to see Mont Blanc, or else it was not visible. Mount Varens and Monte Rosa were seen.

GENEVA, *June* 16.

Here am I in the stern old town, the resort of such various minds, of Calvin, of Rousseau, of Gibbon, of Voltaire, of De Staël, of Byron, on the blue Rhone by the placid Lake Leman. Mont Blanc towers above the Alps on the east sublimely with his three summits; Jura on the west is marking the line of France; and

the lake lies in beauty before me. Everybody
is polite.

Yesterday, to oblige my companions, and pro-
testing all the way upon the unworthiness of his
memory, I went to Ferney to the château, the
salon, the bedchamber, the gardens of Voltaire,
the king of the scorners. His rooms were modest
and pleasing, and hung with portraits of his
friends. Franklin and Washington were there.
The view of the lake and mountains commanded
by the lawn behind the château is superior to that
of Gibbon's garden at Lausanne. The old porter
showed us some pictures belonging to his old
master, and told a story that did full justice to
his bad name. Yet it would be a sin against faith
and philosophy to exclude Voltaire from toleration. He did his work as the bustard[1] and taran-
tula do theirs.

We had a fine ride home, so royally towers
up Mont Blanc with his white, triple top. On
the way we passed the stone which marks the
boundary of France, which made Dr. Stewartson
crow like chanticleer, and the grass he thought
greener. Visited the music-box manufactory, and
the watchmaker's. The music man offered to

1 Thus in the Journal, but probably *buzzard* was what
was really intended. — ED.

make a box with two airs of Beethoven for
50 francs, to be received by me in Paris.

Prices of the best watches that they can make
are 500 francs. Of the second class, without a
compensation, but esteemed as good for all ordinary purposes, 300 francs. S. bought one for
275, the difference of value being in the weight
of the case. They speak of smuggling with perfect simplicity, and offer to send you the watch
to Paris (via smuggler, that is) for a few francs.

Through the Misses Bridgen's acquaintance
in Mr. Wolf's family, I was carried away to hear
M. Gissot, a very worthy Calvinist who has
been ejected from the National Church. His
exercise was a catechism and exhortation of a
large class of children; then I was introduced to
Mr. Cordis and others of their brethren; very
worthy men they seemed. I spent the day at
the house of Mr. Wolf. The daughter told me
that "if I was, as I said, a seeker, she thought
I ought to make it a point of duty to stop longer
at Geneva," and so offered in very pretty broken
English "to intrude me to the minister who
bègun the exercise." She had learned English
because her house was destined to receive boarders, etc., etc. I owed them all much kindness,
but if I had known anything I should have

made acquaintance with M. Chenevière first. After all this kindness it would have been great violence to have gone away to him. The established church of Geneva is now Unitarian, and the three Calvinistic clergymen of the city are ejected.

FRANCE

Left Geneva in the diligence for Paris Monday morning at 4 o'clock, and presently crossed the line of France and began the ascent of Mount Jura. As we rose toward the top, what noble pictures appeared on the Swiss side! The Alps, the Alps and Mont Blanc in all his breadth, towering up so cold and white and dim towards heaven, all uninhabitable and almost inaccessible. Yet more than Saussure have reached the top.

France, France. It is not only a change of name: the cities, the language, the faces, the manners have undergone a wonderful change in three or four days. The running fight we have kept up so long with the *fierté* of postillions and padroni in Italy is over, and all men are complaisant. The face of the country is remarkable; not quite a plain, but a vast undulating champaign without a hill, and all planted like the Connecticutt intervales. No fences, the fields full of working women. We rode in the coupé of a Diligence by night and by day, for three days and a half, and arrived in Paris at noon Thursday.

PARIS

I arrived in Paris at noon on Thursday, 20 June. My companions, who have been in the *belle ville* before, and wished it to strike me as it ought, are scarce content with my qualified admiration. Certainly the eye is satisfied on entering the city with the unquestionable tokens of a vast, rich, old capital. We crossed the Seine by the *Pont Neuf*, and I was glad to see my old acquaintance Henry IV very respectably mounted in bronze on his own bridge; but the saucy faction of the day has thrust a tricolor into his bronze hand, as into a doll's, and in spite of decency the stout old monarch is thus obliged to take his part in the whirligig politics of his city. Fie! Louis Philippe. We were presently lodged in the Hotel Montmorenci on the Boulevard Mont Martre. I have wandered round the city, but I am not well pleased. I have seen so much in five months that the magnificence of Paris will not take my eye to-day. The gardens of the Louvre looked pinched and the wind blew dust in my eyes, and before I got into the

Champs Élysées I turned about and flatly refused to go farther. I was sorry to find that in leaving Italy I had left forever that air of antiquity and history which her towns possess, and in coming hither had come to a loud, modern New York of a place.

I am very glad to find here my cousin Ralph Emerson, who received me most cordially and has aided me much in making my temporary establishment. It were very ungrateful in a stranger to be discontented with Paris, for it is the most hospitable of cities. The foreigner has only to present his passport at any public institution and the doors are thrown wide to him. I have been to the Sorbonne, where the first scientific men in France lecture at stated hours every day, and the doors are open to all. I have heard Jouffroy, Thenard [and Gay Lussac].

Then the *Collège Royale de France* is a similar institution on the same liberal foundation. So with the *Collège du Droit*, and the Amphitheatre of the Garden of Plants.

I have been to the Louvre, where are certainly some first-rate pictures. Leonardo da Vinci has more pictures here than in any other gallery, and I like them well, despite of the identity of the features which peep out of men and women.

I have seen the same face in his pictures I think six or seven times. Murillo I see almost for the first time with great pleasure.

July.

It is a pleasant thing to walk along the Boulevards and see how men live in Paris. One man has live snakes crawling about him, and sells soap and essences. Another sells books which lie upon the ground. Another under my window all day offers a gold chain. Half a dozen walk up and down with some dozen walking sticks under the arm. A little further, one sells cane-tassels at 5 sous. Here sits Boots brandishing his brush at every dirty shoe. Then you pass several tubs of gold fish. Then a man sitting at his table cleaning gold and silver spoons with emery and haranguing the passengers on its virtues. Then a person who cuts profiles with scissors—"shall be happy to take yours, sir." Then a table of card-puppets which are made to crawl. Then a hand-organ. Then a wooden figure called [?] which can put an apple in its mouth whenever a child buys a plum. Then a flower merchant. Then a bird-shop with twenty parrots, four swans, hawks and nightingales. Then the show of the boy with four legs, etc., etc., without end. All these are the mere *boutiques* on the

sidewalk, moved about from place to place as
the sun or rain or the crowd may lead them.

(From Q)

PARIS.

It shall be writ in my memoirs (as Aunt Mary
would say), as it was writ of St. Pachomius, " *Pes
ejus ad saltandum non est commotus omni vita
sua.*" The worse for me in the gay city. Pray
what brought you here, grave sir? the moving
Boulevard seems to say.

" *Aimer, pleurer, mourir, — c'est la vie de la
femme* "; title of a novel just published.

PARIS, *July* 4.

The two gifts of the Old World to the New,
— Columbus and Lafayette.

(From Note-book)

Dined to-day at Lointier's with General Lafayette and nearly one hundred Americans. I
sought an opportunity of paying my respects to
the hero, and inquiring after his health. His
speech was as happy as usual. A certain Lieutenant Levi did what he could to mar the day.[1]

1 Dr. Oliver Wendell Holmes in a letter to his family describes the incident here referred to. (See Morse's *Life and
Letters of Oliver Wendell Holmes*, vol. i, p. 105.)

July 9.

How does everybody live on the outside of
the world! All young persons thirst for a *real*
existence for an object, — for something great
and good which they shall do with all their
heart. Meantime they all pack gloves, or keep
books, or travel, or draw indentures, or cajole
old women.

July 11.

Does any man render written account to himself of himself? I think not. Those who have
anything worth repeating, — ah! the sad confession! Those who are innocent have been employed in tape and pins. When will good work
be found for great spirits? When shall we be
able without a blush and without harm to utter
to the world our inmost thought?

Thus, shall I write memoirs? A man who
was no courtier, but loved men, went to Rome,
— and there lived with boys. He came to France,
and in Paris lives alone, and in Paris seldom
speaks. If he do not see Carlyle in Edinburgh,
he may go to America without saying anything
in earnest, except to Cranch and to Landor.

The errors of traditional Christianity as it
now exists, the popular faith of many millions,

need to be removed to let men see the divine beauty of moral truth. I feel myself pledged, if health and opportunity be granted me, to demonstrate that all necessary truth is its own evidence; that no doctrine of God need appeal to a book; that Christianity is wrongly received by all such as take it for a system of doctrines, — its stress being upon moral truth; it is a rule of life, not a rule of faith.

And how men can toil and scratch so hard for things so dry, lifeless, unsightly, as these famous dogmas, when the divine beauty of the truths to which they are related lies behind them; how they can make such a fuss about the case, and never open it to see the jewel, is strange, pitiful.

PARIS, *July* 12.

Is it not true that in every season of excited thought, when a man has a strong conception of God, it is wholly new to him; he perceives that he has never penetrated so far before into the Holy of Holies? and yet every time —

St. Charles Borromeo, what a man was he! what a priest!

You cannot answer at the hour the argument of little men, which insists on the unavoidableness of sensual pleasure to such constitutions as ours; but St. Charles Borromeo is answer enough, any great and noble man is answer enough, any one who will not be little, who will bestir himself, who will use his faculties and do his duty.

Be cheerful. What an insane habit is this of groping always into the past months, and scraping together every little pitiful instance of awkwardness and misfortune, and keeping my nervous system ever on the rack. It is the disease of a man who is at the same time too idle, and respectful to the opinion of others.

Il tient son affaire.

(From Note-book)

July 13.

I carried my ticket from Mr. Warden to the Cabinet of Natural History in the Garden of Plants. How much finer things are in composition than alone. 'T is wise in man to make cabinets. When I was come into the Ornithological Chambers I wished I had come only there. The fancy-coloured vests of these elegant beings make me as pensive as the hues and forms of a cabinet of shells, formerly. It is a beautiful collection and makes the visitor as calm and genial as a bridegroom. The limits of the possible are enlarged, and the real is stranger than the imaginary. Some of the birds have a fabulous beauty. One parrot of a fellow called *Psittacus erythropterus* from New Holland deserves as special mention as a picture of Raphael in a gallery. He is the beau of all birds. Then the humming birds, little and gay. Least of all is the *Trochilus Niger.* I have seen beetles larger. The *Trochilus pella* hath such a neck of gold and silver and fire! *Trochilus Delalandi* from Brazil is a glorious little tot, *la mouche magnifique.* Among the birds of Paradise I remarked the *Manucode* or *Paradisea regia* from New Guinea, the *Paradisea Apoda*, and *Paradisea rubra.* Forget not the *Veuve à epaulettes*, or *Emberiza longicauda*, black with fine shoulder-knots; nor the *Ampelis cotinga ;* nor the *Phasianus Argus*, a peacock-looking pheasant; nor the *Trogon pavoninus*, called also *Couroncou pavonin.*

I saw black swans and white peacocks; the ibis, the sacred and the rosy ; the flamingo, with a neck like a snake; the toucan rightly called *rhinoceros ;* and a vulture whom to meet in the wilderness would make your flesh quiver, so like an executioner he looked.

In the other rooms I saw amber containing perfect musquitoes, grand blocks of quartz, native gold in all its forms of crystallization,—threads, plates, crystals, dust; and silver, black as from fire. Ah! said I, this is philanthropy, wisdom, taste,—to form a cabinet of natural history. Many students were there with grammar and note-book, and a class of boys with their tutor from some school.

Here we are impressed with the inexhaustible riches of nature. The universe is a more amazing puzzle than ever, as you glance along this bewildering series of animated forms,—the hazy butterflies, the carved shells, the birds, beasts, fishes, insects, snakes, and the upheaving principle of life everywhere incipient, in the very rock aping organized forms. Not a form so grotesque, so savage, nor so beautiful but is an expression of some property inherent in man the observer,—an occult relation between the very scorpions and man. I feel the centipede in me,— cayman, carp, eagle, and fox. I am moved by strange sympathies; I say continually " I will be a naturalist."

There's a good collection of skulls in the Comparative Anatomy Chambers. The best skull seemed to be English. The skeleton of the *Balena* looks like the frame of a schooner turned upside down.

The Garden itself is admirably arranged. They have attempted to classify all the plants *in the ground*, to put together, that is, as nearly as may be, the conspicuous plants of each class on Jussieu's system.

Walk down the alleys of this flower-garden, and you come to the enclosures of the animals where almost all that Adam named or Noah preserved are represented. Here are several lions, two great elephants walking out in the open day, a camelopard seventeen feet high, the bison, the rhinoceros, and so forth, — all manner of four-footed things in air and sunshine, in the shades of a pleasant garden, where all people, French and English, may come and see without money. By the way, there is a caricature in the print-shops respecting the arrival of the giraffe in Paris, exclaiming to the mob, "*Messieurs, il n'y a qu'un bête de plus.*" It is very pleasant to walk in this garden.

As I went out, I noticed a placard posted on the gate giving notice that M. Jussieu would next Sunday give a public herborisation, that is, make a botanical excursion into the country, and inviting all and sundry to accompany him.

July 15.

I have just returned from *Père le Chaise*. It well deserves a visit and does honour to the French. But they are a vain nation. The tomb-stones have a beseeching, importunate vanity and remind you of advertisements. But many are affecting. One which was of dark slate stone had only this inscription, "*Mon Père.*" I prefer the "*Ci gît*" to the "*Ici repose*" as the beginning of the inscriptions, but, take the cemetery through, I thought the Classics rather carried the day. One epitaph was so singular to be read by *me*, that I wrote it off; —

Ici repose Auguste Charles Collignon, mort plein de confiance dans la bonté de Dieu, à l'âge de 68 ans et 4 mois, le 15 Avril, 1830. Il aima et cher-cha à faire du bien, et mena une vie douce et heu-reuse en suivant autant qu'il put la morale et les leçons des essais de Montaigne et des Fables de la Fontaine. I notice that, universally, the French write, as, in the above, "*Here lies Augustus,*" etc., and we write, "*Here lies the body of,*" etc. —a more important distinction than *roi de France* and *roi des Français.*

I live at *pension* with Professor Heari at the corner of *Rue Neuve Vivienne* directly over the entrance of the *Passage aux Panorames.* If I had

companions in the City, it would be something
better to live in the Café and Restaurant. These
public rooms are splendidly prepared for travellers and full of company and of newspapers.

This *Passage aux Panorames* was the first ar-
cade built in Paris and was built by an American, Mr. Thayer. There are now probably fifty
of these passages in the city. And few things
give more the character of magnificence to the
city than the suite of these passages about the
Palais Royal.

Notre Dame is a fine church outside, but the
interior quite naked and beggarly. In general,
the churches are very mean inside.

Young men are very fond of Paris, partly, no
doubt, because of the perfect freedom, — freedom from observation as well as interference, —
in which each one walks after the sight of his
own eyes; and partly because the extent and
variety of objects offers an unceasing entertainment. So long as a man has francs in his pocket
he needs consult neither time, nor place, nor
other men's convenience; wherever in the vast
city he is, he is within a stone's throw of a *patis-
sier*, a *café*, a restaurant, a public garden, a theatre, and may enter when he will. If he wish to
go to the Thuileries perhaps two miles off, let

him stop a few minutes at the window of a print-shop or a book-stall, of which there are hundreds and thousands, and an omnibus is sure to pass in the direction in which he would go, and for six sous he rides two or three miles. Then the streets swarm with *Cabinets de Lecture* where you find all the journals and all the new books. I spend many hours at Galignani's and lately at the English Reading Room in the *Rue Neuve Augustine*, where they advertise that they receive 400 journals in all languages, and have moreover a very large library.

Lastly, the evening need never hang heavy on the stranger's hands, such ample provision is made here for what the newspapers call "*nos besoins recreatifs.*" More than twenty theatres are blazing with light and echoing with fine music every night, from the *Académie Royale de la Musique*, which is the French Opera, down to the Children's Drama; not to mention concerts, gardens and shows innumerable. The theatre is the passion of the French, and the taste and splendour of their dramatic exhibitions can hardly be exceeded. The *Journal*, in speaking of the Opera last night, declares that " Mme. D. was received by the dilettanti of Paris with not less joy than the lost soul by the angels in heaven." I saw the opera *Gustave* performed the other night, and have seen nothing anywhere that could compare with the brilliancy of their scenic decoration. The moonlight scene resembled nothing but Nature's; and as for the masked ball, I think there never was a real fancy-ball that equalled the effect of this.

At the *Théâtre Français*, where Talma played and Madame Mars plays, I heard Delavigne's new piece, *Enfans d'Edouard*, excellently performed; for although Madame Mars speaks French beautifully and has the manners of a princess, yet she scarcely excels the acting of the less famous performers who support her. Each was perfect in his part.

Paris is an expensive place. Rents are very high. All Frenchmen, in all quarters of their dispersion, never lose the hope of coming hither to spend their earnings, and all the men of pleasure in all the nations come hither, which fact explains the existence of so many dazzling shops full of most costly articles of luxury. Indeed, it is very hard for a stranger to walk with eyes forward ten yards in any part of the city.

I have been to the Faubourg St. Martin to hear the Abbé Chatel, the founder of the *Eglise Catholique Française*. It is a singular institution which he calls his church, with newly invented dresses for the priests and martial music performed by a large orchestra, relieved by interludes of a piano with vocal music. His discourse was far better than I could expect from these preliminaries. Sometimes he is eloquent. He is a Unitarian, but more radical than anybody in America who takes that name.

I was interested in his enterprise, for there is always something pathetic in a new church struggling for sympathy and support. He takes upon himself the whole pecuniary responsibilities of the undertaking, and for his chapel in the *Rue St. Honoré* pays an annual rent of 40,000 francs. He gave notice of a grand funeral fête which is to be solemnized on the anniversary of the Three Days at that chapel.

In the print-shops they have a figure of the Abbé Chatel on the same picture with *Père Enfant, Le Templier.*

I went this evening into Frascati's, long the most noted of the gambling houses or hells of Paris, and which a gentleman had promised to show me. This establishment is in a very handsome house on the *Rue Richelieu.* Several servants in livery were waiting in the hall, who took our hats on entering, and we passed at once into the suite of rooms in all of which play was going on. The most perfect decorum and civility prevailed, the table was covered with little piles of napoleons which seemed to change masters very rapidly, but scarce a word was spoken. Servants carry about lemonade, etc., but no heating liquor. The house, I was told, is always one party in the game. Several women were present, but many of the company seemed to be mere spectators like ourselves. After walking round the tables, we returned to the hall, gave the servant a franc for our hats, and departed. Frascati has grown very rich.

Go to the Champs Élysées after sunset and see the manifold show. An orchestra, a roundabout, a tumbler, sugar-plum-gambling-tables, harpers, dancers, and an army of loungers.

I went to the Mazarin Library, and Mr. Warden kindly introduced me to the *séance* of the Class of Science in the Institute, and pointed out to me the conspicuous men. I saw Biot, Arago, Gay Lussac, Jouffroy, and others. Several memoirs were read, and some debate ensued thereon. Visited St. Cloud.

July 18.

Left Paris in the Diligence for Boulogne. Rode all night through St. Denis, Moisselles, Beau-

vais, breakfasted at Abbeville, passed through
Montreuil, Samur, and reached Boulogne about
sunset. At Abbeville we picked up Signore Ales-
sandro, an Italian emigrant.

At Boulogne, on Saturday morn, 19th, took
the steamboat for London. After a rough passage of 20 hours we arrived at London and landed
at the Tower Stairs.

ENGLAND

July 20.

We know London so well in books and pictures
and maps and traditions that I saw nothing surprising in this passage up the Thames. A noble
navigable stream, lined on each side by a highly
cultivated country, full of all manner of good
buildings. Then Greenwich and Deptford, hospital, docks, arsenals, fleets of shipping, and then
the mighty metropolis itself, old, vast, and still.
Scarce anybody was in the streets. It was about
7 o'clock Sunday morning, and we met few persons until we reached St. Paul's. A porter carried
our baggage, and we walked through Cheapside,
Newgate Street, High Holborn, and found lodgings (according to the direction of my friend in
Paris) at Mrs. Fowler's, No. 63 Russell Square.
It was an extreme pleasure to hear English

spoken in the streets; to understand all the
words of children at play, and to find that we
must not any longer express aloud our opinion
of every person we met, as in France and Italy
we had been wont to do.

Went into St. Paul's, where service was saying. Poor church.

LONDON, *July* 24.

Here in the great capital it needs to say something of the creature immortal that swarms on
this spot. Coming to Boulogne, I thought of the
singular position of the American traveller in
Italy. It is like that of a being of another planet
who invisibly visits the earth. He is a protected
witness. He sees what is that boasted liberty of
manners, free of all puritan starch, and sees what
it is worth, how surely it pays its tax. He comes
a freeman among slaves. He learns that old saws
are true, which is a great thing. He is not now to
be answered any longer in his earnest assertions
of moral truth, by the condescending explanation
that these are his prejudices of country and education. He has seen how they hold true through
all the most violent contrasts of condition and
character.

July 28.

Attended divine service at Westminster Abbey. The Bishop of Gloucester preached. It is better than any church I have seen except St. Peter's.

Happy the man who never puts on a face, but receives every visitor with that countenance he has on.

[There are no further notes on London except the following list:] Westminster Abbey; St. Stephen's; Haymarket; Mr. Irving's Chapel; Gallery of Practical Science; London University; Zoölogical Gardens; Regent Street; Athenæum; St. James; Mr. Fox's Chapel; Wilberforce's funeral; Regent's Park; Immense city, very dull city.

July 31.

At Dr. Bowring's, Milton's house; inscription on the wall, "Sacred to Milton, the Prince of Poets."

[Here follows the account of the visit to Wordsworth at Ambleside, which is printed in full in *English Traits*, with but slight alterations.]

Almost nobody in Highgate knew his [Coleridge's] name. I asked several persons in vain; at last a porter wished to know if I meant an elderly gentleman with white hair? Yes, the same. "Why, he lives with Mr. Gillman." Ah yes, that is he. So he showed me the way.

Mr. Bowring says that Wilson and Hogg went to see Wordsworth, and the morning was fine, and then there was a rainbow, and altogether it was genial. So Hogg said to Wordsworth, this is a fit spot for poets to meet in. Wordsworth drew himself up with ineffable disdain saying, "*Poets* indeed!"

[Leaving London, August 9, Mr. Emerson visited Oxford, then Birmingham, but made no records in the Journal.]

MATLOCK, Tuesday evening, 9 o'clock.
August 13.

Beautiful valley! Esteemed the most romantic dell in England. Here sit I close by the Derwent, and under the eaves of the caverns of the Peak of Derbyshire. But it will not do, to visit even these fine things alone. I think I must not stay to visit even Haddon Hall and Chatsworth.

Pleasant it was to me to spend yesterday with Mr. Dewey in such a visit. How reared himself old Kenilworth into the English morning sky. The ruin is as lordly as was the perfect state. I thought, if I had a boy to educate, I would carry him by moonlight into the inner floor of the Lancaster building. It would doom him a poet. The smell of the fresh ground, the cellar smell in a hall so princely as Lancaster's, was tragical.

"The hall of Cyndyllan is gloomy this night,
    Wanting fire, wanting candle.
  I will weep awhile and then be silent."

The visit to Warwick Castle is a proper appendix to the visit to Kenilworth, for Warwick is what Kenilworth was. It overhangs the Avon.

In the interim betwixt these two visits we went to St. Mary's Church and saw "Our Lady's Chapel."

In this day's ride I marked that the botany of England and America is alike. The clematis, the mints, the goldenrods, the gerardias, the wild geranium, the wild parsley, and twenty more better known to my eye than to my ear, I saw and recognized them all. I passed through Tamworth and saw the tower and the town, and thought up the old jingle of my school days : —

> " Largesse, Largesse, Lord Marmion !
>
> . . . .
>
> They hailed him Lord of Fontenaye
> Of Lutterworth and Scrivelbaye,
> Of Tamworth tower and town."

We passed through Ashby-de-la-Zouche, and I saw the ruin of the old castle. We crossed the Trent, we came to Derby. We see throughout Europe the counterparts of the Americans.

I passed Sir Robert Peel's place, then Sir Richard Arkwright's.

[Mr. Emerson then passed Northward, visiting Haddon Hall, through Bakewell, Sheffield, spending a day in York, thence by Newcastle and Berwick to Edinburgh. There are no notes of this part of the journey, nor of his visit to Edinburgh, where he spent four days. The narrative then begins again on some loose sheets, apparently a copy of a letter.]

GLASGOW, *August* 23.

May I send you an account of my romancing from Edinburgh to the Highlands ? I was told it was so easy, at an expense of two days, to see that famous country of Ben Lomond, Loch Katrine and the rest. So up the Forth sailed I, in the steamboat for Stirling, cold, rainy wind in our teeth, all the way. We passed Alloa and Falkirk, yes, close by Bannockburn, I quietly reading my book in the cabin. At Stirling, I saw the ruin of the Abbey of Cambus Kenneth and the view from Stirling Castle.

At night, in a car, being too late for the coach, I rode through the rain ten miles to Doune and Callander. Of the scenery I saw little more than my horse's head. At Callandar I slept hard from 10 till 5, and was then waked to hasten to the Trosachs Inn. This passage was made in an uncovered car again, and the rain wet me through my own coat and my landlord's over that, and though we passed Loch Vennachar, and then Loch Achray, yet the scenery of a shower-bath must be always much the same, and perpendicular rather than horizontal. Once when the flood intermitted, I peeped out from under the umbrella, and it was a pretty place. We dried and breakfasted at the Trosachs Inn. I walked with a party a mile and a half to the head of Loch Katrine. It had cleared up, though the wind blew stoutly, and I had the satisfaction of the Trosachs. The ornament of Scottish scenery is the

heather, which colours the country to the hue
of a rose. In two boats with four oars each we
pushed into the lake, and got as far as Ellen's
Island, the Isle of the Lady of the Lake. Ben
Venue and Ben An rise on either side. The
lake was rough, the wind was strong, and our
party were spattered, and the rowers made such
little way that it seemed impracticable to attempt
to go through the lake, which is nine miles long.
They put into the first cove the shore afforded ;
part of the company returned to the Trosachs,
and a part who were bent on reaching that night
Glasgow, had nothing for it but to walk to the
end of the lake, which, following the windings
of the shore, is fourteen miles. There was no
better road than a sheep-track through every
variety of soil, now sand, now morass, now fern
and brake, now stones. But the day was fine and
on we fared, one of the boatmen acting as guide.

We embarked in the boat at 9 o'clock. Five
out of fifteen reached the little hut at the end of
the lake at 12 ½. Here we dried our shoes and
drank (I drank) whiskey, and eat oat-cake. It
was five miles to Inversnaid, where we must
take the steamboat on Loch Lomond. There
was no conveyance but our legs, which served
us again ; a country as bare almost as a paved

street; mountains, mountains, but I don't remember that I saw a sheep. At Inversnaid, a hut full of Highlandmen and women talking Gaelic, no chimney, and the peat smoke escaped as it could. Behind the house was a roaring cataract. The steamboat came (and through much fear and tribulation on the rough waves) we were transported in a little boat and embarked therein. And so on we fared through this lake about 15 miles to Balloch. The wind blew my cap off, which had travelled with me from Malta where it was made, and it fell into Loch Lomond. My hat was with the baggage all at Glasgow, and the loss not to be repaired, so I shivered, and sweltered when need was, in the rain and wind with a handkerchief on my head. We landed at Balloch, and took coach 5 miles farther to Dumbarton. At Dumbarton we were carried to the steamboat on the Clyde, and went up to Glasgow, where we arrived about ten o'clock at night. My own appearance was no doubt resolute, arriving at an inn (where my baggage had not) in an old surtout, without a hat and without a rag of baggage.

They put me in a little room aloft. I was in no condition to dictate, and crept to bed. This morn came the trunk, and armed with razors and

clean shirt I recovered my courage. I visited the
cathedral of 1123, spared by Knox, and now a
Presbyterian church. In the vaulted cellar of
the same is laid the scene of part of *Rob Roy*.
Then to the Salt Market, and to the Hunterian
Museum, and to the walks behind the College.
A little girl named Jeanie was my guide to the
tower of the church. Broad Scotch she spake,
but she said her name was not Deans.

[A large part of Mr. Emerson's account of
his visit to Carlyle was printed by him in *English Traits* and is therefore omitted here.]

CARLISLE IN CUMBERLAND, *August* 26.

I am just arrived in merry Carlisle from
Dumfries. A white day in my years. I found
the youth I sought in Scotland, and good and
wise and pleasant he seems to me. Thomas
Carlyle lives in the parish of Dunscore, 16
miles from Dumfries, amid wild and desolate
heathery hills, and without a single companion
in this region out of his own house. There
he has his wife, a most accomplished and agreeable woman. Truth and peace and faith dwell
with them and beautify them. I never saw
more amiableness than is in his countenance.

He speaks broad Scotch with evident relish; "in London yonder," "I liked well," "aboot it," "ay, ay," etc., etc. Nothing can be better than his stories, the philosophic phrase: "The Duchess of Queensberry was appointed to possess this estate," — "by God Almighty," added the lady; Wordsworth; the Earl of Lonsdale; the town of Whitehaven; the Liverpool duellist; Coleridge; Allan Cunningham; Hazlitt; Walter Scott, Sheriff of Selkirk. . . . "Mud magazine," "Sand magazine." [1] Coronation of King William. . . .

T. C. was born in Annandale. His reading multifarious, *Tristram Shandy*, *Robinson Crusoe*, Robertson's *America*. Rousseau's *Confessions* discovered to him that he was not such an ass as he had imagined. Ten years ago he learned German. London; heart of the world, wonderful only for the mass of human beings. . . . Splendid bridge from the new world to the old, built by Gibbon. . . .

T. C. had made up his mind to pay his taxes to William and Adelaide Guelph with great cheerfulness as long as William is able to compel the payment, and he shall cease to do so the moment he ceases to compel them. Landor's

1 Carlyle's names for *Fraser's Magazine*, and *Blackwood's*.

principle is mere rebellion, and he fears that is the American principle also. Himself worships the man that will manifest any truth to him.

Mrs. Carlyle told of the disappointment when they had determined to go to Weimar, and the letter arrived from the bookseller to say the book did not sell, and they could not go. The first thing Goethe sent was the chain she wore round her neck, and how she capered when it came! but since that time he had sent many things. Mrs. C. said, when I mentioned the Burns piece, that it always had happened to him upon those papers to hear of each two or three years after. T. C. prefers London to any other place to live in. John S. Mill the best mind he knows, more purity, more force, has worked himself clear of Benthamism. The best thing T. C. thought in Stuart's book was the story of the bootblack that a man can have meat for his labor.

AMBLESIDE, *August* 28.

This morning I went to Rydal Mount and called upon Mr. Wordsworth.

[Here follows the story of this visit, which is printed in *English Traits* almost exactly as in the note-book.

Wordsworth surprised his visitor by offering to repeat some of his verses as they walked in the garden. This amused Mr. Emerson at first, but on reflection he thought it kind, and fitting for a poet to do.]

The poet is always young, and this old man took the same attitudes that he probably had at seventeen, whilst he recollected the sonnet he would recite.

His egotism was not at all displeasing, obtrusive, as I had heard. To be sure it met no rock. I spoke as I felt, with great respect of his genius.

He spoke very kindly of Dr. Channing, who, he said, "sat a long time in this very chair," laying his hand upon an armchair.

He mentioned Burns's sons.

On my return to the inn, he walked near a mile with me, talking, and ever and anon stopping short to impress the word or the verse, and finally parted from me with great kindness and returned across the fields.

His hair is white, but there is nothing very striking about his appearance.

August 29.

From Kendall this morning to Lancaster; thence to Manchester, and there was deposited with my luggage in the coach on the railway to Liverpool. We parted at 11 minutes after six, and came to the 21st milestone at 11 minutes after seven. Strange it was to meet the return cars; to see a load of timber, six or seven masts, dart by you like a trout. Everybody shrinks back when the engine hisses by him like a squib. The fire that was dropped on the road under us all along by our engine looked, as we rushed over it, as a coal swung by the hand in circles, not distinct, but a continuous glare. Strange proof how men become accustomed to oddest things! the laborers did not lift their umbrellas to look as we flew by them on their return at the side of the track. It took about one and one-half hours to make the journey, 32 miles. It has been performed in less than the hour.

LIVERPOOL, *August* 30.

I talked commonplaces to-day with a man at this hotel, who told me he had lived in Boston, until I found out it was Jacob Perkins. He says it is not true that he has failed for want of material strong enough to hold his force. He says he has succeeded in everything he has undertaken, but in making money.

(From Q)

LIVERPOOL, *September* 1.

I thank the Great God who has led me through
this European scene, this last schoolroom in
which he has pleased to instruct me, from Malta's
isle, through Sicily, through Italy, through
Switzerland, through France, through England,
through Scotland, in safety and pleasure, and has
now brought me to the shore and the ship that
steers westward. He has shown me the men I
wished to see, — Landor, Coleridge, Carlyle,
Wordsworth; he has thereby comforted and
confirmed me in my convictions. Many things
I owe to the sight of these men. I shall judge
more justly, less timidly, of wise men forever-
more. To be sure not one of these is a mind
of the very first class, but what the intercourse
with each of these suggests is true of intercourse
with better men, that they never *fill the ear* —
fill the mind — no, it is an *idealized* portrait
which always we draw of them. Upon an intelligent man, wholly a stranger to their names,
they would make in conversation no deep impression, none of a world-filling fame, — they
would be remembered as sensible, well-read,
earnest men, not more. Especially are they all

deficient, all these four,—in different degrees, but all deficient,—in insight into religious truth. They have no idea of that species of moral truth which I call the first philosophy. (Peter Hunt [1] is as wise a talker as either of these men. Don't laugh.)

The comfort of meeting men of genius such as these is that they talk sincerely, they feel themselves to be so rich that they are above the meanness of pretending to knowledge which they have not, and they frankly tell you what puzzles them. But Carlyle — Carlyle is so amiable that I love him.

But I am very glad my travelling is done. A man not old feels himself too old to be a vagabond. The people at their work, the people whose avocations I interrupt by my letters of introduction, accuse me by their looks for leaving my business to hinder theirs. [2]

1 Benjamin Peter Hunt has been already alluded to. He had been one of Mr. Emerson's scholars in the village of Chelmsford, and later, when Mr. Hunt lived in Philadelphia, they sometimes wrote to one another.

2 Mr. Emerson seldom presented a letter of introduction. It was his practice to go to the town where the person he would see lived and write a note to him from the inn. The recipient could judge from the note whether the writer was one whom he cared to see.

These men make you feel that fame is a conventional thing, and that man is a sadly "limitary" spirit. You speak to them as to children, or persons of inferior capacity whom it is necessary to humour; adapting our tone and remarks to their known prejudices and not to our knowledge of the truth.

I believe in my heart it is better to admire too rashly, as I do, than to be admired too rashly, as the great men of this day are. They miss by their premature canonization a great deal of necessary knowledge, and one of these days must begin the world again (as to their surprise they will find needful) poor. I speak now in general, and not of these individuals. God save a great man from a little circle of flatterers. I know it is sweet, very sweet, ratsbane.

To-day I heard Mr. Hinckes, Mr. Martineau, and Mr. Yates, preach: Yates who wrote against Wardlaw. He preached the best sermon I have heard in England,—a great deal the best.

Here at my Hotel, the Star and Garter, Paradise Street, I have found Jacob Perkins the inventor of so many improvements in steam-engines. He has been illuminating me upon the science of heat.

Could not Wordsworth have kept to himself his intimations that his new edition was at the bookseller's and contained some improvements? John Milton was a poet, not a bookmaker, although

The Muse made Shakspear, Milton made his Muse.

True elevation which nothing can bring down is that of moral sentiment. All Carlyle's intellect did not hinder an unpleasant emotion at hearing about his occupation. But Johnson's school or Peter Hunt's are above contempt, and an act of heroism, "A Roman recovery," would have enshrined C. a saint for me. I love his love of truth. The spot is the preference of such a scrub as Mirabeau to Socrates.

LIVERPOOL, *September* 2.

No sailing to-day, so you may know what I have seen and heard in the four days I have been here. Really nothing external, so I must spin my thread from my own bowels. It must be said this is the least agreeable city to the traveller in all England, the old, the rich, the strong nation, full of arts and men and memories; nor can I feel any regret in the presence of the best of its sons that I was not born here.

I am thankful that I am an American as I am thankful that I am a man. It is its best merit to my eye that it is the most resembling country to America which the world contains.

The famous burden of English taxation is bearable. Men live and multiply under it, though I have heard a father in the higher rank of life speak with regret of the increase of his family. That is all I can say ; I am at a dead stand. I can neither write nor read more. If the vessel do sail, they say we shall be drowned on the lee shore; if she do not sail, I perish waiting. What's the odds ? I have plainly said my last word ; it is the prodigality of ink, the wanton destruction of paper to add another syllable, and withal a singular exhibition of what fatuity a man is capable who reckons himself sometimes an educated and thinking man. Yet must I write still. Why ? these lines are the expectants of the dinner ; and it is cold and I cannot go out. Why should I ? I have bid good-bye to all the people. Shall I make them repeal their tears and benedictions ? There are no books in the house, I have digested the newspaper. I have no companion. Even Mr. Perkins, when at home, has finished his communications, and we have got to theology at last.

If it won't rain after the soles and cutlets, I will

brave one family whom I have parted from. Ah me! Mr. Thomas Carlyle, I would give a gold pound for your wise company this gloomy eve. Ah, we would speed the hour. Ah, I would rise above myself—what self-complacent glances casts the soul about in the moment of fine conversation, esteeming itself the author of all the fine things it utters, and the master of the riches the memory produces, and how scornfully looks it back upon the plain person it was yesterday without a thought.

It occurs forcibly, yea, somewhat pathetically, that he who visits a man of genius out of admiration for his parts should treat him tenderly. 'T is odds but he will be disappointed. That is not the man of genius's fault. He was honest and human, but the fault of his own ignorance of the units of human excellence. Let him feel that his visit was unwelcome, and that he is indebted to the tolerance and good nature of his idol, and so spare him the abuse of his own reacting feelings, the back-stroke.

September 3.

No sailing still, but sitting still. I went to the railroad and saw Rocket and Goliath and Pluto and Firefly and the rest of that vulcanian genera-

tion. Mr. Perkins says they should not go faster
than fifteen miles the hour. It racks the engines
to go faster. There are thirty locomotives upon
the road. These only have the circulators. There
is no such thing as latent heat. The thermometer
indicates all the heat that is present. Only when
the particles of the water expand in vapor the
particles of the heat expand also. High pressure
steam-engines are safer than low.

He says that he confidently expects the time
when the ocean will be navigated by merchant-
men by *steam* as the most economical means,
but there is a great deal to be done first; that
now very little advantage is taken of the *expansion*
of steam, its most important property.

Mr. Perkins recited with glee his victory over
one of the directors of the Manchester road. Mr.
Perkins showed that his engine had beat the Sun
(Stephenson's) all last week, doing more work
with less coke. Director said that was because Sun
had been out of order. Mr. P. reminded him of the
quantity of coke which the Director had alleged
was needful always, to the ton and the hour, for
said engine ; to which Director assented. Well,
said Mr. P., I have here certificates of your servants to show that the Sun performed the same
work all last week with a fraction less coke. The

Director acknowledged it could not be much out of order.

(From separate notes)

[The notes which follow were very likely made while waiting in Liverpool, Mr. Emerson perhaps then having in view the writing the lecture which he found opportunity to deliver in November as the introductory discourse before the Boston Society of Natural History. It should be borne in mind that he had turned his back on tradition and turned to Nature as his teacher, and he had already begun his book, *Nature*.]

NATURAL HISTORY

I don't think that we are yet master of all the reasons why we should cultivate it. Natural Magic — Good for society, a diffused taste in natural science; good in a higher degree to the cultivators, —

1. In the knowledge it communicates; pump, natural steam engine, ship, boundaries.

2. In the explanation it gives of moral truth; shells [are] symbols.

3. In the effect upon the character. It makes the intellect exact. It makes the manners simple; makes all boys. It generates enthusiasm.

4. Salutary to the body. Antæus. Higher

questions. Beauty. How old is the pebble? " Is it true? "

Natural history of water; of coal.

It makes every natural event a scientific experiment, — as a snowstorm.

Compare an orrery with the solar system to see how beautiful is nature. Her ropes never entangle, nor crack, nor wear, nor weigh. They are invisible.

So the magnet.

Simplicity of the means. Bees fanning themselves.

Good for the body.

Good for the knowledge it communicates.

Good in its effect upon the mind and character.

Explains moral truth.

Elementary forms of bodies revealed by polarization of light.

Elective affinities.

Polarity of matter. Light. Electricity. Galvanism. Magnetism.

Wednesday, *September* 4.

At 2 o'clock left Liverpool in the New York of N. Y., 14 cabin passengers, 16 steerage. Ship 516 tons.

Thursday [*September*] 5.

Calm fine day. This morn I saw the last lump of England receding without the least regret. I saw too for the first time a piece of Ireland. It was the Wicklow Mountains. As I came down to the waterside in Liverpool, I noticed the announcement of the wind at Holyhead, "At Holyhead, N. E. wind blowing fresh." This communication was telegraphed from Holyhead 60 miles from Liverpool. Noble docks. Heard Mr. Yates preach on Sunday the best sermon I heard in England. "Be clothed with humility." After service I stood waiting for him to come out, when he spoke to me at my side. "Oh," said I surprised, "how do you do, Mr. *Wardlaw*, — I mean Mr. Yates."

Is it not strange that every book begins with "No science deserves more attention than," whether astronomy, geology, civil history, geometry, algebra, commerce, or what not. Even wise Herschel, after a saving flourish, begins with a "no science."

We were towed out of Liverpool Harbor by steamboat. Admirable contrivance for ports in deep bays like this, or Philadelphia, or Baltimore, for they might lie weeks waiting to get out with the wind fair for the voyage all the time.

At one moment the boat and the ship had nearly struck. Every ship, every man, has all but struck, been within an inch of destruction a thousand times. It is such a narrow line that divides an awkward act from the finish of gracefulness. Every man eats well alone. Let a stranger come in, and he misses his mouth, and spills his butterboat, and fails of finding the joint in carving, and that by so little.

I wrote above something concerning the golden mean wherein grace and safety lies. In peaceful pursuits, in cities, we do not consider how great is the distance between danger and death. A man in his parlor thinks that to meet a lion in the desert, or to stumble over an alligator in wading through a watered savannah, is certain destruction. They who are familiar with these *rencontres* think no such thing, and in that discrimination their safety lies. See the story of the Indian girl who put out the Cayman's eyes; and, in the accurate Dampier, the account of the Irishman whose knee was seized by an alligator, — he quietly waited till the animal loosened his teeth to take a new and surer hold, and when it did so, snatched away his knee, interposing the butt end of his gun in its stead, which the animal seized so firmly that it was jerked out of the man's hand and carried off. See also the marvellous expedient of righting the ship when lying in the trough of the sea by going up the fore-shrouds and spreading out their coats. (Early English Navigation Cabinet Library.)

When the French fleet under Count d'Estrées was wrecked, those of the ordinary seamen who got ashore died of fatigue and famine, while those who had been Buccaneers were wrecked here, being used to such accidents, lived merrily ; for they kept a gang by themselves and watched when the ships broke up to get the goods that came out of them, and though much was staved against the rocks, yet abundance of wine and brandy floated over the reef where they waited to take it up. . . . In the selecting unknown wild fruits they were guided by birds, freely eating whatever kind had been pecked.

Friday, 6.

Fair ; fine wind; still in the Channel, off the coast of Ireland, but not in sight of land. This morning 37 sail in sight.

I like my book about Nature, and wish I knew where and how I ought to live. God will show me. I am glad to be on my way home, yet not so glad as others, and my way to the bottom I could find perchance with less regret, for I think it would not hurt me, — that is, the ducking or drowning.

Saturday, 7.

Gentle airs. Wind still, and, what is perhaps good, no events. At 12 o'clock, south of Cape Clear.

Sunday, 8.

The solitary keeper of the lighthouse of the Smalls in the English Channel, which stands on three pillars of cast iron, the waves washing through them : there were two, one sickened and died, the other kept his body, lest they should say he murdered him, until somebody came to the spot ; and the body was quite rotten.

Bread must be well mixed to keep sweet ; man well tempered to keep his spirit clear.

"A rum place," says an Englishman.

It is pleasant to know that our ship is renowned for fast sailing. Captain Hoxie tells me that in three successive days he sailed in this ship 275, 273 and 276 miles = 824.

Astronomy, I thank Herschel, promises everything. It refers me to a higher state than I now occupy. I please myself rather with contemplating the penumbra of the thing than the

thing itself. But no moralities now, the good,
the holy day.

(From Q)

At Sea. Sunday, *September* 8.

I wrote above my conviction that the great
men of England are singularly ignorant of religion. They should read Norton's preface to his
new book,[1] who has stated that fact well. Carlyle
almost grudges the poor peasant his Calvinism.
Must I not admit in the same moment that I
have practical difficulties myself. I see or believe
in the wholesomeness of Calvinism for thousands and thousands. I would encourage, or
rather I would not discourage, their scrupulous
religious observances. I dare not speak lightly
of usages which I omit. And so with this hollow
obeisance to things I do not myself value. I go
on not pestering others with what I do believe,
and so I am open to the name of a very loose
speculator, a faint, heartless supporter of a frigid
and empty theism, a man of no rigor of manners, of no vigor of benevolence. Ah me! what
hope of reform, what hope of communicating
religious light to benighted Europe, if they who
have what they call the light are so selfish and
timid and cold, and their faith so unpractical and,

1 Prof. Andrews Norton's attack on Trinitarian doctrines.

in their judgment, so unsuitable for the middling classes. I know not, I have no call to expound, but this is my charge plain and clear, to act faithfully upon my own faith, to live by it myself, and see what a hearty obedience to it will do.

(Carlyle deprecated the state of a man living in rebellion, as he termed it, with no worship, no reverence for anybody. Himself, he said, would worship anyone who showed him more truth. And Unitarians, he thought, were a tame, limitary people, who were satisfied with their sciolistic system, and never made great attainments, — incapable of depth of sentiment.)

Back again to myself. I believe that the error of religionists lies in this, that they do not know the extent or the harmony or the depth of their moral nature; that they are clinging to little, positive, verbal, formal versions of the moral law, and very imperfect versions too, while the infinite laws, the laws of the Law, the great circling truths whose only adequate symbol is the material laws, the astronomy, etc., are all unobserved, and sneered at when spoken of, as frigid and insufficient. I call Calvinism such an imperfect version of the moral law. Unitarianism is another, and every form of Christian and of Pagan faith in the hands of incapable teachers is such a version. On the contrary, in the hands of a true Teacher, the falsehoods, the pitifulnesses, the sectarianisms of each are dropped, and the sublimity and the depth of the Original is penetrated and exhibited to men. I say also that all that recommends each of these established systems of opinion to men is so much of this Moral Truth as is in them, and by the instructive selection of the preacher is made to shine forth when the system is assailed.

And because of this One Bottom it is that the eminent men of each church, Socrates, À Kempis, Fénelon, Butler, Penn, Swedenborg, Channing, think and say the same thing.

But the men of Europe will say, Expound; let us hear what it is that is to convince the faithful and at the same time the philosopher? Let us hear this new thing. It is very old. It is the old revelation, that perfect beauty is perfect goodness, it is the development of the wonderful congruities of the moral law of human nature. Let me enumerate a few of the remarkable properties of that nature. A man contains all that is needful to his government within himself. He is made a law unto himself. All real good or evil that can befal him must be from himself. He only can do himself any good or any harm. Nothing can be given to him or taken from him but always there is a compensation. There is a correspondence between the human soul and everything that exists in the world; more properly, everything that is known to man. Instead of studying things without the principles of them, all may be penetrated unto within him. Every act puts the agent in a new condition. The purpose of life seems to be to acquaint a man with himself. He is not to live to the future as described to him, but to live to the real future by living to the real present. The highest revelation is that God is in every man.

(From separate notes)

Monday, *September* 9.

The road from Liverpool to New York, as they who have travelled it well know, is very long, crooked, rough, and eminently disagreeable. Good company even, Heaven's best gift, will scarce make it tolerable. Four meals a day is the usual expedient (and the wretchedness of the expedient will show the extremity of the case) and much wine and porter,— these are the amusements of wise men in this sad place. The purest wit may have a scurvy stomach.

The letter-bag is our captain's best passenger. He neither eats nor drinks, and yet pays, at

least in Liverpool, a passenger's fare. Captain
Hoxie tells me that he usually carries between
4000 and 5000 letters each way. At the New
York Post Office they count his letters and
pay him two cents for every one. At Liverpool two pence. The last time he received in
Liverpool £39 for them.

Fraser's Magazine states that Lord Claren-
don wrote a sketch of the life of Charles Cotton, father of Charles Cotton, doubtless the
translator of Montaigne. I have never seen it.

(From Q)

LIVERPOOL, *September* 10.

I have heard the proverb that there is no
evil but can speak. Especially in these days
when every sentiment and every class of opinions and interests has its organ and voice, is
there no evil but speaks. Also consider that
every week Europe sends this voice of all its
opinions and interests by its periodical press or
occasional works into America; it follows that
one can better know what transpires there by
reading here (with more accuracy and in a
shorter time) than by the slow and partial
method of personal observation in travelling.
It seems to argue great simplicity then for a

traveller to undertake to inform us upon Europe because he has seen it. So it would. You have learned more by contenting yourself with this abbreviated tabulated method. I will then say what I have to say, merely in confirmation of your results, and by no means pretending to state new views or theories.

The whole creation groaneth until now, waiting for that which shall be revealed.

Loud winds last night, but the ship swam like a waterfowl betwixt the mountains of sea. The wise man in the storm prays God, not for safety from danger, but for deliverance from fear. It is the storm within which endangers him, not the storm without. But it is a queer place to make one's bed in, the hollows of this immense Atlantic; Mazeppa-like we are tied to the side of these wild horses of the Northwest. But this rough breath of Heaven will blow me home at last, as once it blew me to Gibraltar. The powerful trumpet of the blast finds a response to all its stops in the bottom of the heart of the men in the cabin.

(From separate notes)

Friday, *September* 13.

The sea to us is but a lasting storm. How it blows, how it rocks! My sides are sore with

rolling in my berth. The coverlet is not wide
enough that a man should wrap himself in it.
It is only strange that with such a sea and wind
and rain, such wild, distressful, noisy nights, no
harm should befal us. We have torn a sail and
lost a hencoop and its inmates, but the bulwarks are firm, and I often hear of the sea
breaking the bulwarks of ships. Captain Fox,
who went in 14 days from Liverpool to Boston,
slept in the cable tier to keep the mate from
taking in sail. Running in for Boston Harbor
it was very misty and the passengers besought
him to lay to, in vain. Presently the man before
cried, "A sail!" "Pooh!" said Captain Fox,
"'t is the lighthouse; starboard helm!" It was
the light, and he ran round it and came to anchor within the bay.

What a machine is a ship, changing so fast
from the state of a butterfly, all wing, to the
shape of a log, all spar.

Poor Ireland! They told a story of an Irish
boy at school asking a holiday to go to the
market town. "What to go for?" "To see
Uncle hanged."

Monday, 16.

Gale and calm, pitch and rock, merrily swim
we, the sun shines bright. The mate says they

took up, about where we are now, a year ago, the crew of the Leonidas, a Portland vessel loaded with salt, which sprang a leak. The Captain would not leave the ship, after putting quadrant and compass and his own things in a boat, and saw the boat leave the ship. One of this line of packets struck an island of ice, and the whole company with 35 passengers escaped in the boat.

Dull stormy day yesterday. I kept Sunday with Milton, and a Presbyterian magazine. Milton says, if ever any was ravished with moral beauty, he is the man.

It occurred with sad force how much we are bound to be true to ourselves (the old string) because we are always judged by others as *ourselves*, and not as those whose example we would plead. A. reads in a book the praise of a wise man who could unbend and make merry, and so he tosses off his glass whilst round him are malicious eyes watching his guzzling and fat eating. The truth is, you can't find any example that will suit you, nor could, if the whole family of Adam should pass in procession before you, for you are a new work of God.

"Time and the hour wear through the roughest day."

[IMPROVISATIONS]

(From a Verse book)

America, my country, can the mind
Embrace in its affections realms so vast
(Unpeopled, yet the land of men to be)
As the great oceans that wash thee enclose?
'T is an ambitious charity that makes
Its arms meet round —
And yet, the sages say, the preference
Of our own cabin to a stranger's wealth,
The insidious love and hate that curls the lip
Of the frank Yankee in the tenements
Of ducal and of royal rank abroad,
His supercilious ignorance
Of heraldry and ceremony,
And his tenacious recollection
Amid the coloured treasuries of art
That circle the Louvre or the Pitti house, —
Tuscany's unrivalled boast, —
Of the brave steamboats of New York,
The Boston Common, and the Hadley farms
Washed by Connecticut;
Yea, if the ruddy Englishman speak true,
Of the vast Roman church, and underneath
The frescoed sky of its majestic dome,
The American will count the cost
And build the shrine with dollars in his head;
And all he asks, arrived in Italy,

Has the star-bearing squadron left Leghorn?
Land without history, land lying all
In the plain daylight of the temperate zone,
　　　　Thy plain acts
Without exaggeration done in day;
Thy interests contested by their manifest good sense,
In their own clothes without the ornament
Of bannered army harnessed in uniform.
Land where — and 't is in Europe counted a re-
　　　proach —
Where man asks questions for which man was made.
A land without nobility, or wigs, or debt,
No castles, no cathedrals, and no kings;
Land of the forest. . . .

In this world, if a man sits down to think, he
is immediately asked if he has the headache?

(From Q)

AT SEA. *September* 17.

Yesterday I was asked what I mean by
morals. I reply that I cannot define, and care
not to define. It is man's business to observe, and the definition of moral nature must
be the slow result of years, of lives, of states,
perhaps of being. Yet in the morning watch on
my berth I thought that morals is the science
of the laws of human action as respects right

and wrong. Then I shall be asked, And what is Right? Right is a conformity to the laws of nature as far as they are known to the human mind. These for the occasion, but I propound definitions with more than the reserve of the feeling above-named,—with more, because my own conceptions are so dim and vague. But nevertheless nothing darkens, nothing shakes, nothing diminishes my constant conviction of the eternal concord of these laws which are perfect music, and of which every high sentiment and every great action is only a new statement, and therefore and insomuch speaks aloud to the whole race of man. I conceive of them by no types, but the apparent hollow sphere of the whole firmament wherein this ball of the earth swims. Not easy are they to be enumerated, but he has some idea of them who considers such propositions as St. Bernard's,—Nobody can harm me but myself,—or who developes the doctrine in his own experience that nothing can be given or taken without an equivalent.

Milton describes himself in his letter to Diodati as enamoured of moral perfection. He did not love it more than I. That which I cannot yet declare has been my angel from childhood until now. It has separated me from men. It has watered my pillow, it has driven sleep from my bed. It has tortured me for my guilt. It has inspired me with hope. It cannot be defeated by my defeats. It cannot be questioned, though all the martyrs apostatize. It is always the glory that shall be revealed; it is the "open secret" of the universe; and it is only the feebleness and dust of the observer that makes it future, the whole *is* now potentially in the bottom of his heart. It is the soul of religion. Keeping my eye on this, I understand all heroism, the history of loyalty and of martyrdom and of bigotry, the heat of the Methodist, the nonconformity of the Dissenter, the patience of the Quaker.

But what shall the hour say for distinctions such as these, this hour of southwest gales and rain-dripping cabin? As the law of light is, fits of easy transmission and reflexion, such is also the soul's law. She is only superior at intervals to pain, to fear, to temptation, only in raptures unites herself to God; and Wordsworth truly said, —

"'T is the most difficult of tasks to keep
  Heights which the soul is competent to gain."

What is this they say about wanting mathematical certainty for moral truths. I have always affirmed they had it. Yet they ask me whether I know the soul immortal. No. But do I not know the Now to be eternal?

Is it not a sufficient reply to the red and angry worldling, colouring as he affirms his unbelief, to say, Think on living, I have to do no more than you with that question of another life? I believe in this life. I believe it continues. As long as I am here I plainly read my duties as writ with pencil of fire; they speak not of death. They are woven of immortal thread.

Men seem to be constitutionally believers and unbelievers. There is no bridge that can cross from a mind in one state to a mind in the other. All my opinions, affections, whimsies, are tinged with belief,—incline to that side. All that is generous, elegant, rich, wise, looks that way. But I cannot give reasons to a person of a different persuasion that are at all adequate to the force of my conviction. Yet when I fail to find the reason, my faith is not less.

Unpalatable must be always the argument based upon the text, "If ye do my Father's will, ye shall know of the doctrines," and almost incapable of being used in conversation. It is felt as a gross personality. Yet it is a good topic for the preacher, and a better topic for the closet.

I believe that virtue purges the eye, that the abstinent, meek, benevolent, industrious man is in a better state for the fine influences of the great universe to act upon him than the cold, idle, eating disputant. The rocky, dry, fallow ground says, "I can produce nothing, nothing will grow; yet I see the sun and feel the rain as much as you." "Aye," replies the cornfield, "but they have plucked away my stones and turned up my surface and let in the watercourses, and now the sun and the air, the heat and the snow all serve me."

Is it not singular and not at all unpleasing, the fact that almost all great men have been so yoked together by the accidents of their lives, and few or none stand alone, but all in a genial constellation? John Evelyn gave a pension to Jeremy Taylor. Jeremy Taylor and John Milton both did homage to the same lady, Countess of Carbery, one in his *Dedication*, the other in his *Comus*. Milton and Galileo, Clarke, Butler, and Hume, Cervantes and Shakespear. Sir Henry Wotton was a hoop of gold to what a company! Dante died at Ravenna, 1321; fifty-one years after, Boccaccio was made professor at Florence to lecture upon the Divine Comedy, and in 1351 Boccaccio was sent by the Floren-

tines to Padua to entreat Petrarch to return and
end his days in his native city. These are God's
mnemonics. Newton was born the year Galileo
died. Cuvier, Scott and Mackintosh were born
and died in the same years.

It were a good topic for a sermon, to preach
upon serenity of mind, manners, countenance;
according to the sentiment of some pretty verses
on "Consider the lilies of the field how they
grow," verses contained in *The Pious Minstrel*
and which also have the fine line,

"Christ's blessing at your heart is warm";

and, according to the sentiment of Herbert's
Verses upon Rest, "Study to be quiet."

> I will not hesitate to speak the word
> Committed to me. It is not of men;
> It is not of myself, no vain discourse
> Empty oration, tinkling, soulless talk.
> My heart lies open to the universe,
> I read only what there is writ. I speak
> The sincere word that 's whispered in my ear.
> I am an organ in the mouth of God,
> My prophecy the music of his lips.
> Tho' harsh in evil ears, 't is harmony
> To patient, wise and faithful hearts whose love
> Coöperates with his

Concord of heaven and earth. Author divine
Of what I am and what I say, vouchsafe
To cleanse me, that my folly may not hide
Thy truth, nor my infirmity disguise
The omnipotence that animates my clay.
Thou, Lord, dost clothe thy attributes with flesh,
And named it man, a morning spectacle
Unto the universe exhibiting,
A manifold and mystic lesson.

(From separate notes)

Sunday, *September* 22.

Gales and headwinds producing all the variety of discomfort and ennui in the cabin. We try in vain to keep bright faces and pleasant occupation below, heedless of the roar of the tempest above. We are too nearly interested in every rope that snaps and every spar that cracks overhead, to hear the ruin with philosophy. We may keep our eyes on the Cicero or Addison in our hands, but that noise touches our life. I would I were in the bushes at Canterbury,[1] for my part. Yesterday was too fine a day to lose at sea. Calm shining after the wild storm of two preceding days. This time I have not drawn the golden lot of company, and yet far better than the last voyage. But that little one to Charleston

[1] The home in Roxbury during school-keeping days.

from St. Augustine with Murat was worth all the rest. Yet thanks to the good God, who leads and protects me, for the measure of comfort and intellectual occupation that is possible in the valleys of the sea by means of this wonderful *chef d'œuvre* of human art, the ship. Sad for the steerage passengers; old women and children sitting up all night or lying in wet berths. The poor cow refuses to get up and be milked, and four dogs on board shiver and totter about all day, and bark when we ship a sea.

September 25.

It was a good jest which a passenger quoted from a sea-song in which two sailors in a storm at sea express their pity for the poor landsmen : —

> " My eyes ! what tiles and chimney pots
> About their heads are flying,
> Whilst you and I upon the deck
> Are comfortably lying."

It is like the being thankful for the board blanket.[1] What a gale that was on the night of the 19th ! The second mate says that if an

1 A story of which Mr. Emerson was fond, of a widow so poor that she eked out the thin blanket by laying an old door over herself and her little children. One of these piped up, " Mamma, what do those poor little children do who have n't got a door to cover them ? "

18-pounder had been fired on deck it could not have been heard aloft, and the only way he got the captain's orders was by putting his ear to his mouth.

Dear Brother [1] would you know,
Sitting under a gold September sun,
How we plough the Atlantic wave
Under the stars and under the clouds,
With swimming deck and singing shrouds,
Climbing the steep slope of the cabin floor,
Or peeping timid into the rain
Out of the round-house door?
Shall I not tell you, to kill the time,
How we spend the day?
Dull the bard, and sad the lay.
Uneasy rolls the ship,
Uneven runs the rhyme.
Dimly the morning breaks
Upon the skylight of my berth,
Where I had dreamed myself at peace,
My feet upon my Maker's earth.
But the Muse doth refuse
To recollect these trumpery cares, —
The waking bell, that tragic knell
That calls us back to recognition
Of our deplorable condition.

1 This letter in verse was probably sent to Edward at Porto Rico.

Out we come, unshaven faces,
And with what look forlorn
Pass the greetings of the morn
Each to the other in the well-known places.
We climb the gangway, walk the deck,
Survey the wide horizon round —
There's not a sail, there's not a wreck,
There's not a wreck, there's not a sail,
Nor land, nor waterspout, nor whale:
The only living thing,
Sometimes a gull with snowy wing.
A shoal of porpoises come wheeling
Across the bows thro' the grey waves,
Or Mother Carey's chickens, stealing
On wings that never rest their forlorn food.
Poor little wanderers, outcasts of nature,
Where have you been in the drowning storm?
Here is no bush to hide you from whirlwinds,
Here is no perch to rest your little footies,
Going alway
By night and by day,
Under starlight, under clouds,
With swimming deck and singing shrouds.
I have read what Shakespeare wrote
Of bloated Falstaff, royal Lear.
There is a dulness proper to great wit,
And Jonson hath his ample share of it.
It needs much skill to write so dull a piece,
Draw learned faults from Italy and Greece —

Beautiful songs Ben Jonson can write, and his vocabulary is so rich, and when he pleases, so smooth, that he seems to be prosing with a design to relieve and display better the bright parts of the piece. Then he shows himself master of the higher, the moral taste, and enriches himself occasionally with those unquestionable gems which none but the sons of God possess. Strange that among his actors, and not the first, is Will Shakspeare. He never was dull to relieve his brilliant parts. He is all light, sometimes terrestrial, sometimes celestial, but all light.

"Take away that empty marine," said the Duke of York. "What do you mean, sir?" said an officer of marines. "I mean that fellow who has done his duty and is ready to do it again," replied the Duke.

"O, c'est grande! magnifique! dat is, vat you call pretty well," said Monsieur, arrived in London.

Thursday, September 26. Long. 49, lat. 44.
On the Banks; found bottom at 49 fathoms, and fished in vain with 70 fathoms of line. Saw a fishing schooner. They fish from June to

October. It may take two months to get full and they bring home 20,000 or 25,000 fish. The colour of the water has changed, the birds fly about and we have fogs. Yesterday a little petrel caught in the end of a rope and was drowned; web-footed, a pretty bird with a white belt upon the tail.

September 29.

Storm, storm, storm, but only this can show the virtues of the ship, which behaves well and carries these tender bodies tucked up in boxes along its side without injuring a hair through these wild, cold, savage waters. Strange that anybody who has hands to work should be willing to spend two months on that Bank exposed to such storms as yesterday's. " That fellow has got a bleak place," said the Captain.

Much indebted to Mr. H.'s conversation. Story of the Duc de Bourdeaux, infant son of the Duc de Berri, being carried to Louis XVIII. "*Le roi pue.*" " *L'enfant a raison; ôtez l'enfant.*"

Qui pius est, summe philosophatur. I notice that we always judge of the length of the passage by the weather of the present moment.

Friday, *October* 4. Long. 67, *je crois.*

Our month expires to-day, and therefore 't is time to look for land. The poor Malay saith to the wind in his petulance, " Blow, me do tell you blow," but not of that mind are we, but contrariwise, very glad of this fine weather. Captain's merry account of his capture by pirates in South America in 1822 when they cut up his sails for trousers and ripped off the copper sheathing of the vessel for French horns and appointed him fifer. He played in that capacity the dead march of two priests, whom the worthy lieutenant general shot for smuggling.

" Chap from Wiggin, Manchester man, and a gentleman from Liverpool," said Coachey. Sea of all colours. To-day indigo, yesterday grass green, and day before grey.

October 8.

My God, who dost animate and uphold us always on the sea and on land, in the fields, in cities, and in lonely places, in our homes, and among strangers, I thank thee that thou hast enlightened and comforted and protected me to this hour. Continue to me thy guard and blessing. May I resist the evil that is without by the good that is within. May I rejoice evermore in the consciousness that it is by thee I live. May I rejoice in the Divine Power, and be humble. Oh that I might show forth thy gift to me by purity, by love, by unshrinking industry and unsinking hope, and by unconquerable courage. May I be more thine, and so more truly myself every day I live.

[Mr. Emerson landed in New York, October 9, and went by stage to Boston, thence to Newton Upper Falls where his mother was living for the time, probably on the farm of Mr. Ladd, who had married the sister of Mr. Emerson's father.]

(From Q)

NEWTOWNE, *October* 20.

A Sabbath in the country, but not so odoriferous as I have imagined. Mr. B., a plain serious Calvinist, not winning, but not repelling : one of the useful police which God makes out of the ignorance and superstition of the youth of the world. I dare not and wish not to speak disrespectfully of these good, abstemious, laborious men, yet I could not help asking myself how long is the society to be taught in this dramatic or allegorical style? When is religious truth to be distinctly uttered, what it is, not what it resembles? Thus every Sunday ever since they were born this congregation have heard tell of *salvation*, and of going to the door of Heaven and knocking, and being answered from within, " Depart, I never knew you," and of being sent away to eternal ruin. What hinders that, instead of this parable, the naked fact be stated to them? namely that as long [as] they offend against their conscience they will seek to be happy, but they shall not be able, they shall not come to any true knowledge of God, they shall be avoided by good and wise men, they shall become worse and worse.

God defend me from ever looking at a man as an animal. God defend me from the vice of my constitution, an excessive desire of sympathy. Let me be content with the consciousness of innocency and the desire of worth, without stretching myself upon the rack whenever any man, woman, or child passes by until he, she or it is possessed of my intention. The nine solids.

An impulse as irresistible as is the acorn to germinate is in the soul of the prophet to speak.

Mr. Blanchard said that labor had kept him well eleven years at the desk.

October 21.

I am sure of this, that by going much alone a man will get more of a noble courage in thought and word than from all the wisdom that is in books. He will come to hear God speak as audibly through his own lips as ever He did by the mouth of Moses or Isaiah or Milton. "For Nature never did betray the heart that loved her." Such revelations as were made to George Fox or Emanuel Swedenborg are only made in the woods or in the closet. They were no common madmen. They wanted but little, or, if you please, they exceeded but little, of being true prophets.

E. B. E.[1] quotes from St. Pierre the saying that "when the chain is put upon a slave, the other end is rivetted around the neck of the master," and sanctions warmly the observation.

When a man goes into the woods he feels like a boy without loss of wisdom. To be sure a dandy may go there, and Nature will never speak to a dandy.

It seems to me that the perspective of time, as it sets everything in the right point of view, does

[1] His brother.

the same by Christianity. We learn to look at it now as a part of the history of the world, to see how it rests in the broad basis of man's moral nature, and is not itself that basis. I cannot but think that Jesus Christ will be better loved by being less adored. He has had an unnatural, an artificial place for ages in human opinions — a place too high for love. There is a recoil of the affections from all authority and force. To the barbarous state of society it was thought to add to the dignity of Christ to make him king, to make him God. Now that the scriptures are read with purged eyes, it is seen that he is only to be loved for so much goodness and wisdom as was in him, which are the only things for which a sound human mind can love any person. As the world waxes wiser, he will be more truly venerated for the splendor of the contrast of his character to the opinions and practices of his age, he will attract the unfeigned love of all to whom moral nature is dear because he planted himself in the face of the world upon that sole ground, showing that noble confidence in the reality and superiority of spiritual truths, that simplicity and at the same time enthusiasm in declaring them which is itself one of the highest merits and gives confidence to all thinkers that come after.

But will not this come to be thought the chief value of his teaching, that is, of Christianity, to wit, that it was a great stand made for man's spiritual nature against the sensualism, the forms, and the crimes of the age in which he appeared and those that preceded it? Like every wise and efficient man, he spoke to the [men of] his times in all their singular peculiarities. His instruction is almost as local, as personal, as would be the teaching in one of our Sunday Schools. He speaks as he thinks, but he is thinking for them. Yet such is the extraordinary truth of his mind that his sentences have a fulness of meaning, a fitness to human nature, and an universality of application, that has commended them to the whole world.

They must be looked upon as one affirmation, proclamation glorious of moral truth, but not as the last affirmation. There shall be a thousand more. Very inconsistent would it be with a soul so possessed of this love as his to set bounds to that illimitable ocean. None knew better than he that every soul occupies a new position, and that if the stars cannot be counted, nor the sands of the sea, neither can those moral truths be numbered and ended of which the material creation is only the shadow.

NEWTON, *October* 24.

The teacher of the coming age must occupy himself in the study and explanation of the moral constitution of man more than in the elucidation of difficult texts. He must work in the conviction that the scriptures can only be interpreted by the same spirit that uttered them. And that as long as the heart and the mind are illumined by a spiritual life, there is no dead letter, but a perpetual scripture.

I expect everything good and auspicious from the studies and the actings of good men in the course this thought shall guide them. It will be inspiration to prophet and to heroes. It will bring the heavens near and show a calm sky always overhead.

[*October*]¹ 31.

Sir J. Mackintosh has well said that every picture, statue, poem is an experiment on the human mind. And if such slight and transient things often produce in us deepest results, if a paragraph of a newspaper or an eloquent word touch us so to the quick, as now they often do, what may we not expect from a familiar and full comprehension of the amazing discoveries that the naturalists of this day have made, from

1 " 31 November " in Journal, by mistake.

the wonderful application of polarized light to the discovery of periodical colours in refrangible substances, and so to the uncovering of nature's primary forms in the secret architecture of bodies, or the great, long-expected discovery of the identity of electricity and magnetism lately completed by Dr. Faraday's obtaining the spark from the magnet, and the opening almost a door to the secret mechanism of life and sensation in the relation of the pile of Volta to the electrical fish.

November 2.

Bacon said man is the minister and interpreter of nature : he is so in more respects than one. He is not only to explain the sense of each passage, but the scope and argument of the whole book. He is to explain the attractiveness of all.

There is more beauty in the morning cloud than the prism can render account of. There is something in it that resembles the aspects of mortal life, its epochs and its fate. There is not a passage in the human soul, perhaps not a shade of thought, but has its emblem in nature. And this does not become fainter, this undersong, this concurrent text, with more intimate knowledge of nature's laws, but the analogy is felt to be deeper and more universal for every law that is revealed. It almost seems as if an unknown intelligence in us expressed its recognition of each new disclosure.

Let a man under the influence of strong passion go into the fields, and see how readily every thought clothes itself with a material garment. (Is it not illustration to us of the manner in which every spirit clothes itself with body?) Now I say, is it not time that something was done to explain this attractiveness which the face of Nature has for us, — renewed this 2d day of November of the 6000th year of the world, as it has been every day of the 6000 years, — to the reality of which every age has testified?

Nature is a language, and every new fact that we learn is a new word; but rightly seen, taken all together, it is not merely a language, but the language put together into a most significant and universal book. I wish to learn the language, not that I may learn a new set of nouns and verbs, but that I may read the great book which is written in that tongue.

The glutton wrote for his epitaph: —

" What I have eat is mine; in words my will
    I 've had, and of my lust have ta'en my fill."

Crates, the philosopher, altered it for himself:

" What I have learned is mine, I 've had my thought,
    And me the Muses noble Truths have taught."

To an instructed eye the universe is transparent. The light of higher laws than its own shines through it.

NEW BEDFORD, *November* 19.

Stubler said the difference between Brother Witherlee's preaching and his was this : Brother W. said, " If you do not become good you shall be whipt," and himself said, " If you will become good, you shall not be whipt." [1]

Wrote to Charles yesterday of the amount of meaning in life : *dum tacet, clamat*. He would feel it, if he should suppose Shakspear should go with him to Mr. Peabody's or Aunt Cook's. If a susceptible man should lay bare his heart, it would show theories of life, thoughts of unutterable tenderness, and visions of beauty that were suggested from the most seemingly inadequate and mean occasions, from hearing an unwashed boy spell or cipher in his class, or

1 Stubler, the Quaker, has been already mentioned in the Journals, a serious-minded man whom Mr. Emerson met in travelling.

seeing the blush upon the cheek of a school-
girl, or watching the transmission of the candle-
light through his closed fingers, or listening
long to the sound made by tinkling a glass tumbler or touching the key of a piano. Is it not
true that no persons meet, of what inequality
soever, but a quick apprehension can straightway bridge over the distance between them and
see how they may stand in most strict and amiable relations?

[QUAKER CONVERSATIONS][1]

"Thomas, I know what thee is thinking of."
"If you do, Micah, you don't feel flattered."

"Mary, it has been revealed to me that I
should marry thee." "Abner, when it is revealed to me I will tell thee."

"William, I am sent to tell thee thou hast a
divided heart."

(From Note-book)

I much regret that in all my sauntering in
London streets, where I suppose I felt much
like an English boy on his first visit from the

1 Mr. Emerson in the autumn accepted an invitation to
preach in Dr. Dewey's church in New Bedford. He made
pleasant acquaintances among the more liberal Quakers there,
from whom he heard these anecdotes.

country, — the names were so familiar and the things so new, yet tallying so well with their pictures, — I did not chance upon Great Cheyne Row, Chelsea, for I should gladly know all, even to the peach-coloured doublet. The bounds of friendship, where are they? The good soul meekly defies all the angels to strip it of its state and reputation, and can even make the pure beam permeate the meanness of man's state and behold it as a god, put gentle charitable hands under the faults, as separate as is every loathed symptom of a diseased friend from the friend. It transmutes blood to ichor and transubstantiates flesh. . . . Will God grant me your society, fear not that I am to eat up your time. You shall make your own laws and, idler as I am, I have mine. I feel assured that though I am searching in a mine not quickly exhausted, — say boldly, *inexhaustible*, for though talent is finite, character is not, and who has that great spiritual force from God, which we denominate character, is endless study, surprise, solace and support, — I do not know seven in the world.

"It is not permitted to a man to corrupt himself for the sake of mankind." ROUSSEAU.

"Who is discreet is seldom betrayed." BUL-
WER.

"Character is the only rank. Principle is a
passion for truth." HAZLITT.

The old jail in Cambridge was immediately
back of Mrs. Kneeland's house. The inmates
of the prison were very bad neighbors and used
to take delight in pestering Mrs. Kneeland with
foul names and profane language. Professor
Hedge took great pains to get the nuisance removed, and at last the old jail was pulled down.
Someone congratulated Mrs. K. upon the
happy deliverance, but found her quite sad at
the loss of her stimulus. "She kind o' missed
'em," she said.

Wise moments are years, and light the coun-
tenance ever. They are the good moments.
They do not belong to genius, but to man.
They refuse to be recorded.

The suicide is beside himself, yet is his act no
more unreasonable than the thief's or the fop's.

Old tree in the Common, circumference
twenty-four feet at base; 17 at 6 feet from
ground.

I will not refer, defer, confer, prefer, differ. I renounce the whole family of *fero*.[1] I embrace absolute life.

I nor you can feel the chain that draws us together. Perhaps continents, tongues, ages intervene, a prejudice may be an age, and yet all be nothing against that strong sympathy.

(From "A")

Tuesday, *December* 10.

Took possession of my chamber at Mr. Pelletier's.[2]

Boston, *December* 11.

The call of our calling is the loudest call. There are so many worthless lives, apparently, that to advance a good cause by telling one anecdote or doing one great act, seems a worthy reason for living. When a poor man thanked Richard Rey-

1 In a lecture called "Art and Criticism," given by Mr. Emerson in a course in Boston in 1859, a portion of which is printed for the first time in the Centenary Edition of *Natural History of Intellect,* he bids young writers "Beware of the whole family of *Fero*" (including of course its participle *latus*) perhaps because "choose," "give way," "gather," "bring together," and "remove," are less pedantic than "prefer," "defer," "infer," "collate," and "translate."

2 Probably in Boston.

nolds for his goodness, he said, " Do you thank
the clouds for rain ? " The elder Scipio said, he
had given his enemies as much cause to speak
well of him as his friends. Fontenelle said, " I
am a Frenchman, I am sixty years old, and
I never have treated the smallest virtue with
the smallest ridicule."

December 14.

I please myself with contemplating the felicity
of my present situation. May it last. It seems to
me singularly free, and it invites me to every
virtue and to great improvement.

" In being silent, and hoping, consisteth our
strength," — so Luther quotes Isaiah.

For every gift of noble origin
Is breathed upon by hope's perpetual breath.

WORDSWORTH.

Alexander gave away the Conquered Prov-
inces, — "And what have you left for yourself ?"
" Hope," replied the hero. " How do the wise
differ from the unwise ? " was the question put
to Bias. He replied, "In a good hope." It is the
true heroism and the true wisdom, Hope. The
wise are always cheerful. The reason is (and it
is a blessed reason), that the eye sees that the

ultimate issues of all things are good. There is always a presumption in favor of a cheerful view.

[Here follow some notes on hints taken by engineers and architects from Nature, printed in " Art," *Society and Solitude*.]

(From small Note-book)

My children, said my Grandfather,[1] you will never see anything worse than yourselves. Why can we find a spiritual meaning in every natural fact?

The young bee, up to the time he leaves the hive, has never seen light. Yet he launches at once into the air, flies far from home, wanders to many flowers, yet comes back with unerring certainty to the hive. Who pilots him?

(From "A")

December 19.

The moral of your piece should be cuneiform and not polygonal. Judge of the success of the piece by the exclusive prominence it gives to the subject in the minds of all the audience.

1 William Emerson, Minister of Concord, or his father, Reverend Joseph of Malden, or possibly John Haskins of Boston.

[The following, probably written in 1833, are from a smaller note-book.]

The *first* Philosophy, that of mind, is the science of what *is*, in distinction from what *appears*. It is one mark of its laws that their enunciation awakens the feeling of the moral sublime, and *great men* are they who believe in them. They resemble great circles in astronomy, each of which, in what direction soever it be drawn, contains the whole sphere. So each of these seems to imply all truth. These laws are Ideas of the Reason, and so are obeyed easier than expressed. They astonish the Understanding, and seem to it gleams of a world in which we do not live.

Our compound nature differences us from God, but our Reason is not to be distinguished from the divine Essence. We have yet devised no words to designate the attributes of God which can adequately stand for the universality and perfection of our own intuitions. To call the Reason "ours" or "Human" seems an impertinence, so absolute and unconfined it is. The best we can say of God, we mean of the mind as it is known to us. Thus when you say,

" The gods approve
The depth, but not the tumult of the soul
(A fervent, not ungovernable love),"

the sublime in the sentiment is, that to the soul itself depth, not tumult, is desirable. When you say (Socrates said it), " Jupiter prefers integrity to charity," your finest meaning is the "soul prefers," etc. When Jesus saith, " Who giveth one of these little ones a cup of cold water shall not lose his reward," is not the best meaning the love at which the giver has arrived? And so on throughout the New Testament there is not a volition attributed to God considered as an external cause but gains in truth and dignity by being referred to the soul.

Reason, seeing in objects their remote effects, affirms the effect as the permanent character. The Understanding, listening to Reason, on the one side, which says *It is*, and to the senses on the other side, which say *It is not*, takes middle ground and declares *It will be*. Heaven is the projection of the Ideas of Reason on the plane of the understanding.

Jesus Christ was a minister of the pure Reason. The beatitudes of the Sermon on the Mount are all utterances of the mind contemning the phenomenal world. " Blessed are the righteous poor, for theirs is the kingdom of heaven. Blessed are ye when men revile you," etc. The Understanding can make nothing of it. 'T is all nonsense. The Reason affirms its absolute verity.

Various terms are employed to indicate the counteraction of the Reason and the Understanding, with more or less precision, according to the cultivation of the speaker. A clear perception of it is the key to all theology, and a theory of human life. St. Paul marks the distinction by the terms natural man and spiritual man.

When Novalis says, " It is the instinct of the understanding to counteract the Reason," he only translates into a scientific formula the sentence of St. Paul " The Carnal mind is enmity against God."

The mind is very wise, could it be roused into action. But the life of most men is aptly signified by the poet's personification, " Death in Life." We walk about in a sleep. A few moments in the year, or in our lifetime, we truly live; we are at the top of our being; we are pervaded, yea, dissolved by the Mind ; but we fall back again presently. Those who are styled Practical Men are not awake, for they do not exercise the Reason ; yet their sleep is restless. The most active lives have so much routine as to pre-

clude progress almost equally with the most inactive. We bow low to the noted merchants whose
influence is felt, not only in their native cities,
but in most parts of the globe; but our respect
does them and ourselves great injustice, for their
trade is without system, their affairs unfold themselves after no law of the mind, but are bubble
built on bubble without end; a work of arithmetic, not of commerce, much less of humanity.
They add voyage to voyage, and buy stocks,—
that they may buy stocks,—and no ulterior purpose is thought of. When you see their dexterity in particulars, you cannot overestimate the
resources of good sense; and when you find how
empty they are of all remote aims, you cannot
underestimate their philosophy.

The man of letters puts the same cheat upon
us, bestirring himself immensely to keep the
secret of his littleness. He spins his most seeming surface directly before the eye, to conceal the
universe of his ignorance. To what end his languages, his correspondence, his academic dis-
courses, his printed volumes? Newton said that
if this porous world were made solid, *it would
lie in a nutshell.*

All our writings are variations of one air. Books
for the most part are such expedients as his who

makes an errand for the sake of exercise. And
for the sincere great men the wisest passages they
have writ, the infinite conclusions to which they
owe their fame, are only confessions. Throughout their works, the good ear hears the undersong of confession and amazement, the apothegm
of Socrates, the recantation of man.

Such is the inaction of men. We have an obscure consciousness of our attributes. We stand
on the edge of all that is great, yet are restrained
in inactivity and unconscious of our powers, like
neuters of the hive, every one of which is capable of transformation into the Queen bee. We
are always on the brink, etc.

Much preparation, little fruit. But suddenly
in any place, in the street, in the chamber, will
the heavens open and the regions of wisdom be
uncovered, as if to show how thin the veil, how
null the circumstances. As quickly, a Lethean
stream washes through us and bereaves us of
ourselves.

*What a benefit if a rule could be given whereby
the mind, dreaming amid the gross fogs of matter,
could at any moment* CAST ITSELF *and* FIND THE
SUN! But the common life is an endless succession of phantasms; and long after we have

deemed ourselves recovered and sound, light breaks in upon us and we find we have yet had no sane hour. Another morn rises on mid-noon.

LEGENDA

Article, "Croker's Boswell's Johnson," in *Edinburgh Review*.

Essays on Pursuit of Truth.

Hazlitt's *Essays on Principles of Human Action*.

Hobbes' *Treatise on Human Nature*.

Hume's *Dissertation on the Passions;* and *Enquiry*.

Shaftesbury's *Enquiry*.

Sir Charles Bell's *Animal Mechanics*.

Sir Samuel Romilly's article on "Codification."

Hartley.

Tucker's chapter on "Pleasure," and Paley's on "Happiness."

Cousin's [Translation of] *Tennemann*.

Turner's *Elements of Chemistry*. Affinity.

AUTHORS OR BOOKS QUOTED OR REFERRED TO IN JOURNAL OF 1833

Homer; Cicero;

Petrarch; Montaigne;

Sir Henry Wotton; George Herbert, *Verses upon Rest;*

Milton, *Lycidas, Letter to Diodati* ; Jeremy Taylor ;

Dampier, *Voyage round the World, apud Early English Navigators;*

Addison ; Bossuet ; Voltaire ; Johnson, *apud* Boswell ;

Abela, *Melita Illustrata;* Goldoni, *Scelta di;* Rousseau ; Gibbon ;

Alfieri ; Goethe, *Travels in Italy, Wilhelm Meister;* Herschel ; Sismondi, *La Littérature du Midi de l'Europe;* Byron, *Childe Harold;* Scott, *Marmion, Rob Roy, Heart of Midlothian;*

Wordsworth ; Hazlitt ; Mackintosh ;

Manzoni, *I Promessi Sposi;*

Andrews Norton ; *A Statement of Reasons for not believing the Doctrines of Trinitarians concerning the Nature of God and the Person of Christ.*

Carlyle, *Sartor Resartus* and various articles in English and Scotch Reviews.

Bulwer.

JOURNAL

NEWTON

LECTURES IN BOSTON

PREACHING AT NEW BEDFORD
AND PLYMOUTH

THE OLD MANSE, CONCORD

JOURNAL XXV

1834

(From Journal A)

Not of men, neither by man.

"May I consult the auguries of time,
    And through the human heart explore my way,
    And look and listen."

"Ch' apporta mane, e lascia sera." [1]

[So far as the headquarters of the Emerson family could be determined by the presence of Madam Emerson, it might have been considered at the farm of their kinswoman Mrs. Ladd, near Newton Upper Falls. Charles may have been there too, but more probably at the Manse in Concord, as then, or soon after, he was studying law in the office of that fine old Roman, Samuel Hoar. Waldo came and went, for dur-

1 It was Mr. Emerson's custom after this time to write one or more mottoes at the beginning of each journal.

ing most of the winter he was filling the pulpit of his kinsman, the Rev. Orville Dewey, in New Bedford, occasionally preaching in Plymouth, where he made the acquaintance of Miss Lydia[1] Jackson, a lady slightly older than himself, whose spiritual mind, refined character and distinguished bearing caused her to be regarded almost as a lady-abbess among her generation and the younger people there. The next year she became his wife. . In New Bedford Mr. Emerson made many friends among the liberal Quakers.

In January he delivered a lecture at the Athenæum in Boston before the Mechanics' Institute. The subject was "Water," very freely treated, after his wont. Later in the winter he gave two lectures on Italy, in Boston, and, in May, one called "Naturalist" at the annual meeting of the Boston Natural History Society.]

This Book is my Savings Bank. I grow richer because I have somewhere to deposit my earnings; and fractions are worth more to me because corresponding fractions are waiting here that shall be made integers by their addition.

1 After her marriage, at Mr. Emerson's request, she changed her name to Lidian.

January 2, 1834.

The year, the year, but I have no thought for time. It occurs that a selection of natural laws might be easily made from botany, hydraulics, natural philosophy, etc., which should at once express also an ethical sense. Thus, 'water confined in pipes will always rise as high as its source.' 'A hair line of water is a balance for the ocean if its fount be as high.' 'Durable trees make roots first,' Charles reads. 'A cripple in the right road beats a racer in the wrong road.' 'Fractures well cured make us more strong.' 'Action and reaction are equal.' Concentrated nourishment is unhealthy ; there must be mixture of excrement.

January 3.

To Goethe there was no trifle. Glauber picked up what everybody else threw away. Cuvier made much of humblest facts. The lower tone you take, the more flexible your voice is. The whole landscape is beautiful, though the particulars are not. 'You never are tired whilst you can see far.'

There is no weakness, no exposure, for which we cannot find consolation in the thought,— Well, 't is a part of my constitution, part of my relation and office to my fellow creature. I like to see the immense resources of the creature.

January 5.

"Newton," says Fourier, "knew not yet the perfections of the universe." "What La Place called great was really great." I read in Herbert a beautiful verse, a high example of what the rhetorician calls the moral sublime:—

"Ah, my dear God! though I am clean forgot,
   Let me not love thee, if I love thee not."

January 12.

I was well pleased with Dr. Bradford's view of judgment the other day.[1] Particular men are designated as persons of good judgment. It is merely that they are persons of experience in such affairs as interest most men. Their opinion on any question where they have not experience is worthless. Men of good sense act in certain conjunctures in a most imbecile manner. It is because it is their first trial. Others act with decision and success. It is because they have made many trials before, and of course got through their failures. Then some men reserve their opinion, and so never speak foolishly. Others publish

1 Dr. Gamaliel Bradford of Boston, brother to Mrs. Ripley and Mr. George P. Bradford.

every opinion they hold, and so, though the first thoughts of all were equally ineffectual and foolish, yet the abstemious have the credit of forming sound opinions the first time, and the prompt speakers, if of active and advancing minds, are always uttering absurdities.

January 19.

What is it that interests us in biography? Is there not always a silent comparison between the intellectual and moral endowments portrayed, and those of which we are conscious? The reason why the Luther, the Newton, the Bonaparte, concerning whom we read, was made the subject of panegyric, is, that in the writer's opinion, in some one respect this particular man represented the idea of Man. And as far as we accord with his judgment, we take the picture for a Standard Man, and so let every line accuse or approve our own ways of thinking and living by comparison. At least I thought thus in reading Jeffrey's fine sketch of Playfair the other evening.

January 21.

Is not the use of society to educate the Will, which never would acquire force in solitude? We mean Will, when we say that a person has a good deal of character. Women generally have weak wills, sharply expressed perhaps, but capricious, unstable. When the will is strong, we inevitably respect it in man or woman. I have thought that the perfection of female character seldom existed in poverty, at least where poverty was reckoned low. Is not this because the rich are accustomed to be obeyed promptly, and so the will acquires strength and yet is calm and graceful? I think that involuntary respect which the rich inspire in very independent and virtuous minds, arises from the same circumstance, the irresistible empire of a strong will. There is not nor ever can be any competition between a [will] of words and a real will. Webster, Adams, Clay, Calhoun, Chatham, and every statesman who was ever formidable are wilful men. But Everett and Stanley and the Ciceros are not; want this backbone. Meantime a great many men in society speak strong, but have no oak, are all willow. And only a virtuous will is omnipotent.

(*January* 31. I add that in a former age the men of might were men of will, now the men of wealth.)

January 22.

Luther and Napoleon are better treatises on the Will than Edwards's. Will does not know if it be cold or hot or dangerous, he only goes on to his mark, and leaves to mathematicians to calculate whether a body can come to its place without passing through all the intermediates. "Men have more heart than mind."

Different faces things wear to different persons. Whole process of human generation how bifronted! To one it is bawdry, to another pure. In the mother's heart every sensation, from the nuptial embrace, through the uncertain symptoms of the quickening, to the birth of her child, is watched with an interest more chaste and wistful than the contemplations of the nun in her cloister; yet the low-minded visitor of a woman in such circumstances has the ignorant impertinence to look down and feel a sort of shame.

Akin to the pathetic sublime of the two lines of Herbert on the last leaf, are the lines in the last Canto of *Il Paradiso*, thus translated:—

> "O virgin mother, daughter of thy Son!
> Created beings all in loveliness
> Surpassing, as in height above them all."

January 23.

I cannot read of the jubilee of Goethe, and of such a velvet life, without a sense of incongruity. Genius is out of place when it reposes fifty years on chairs of state, and inhales a continual incense of adulation. Its proper ornaments and relief are poverty and reproach and danger, and if the grand-duke had cut Goethe's head off, it would have been much better for his fame than his retiring to his rooms, after dismissing the obsequious crowds, to arrange tastefully and contemplate their gifts and honorary inscriptions.[1]

NEW BEDFORD, *January* 29.

Michel Angelo's life, in the *Library of Useful Knowledge*; and his poverty, by Signor Radici in the *Retrospective Review*, volume xiii. These elevate my respect for the artist. His life, they say, too, was a poem. Beautiful is his Platonic passion, before that word had been perverted by affectation and hypocrisy.[2] . . .

Berni said of him, *Ei dice cose, e voi dite parole.* He sought to penetrate by just degrees to the centre of that eternal radiance, in which is hidden

"*l'amor che move il sole e l'altre stelle.*"

1 Compare Emerson's letter to Carlyle of November 20, 1834, in their *Correspondence*, I, 27.

2 Here follow passages used in the lecture on Michael Angelo given, a year later, before the Society for the Diffusion of Useful Knowledge in Boston, in a course on Biography. The lectures were, "Tests of Great Men," "Michel Angelo," "Luther," "George Fox," "Milton," "Edmund Burke."

Are not his struggles and mortifications a more beautiful wreath than the milliners made for Goethe?

In reference to this appetite for death, shall I say it is sometimes permissible? that the object of life is answered when the uses of time are discovered; when the soul has so far discovered its relation to external truth, that time can never more be a burden, and nothing but the evils inseparable from human condition prevent it from being a heaven?

February 1.

In viewing the greatness of men of the first ages, Homer and Alfred equal to Goethe and Washington, does it not seem that a little additional force of Will in the individual is equivalent to ages-ful of the improvements we call civilization? But these Anakim do yet yield to the sad observer of his race real and great consolation (I am thinking now of Michel Angelo and his Platonism), for they seem to him, himself without his faults and in favorable circumstances; he recognizes their lofty aspirations as the thoughts of his own childhood; he looks at these heroes as nothing peculiar and monstrous, but as only more truly men, and he perceives that a heaven of truth and virtue is still possible.

Some thoughts always find us young, and keep us so.[1] Such a thought is the love of the universal and eternal beauty. Every man leaves that contemplation with the feeling that it rather belongs to ages than to mortal life.

February 2.

How often our nature is conscious of and labours with its own limits! In the very act of pretension it is oppressed with secret humiliation.

February 3.

I have read *Corinne* with as much emotion as a book can excite in me.[2] A true representation of the tragedy of woman, which yet (thanks to the mysterious compensation which nature has provided) they rarely feel. The tragedy of genius also. The story labours with the fault of an extravagant, I may say ridiculous, filial passion in Oswald, which no man of such intelligence can carry so far, and then with the second impossibility of his rapid marriage. No matter; though

[1] Olympian bards who sung
     Divine ideas below,
     Which always find us young,
     And always keep us so.
                    Poems: "Ode to Beauty."
[2] *Corinne, ou l' Italie,* by Mme. de Staël.

the circumstances are untrue, the position and
the feelings of Corinne are possible, and, as Plato
would say, more true than history.

NEW BEDFORD, *February* 7.

I have been to Plymouth and stood on the
Rock, and felt that it was grown more important
by the growth of this nation in the minutes that
I stood there. But Barnabas Hedge ought not —
no man ought — to own the rock of Plymouth.

Mr. Bond said he had learned that men can
never learn by experience. In the last depression
of trade he had resolved never to be caught
again; and now, amid his perplexities, resolves
again. At sea we always judge by the present
weather the probable length of the voyage.

February 10.

The newspapers say they might as well publish a thunderstorm as a report of Webster's
speech in answer to Wright.[1] His tones were

1 Mr. Emerson had been chosen Poet for the annual meeting of the Phi Beta Kappa Society at Cambridge. The two
best passages in the poem, otherwise not remarkable, were
those on Lafayette, who had just died, and on Webster. The
latter is given in the Appendix to the *Poems* (Riverside and
Centenary Editions).

like those of a commander in a battle. Times of eloquence are times of terror. I wrote to Charles last night that the obstinate retention of simple and high sentiments in obscurest duties is hardening the character to that temper that will work with honor, if need be, in the tumult, or on the scaffold. Yet perhaps the courage of heroes in revolutions is extemporary, and what seems superhuman fortitude is the effect of an ecstasy of sorrow. Evil times have the effect of making men think. I suppose in the last few weeks men have thrown more searching glances at the structure and interdependence of society than in years of prosperous times. They begin to trace the path of an ear of corn from its stalk to their table.

G. A. S.[1] confirms the views of the education of the Will (see January 21) by saying, that in his experience a very great change is produced in men by the possession of property, a great addition of force, which would remain to them if their property were taken away. It is not the possession of luxuries, but the exercise of power, which belongs to wealth that has wrought this effect. The possession of office has the same

1 George A. Sampson.

effect. What a pepper-corn man is — if he had been poor. By this education of things and persons he is now a person of decision and influence. How imbecile is often a young person of superior intellectual powers for want of acquaintance with his powers; bashful, timid, he shrinks, retreats before every confident person, and is disconcerted by arguments and pretensions he would be ashamed to put forward himself. Let him work, as many merchants do, with the forces of millions of property for months and years upon the wills of hundreds of persons, and you shall see him transformed into an adroit, fluent, masterful gentleman, fit to take and keep his place in any society of men. This is the account to be given of the fine manners of the young Southerners brought up amidst slaves, and of the concession that young Northerners make to them, — yes, and old Northerners to old Southerners. . . . This part of education is conducted in the nursery and the playground, in fights, in frolics, in business, in politics. My manners and history would have been very different, if my parents had been rich, when I was a boy at school. Herein is good ground for our expectation of the high bearing of the English nobleman.

B[enjamin] R[odman] called his friend, the naval architect, a perfect ship. Mr. Hillman.

NEW BEDFORD, *February* 12.

The days and months and years flit by, each with his own black riband, his own sad reminiscence. Yet I looked at the almanack affectionately as a book of Promise. These three last years of my life are not a chasm — I could almost wish they were—so brilliantly sometimes the vision of Ellen's beauty and love and life come out of the darkness. Pleasantly mingled with my sad thoughts the sublime religion of Miss Rotch yesterday. She was much disciplined, she said, in the years of Quaker dissension, and driven inward, driven home, to find an anchor, until she learned to have *no choice*, to acquiesce without understanding the reason when she found an obstruction to any particular course of acting. She objected to having this spiritual direction called an impression, or an intimation, or an oracle. It was none of them. It was so simple it could hardly be spoken of. It was long, long, before she could attain to anything satisfactory. She was in a state of great dreariness, but she had a friend, a woman, now deceased, who used to advise her to dwell patiently with this dreariness and absence, in the confidence that it was necessary to the sweeping away of all her dependence upon traditions, and that she would finally attain to something better. And when she attained a better state of mind, its beginnings were very, very small. And now it is not anything to speak of. She designed to go to England with Mr. and Mrs. Farrar, and the plan was very pleasant, and she was making her preparations, and the time was fixed, when she conceived a reluctance to go for which she could not see any reason, but which continued; and she therefore suspended her purpose, and suffered them to depart without her. She said she had seen reason to think it was best for her to have staid at home. But in obeying it, she never felt it of any importance that she should know now or at any time what the reasons were. But she should feel that it was presumption to press through this reluctance and choose for herself. I said it was not so much any particular power as a *healthful state of the mind;* to which she assented cordially. I said, it must produce a sublime tranquillity in view of the future — this assurance of higher direction; and she assented.[1]

[1] In the essay "Greatness" (*Letters and Social Aims,* p. 309, Cent. Ed.) Mr. Emerson gives this doctrine of the Quakers.

Can you believe, Waldo Emerson, that you may relieve yourself of this perpetual perplexity of choosing, and by putting your ear close to the soul, learn always the true way? I cannot but remark how perfectly this agrees with the Daimon of Socrates, even in that story which I once thought anomalous, of the direction as to the choice of two roads; and with the grand unalterableness of Fichte's morality. Hold up this lamp and look back at the best passages of your life. Once there was choice in the mode, but obedience in the thing. In general there has been pretty quiet obedience *in the main*, but much recusancy *in the particular*.

"HAMLET. But thou wouldst not think how ill all's here about my heart, — but it is no matter.

"HORATIO. If your mind dislike anything, obey it."

"The barber learns his art on the orphan's face." [1]

                    ARABIAN PROVERB.

---

1 This proverb was a favorite one of Mr. Emerson's. He used to say, "When a village Lyceum Committee asks me to give a lecture, and I tell them I will read one I am just writing, they are pleased. Poor men, they little know how

The walls of houses are transparent to the architect.

Providence; men apply themselves to events, and according to their affinities, that is sweet or bitter. [The] good man is obedient to the laws of the world, and so successful. The angel rather.

Conversation with William W. Swain.

BOSTON, *February* 19.

A seaman in the coach told the story of an old sperm-whale, which he called a white whale, which was known for many years by the whalemen as Old Tom, and who rushed upon the boats which attacked him, and crushed the boats to small chips in his jaws, the men generally escaping by jumping overboard and being picked up. A vessel was fitted out at New Bedford, he said, to take him. And he was finally taken somewhere off Payta Head by the *Winslow* or the *Essex*. He gave a fine account of a storm, which I heard imperfectly, only " the whole ocean was all feather white." A whale sometimes runs off three rolls of cord, three hundred fathom in length each one.

different that lecture will be when it is given in New York, or is printed. I 'try it on' on them; '*The barber learns his trade on the orphan's chin.*'"

February 20.

Self-contradiction is the only wrong;
For, by the laws of spirit, in the right
Is every individual character
That acts in strict consistence with itself.

COLERIDGE's *Wallenstein.*

February 21.

The true reasons for actions are not given.
George P. Bradford says that he is so well understood at Plymouth that he can act naturally
without being reckoned absurd. That is a valid
reason for going there. But how many would
not understand it, and how many, understanding it, would hoot at it. They think a cheaper
board is a good reason for going to one house,
or the prospect of making acquaintance that give
parties, or the like; but such a reason as this,
which affects happiness and character, seems unworthy attention. As George says, it is agreed
in society to consider realities as fictions, and
fictions realities.

February 22.

It were well to live purely, to make your word
worth something. Deny yourself cake and ale
to make your testimony irresistible. Be a pure
reason to your contemporaries for God and

truth. What is good in itself can be bad to nobody. As I went to church I thought how seldom the present hour is seized upon as a new
moment. To a soul alive to God every moment
is a new world. A new audience, a new Sabbath, affords an opportunity of communicating
thought and moral excitement that shall surpass
all previous experience, that shall constitute an
epoch, a revolution, in the minds on whom you
act and in your own. The awakened soul, the
man of genius, makes every day such a day,
by looking forward only ; but the professional
mob look back only to custom and their past
selves.

February 25.

"The day is immeasurably long to him who
knows how to value and to use it," said Goethe.

March 2.

It is very seldom that a man is truly alone.
He needs to retire as much from his solitude
as he does from society, into very loneliness.
While I am reading and writing in my chamber
I am not alone, though there is nobody there.
There is one means of procuring solitude which
to me, and I apprehend to all men, is effectual,
and that is to go to the window and look at the

stars. If they do not startle you and call you off from vulgar matters I know not what will. I sometimes think that the atmosphere was made transparent with this design, to give man in the heavenly bodies a perpetual admonition of God and superior destiny. Seen in the streets of cities, how great they are![1] When I spoke of this to G. A. S. he said, that he had sought in his chamber a place for prayer and could not find one till he cast his eye upon the stars.

New Bedford, *March* 15.

I have been again to Plymouth, and the families and the faces are almost as tranquil as their pines. The blue ocean reminded me of Goethe's fine observation that " Nature has told everything once "; one illustration of it . . . was to me this noble line of sea by which Nature is pleased to reveal to the asking eye the dimensions of the globe by showing the true outline of the world.

Fine objects in Plymouth from men and women down to vegetables. I saw and relished all even to the *Epigæa* and the *Byssus* or *Pul-*

1 One or two sentences in this paragraph occur in the opening passage of *Nature*.

vis simplicissimus, ground-pine, *Sabbatia*, and *Empetrum*.[1]

"Nature tells everything once." Yes, our microscopes are not necessary; they are a mechanical advantage for chamber-philosophers; she has magnified everything somewhere.[2] Each process, each function, each organ, is disproportionately developed in some one individual. Go study it there, instead of wearing your eyes out in your 6-million magnifier.

I count no man much because he cows or silences me. Any fool can do that. But if his conversation enriches or rejoices me, I must reckon him wise.

NEW BEDFORD, *March* 21.

I have been much interested lately in the MS. Record of the debates in the Quaker Monthly Meetings here in 1823, when Elizabeth Rodman and Mary Rotch were proposed to be removed from the place of Elders for uniting in the prayers of Mary Newhall. I must quote a sentence or two from two of these speakers. " Febru-

1 *Byssus* (?) *Epigæa repens* (mayflower), *Sabbatia chloroides, Corema Conradii* (Gray).

2 These two sentences occur in " Country Life," in *Natural History of Intellect*, Centenary Edition, p. 160.

ary, 1823: M. N. rose in the meeting and began with, 'As the stream does not rise higher than the fountain,' etc.; spoke of the Mosaic dispensation in which the performance of certain rituals constituted the required religion; the more spiritual dispensation of our Saviour; of the advent of Christ; and the yet more inward and spiritual dispensation of the present day. These dispensations she compared to the progressive stages of the human heart in the work of religion, from loving our neighbor as ourselves to loving our enemies, and lastly arriving at that state of humility when self would be totally abandoned and we could only say, Lord be merciful to me a sinner."

NEW BEDFORD.

My Swedenborgian friend Dr. Stebbins tells me that he esteems himself "measureably excused for not preaching whilst I remain here, as I am giving as much New Jerusalem doctrine as the people will bear."

Fine thought in the old verse by Barbour describing Bruce's soldiers crowding around him as with new unsated curiosity after a battle: —

"Sic wordis spak they of their king;
  And for his hie undertaking
  Ferleyit and gernit him for to see,
  That with him ay was wont to be."

March 22.

The subject that needs most to be presented, developed, is the principle of Self-reliance, what it is, what is not it, what it requires, how it teaches us to regard our friends. It is true that there is a faith wholly a man's own, the solitary inmate of his own breast, which the faiths of all mankind cannot shake, and which they cannot confirm. But at the same time, how useful, how indispensable, has been the ministry of our friends to us, our teachers — the living and the dead!

I ask advice. It is not that I wish my companion to dictate to me the course I should take. Before God, No. It were to unman, to un-god myself. It is that I wish him to give me information about the facts, not a law as to the duty. It is that he may stimulate me by his thoughts to unfold my own, so that I may become *master of the facts* still. My own bosom will supply, as surely as God liveth, the direction of my course.

This truth constitutes the objection to *pledges*.

They are advocated on the principle that men are not to be trusted. They are to be trusted. They can never attain to any good, until they are trusted with the whole direction of themselves, and therefore it is pernicious, it is postponing their virtue and happiness, whenever you substitute a false principle for the true, in a mind capable of acting from a right motive.

March 23.

It occurs that the distinction should be drawn in treating of Friendship between the *aid of commodity* which our friends yield us, as in hospitality, gifts, sacrifices, etc., and which, as in the old story about the poor man's will in Montaigne, are evidently esteemed by the natural mind (to use such a cant word) the highest manifestations of love; and, secondly, the spiritual aid, — far more precious and leaving the other at infinite distances, — which our friends afford us, of confession, of appeal, of social stimulus, mirroring ourselves.

March 26.

As the flower precedes the fruit, and the bud the flower, so, long before the knowledge, comes the opinion, long before the opinion comes the instinct, that a particular act is unfriendly,

unsuitable, wrong. We are wonderfully protected. . . .

March 28.

Wherever the truth is injured, defend it. You
are there on that spot within hearing of that word,
within sight of that action, as a Witness, to the
end that you should speak for it.

" My Heritage how long and wide, —
    Time is my heritage, my field is Time."

Boston, *April* 10.

Is it possible that, in the Solitude I seek, I
shall have the resolution, the force, to work as
I ought to work, as I project in highest, most
far-sighted hours? Well, and what do you project? Nothing less than to look at every object
in its relation to myself.

Edward wrote on the back of Alexander's portrait of Mother, taken in 1825 at the age of
57, —

*Feminæ, uxoris, viduæ, matris optimæ, laudatæ,
benedictæ, vita pulchra, similitudo tam similis pre-
tiosa. Ipsa mulier ad cœlum ibit: umbra picta inter
amicos, Deo volente, numquam inter inimicos, quia
tales non sunt, vivis descriptionem sine errore mortalis quondam, tunc angeli, dabit.*

C. C. E. proposes an improved reading of the second sentence : — *Ipsa mulier in cœlum ibit : umbra picta inter amicos, Deo volente, non umquam, cum tales nulli sint, inter inimicos, errore puræ mortalis quondam, tunc animæ beatæ, imaginem servabit.*

Placuit omnibus cui satis uni placuisse ; epitaph on Olivia Buckminster Emerson.

April 11.

Went yesterday to Cambridge and spent most of the day at Mount Auburn; got my luncheon at Fresh Pond, and went back again to the woods. After much wandering and seeing many things, four snakes gliding up and down a hollow for no purpose that I could see — not to eat, not for love, but only gliding; then a whole bed of *Hepatica triloba,* cousins of the Anemone, all blue and beautiful, but constrained by niggard nature to wear their last year's faded jacket of leaves; then a black-capped titmouse, who came upon a tree, and when I would know his name, sang *chick-a-dee-dee;* then a far-off tree full of clamorous birds, I know not what, but you might hear them half a mile. I forsook the tombs, and found a sunny hollow where the east wind would

not blow, and lay down against the side of a tree
to most happy beholdings. At least I opened my
eyes and let what would pass through them into
the soul. I saw no more my relation, how near
and petty, to Cambridge or Boston; I heeded
no more what minute or hour our Massachusetts
clocks might indicate — I saw only the noble
earth on which I was born, with the great Star
which warms and enlightens it. I saw the clouds
that hang their significant drapery over us. It
was Day — that was all Heaven said. The pines
glittered with their innumerable green needles in
the light, and seemed to challenge me to read
their riddle. The drab oak-leaves of the last year
turned their little somersets and lay still again.
And the wind bustled high overhead in the forest top. This gay and grand architecture, from
the vault to the moss and lichen on which I lay,
— who shall explain to me the laws of its proportions and adornments?

See the perpetual generation of good sense:
nothing wholly false, fantastic, can take possession of men who, to live and move, must
plough the ground, sail the sea, have orchards,
hear the robin sing, and see the swallow fly.

To-day I found in Roxbury the *Saxifraga
vernalis.*

April 12.

Glad to read in my old gossip Montaigne some robust rules of rhetoric: I will have a chapter thereon in my book. I would Thomas Carlyle should read them. "In good prose," said Schlegel (?), "every word should be underscored." Its place in the sentence should make its emphasis. Write solid sentences, and you can even spare punctuation. The passages in Montaigne are in volume iii, pages 144–146.' We are always on the brink of an ocean of thought into which we do not yet swim. We are poor lords, — have immense powers which we are hindered from using. I am kept out of my heritage. . . .

. . . Are we not ever postponing great actions and ineffable wisdom. We are ever coming up with a group of angels still in sight before us,² which we refer to when we say " the Truth " and the Wise Man, and the corrections these shall make in human society. All the mistakes I make arise from forsaking my own station and trying to see the object from another person's point of view. I read so resolute a self-thinker as Carlyle, and am convinced of the riches of wisdom that

1 Probably Cotton's translation.
2 The thought of his poem, "The Forerunners."

ever belong to the man who utters his own
thought with a divine confidence that it must
be true if he heard it there.

We live, animals in the basement story, and
when Shakspeare or Milton, or even my fan-
tastical Scotchman who fools his humor to the
top of his bent, call us up into the high region,
we feel and say, "this is my region, they only
show me my own property. I am in my element.
I thank them for it." Presently we go about our
business into the basement again, cumbered with
serving; and assured of our right to the halls
above, we never go thither.

I had observed long since that, to give the
thought a just and full expression, I must not
prematurely utter it. Better not talk of the matter you are writing out. It was as if you had let
the spring snap too soon. I was glad to find Goethe
say to the same point, that "he who seeks a
hidden treasure must not speak."

Sabbath, *April* 13.

There are some duties about courtesy: and
were it not lawful for the discontented spirit
sometimes to cry out, Husks, Husks! Ye feed
the people with words, even in their solemn

assembly ? They distress me by their prayers, and all the discourse was an impertinence. There sat, too, the gifted man, and if he unlawfully withheld his word, this wearisome prose was his just punishment.

Elsewhere,—certainly not there, but from M. M. E., from Carlyle, or from this delicious day, or whatever celestial fingers touched the divine harp,—I woke to a strain of highest melody. I saw that it was not for me to complain of obscurity, of being misunderstood; it was not for me, even in the filthy rags of my unrighteousness, to despond of what I might do and learn. Can you not do better than clear your action to the highest of these puppets or these potentates around you, by clearing it to your Creator, by being justified to yourself? Absolve yourself to the universe, and, as God liveth, you shall ray out light and heat,—absolute good. Were it not noble gratitude, since we are the fruit of Time and owe all to the immeasurable Past— its nations and ages guide our pen—to live for the world; to inspect the present and, in the present, report of the future for the benefit of the existing race; and having once seen that Virtue was beautiful, count that portion enough, without higgling for our particular Commodity to

boot? Down with that fop of a Brutus![1] Peace
to the angel of Innocency for evermore!

SEEMING DISPROPORTIONATE

It occurs how much friction is in the machinery of society. The material is so much that
the spiritual is overlaid and lost. A man medi-
tates in solitude upon a truth which seems to
him so weighty that he proposes to impart it to
his fellow men. Immediately a society must be
collected, and books consulted, and much paper
blotted in preparation of his discourse. Alien
considerations come in, personal considerations
— and finally when he delivers his discourse, 'tis
quite possible it does not contain the original
message, so that it was no superfluous rule he
gave who said, "When you write, do not omit
the thing you meant to say." The material in-
teguments have quite overlaid and killed the
spiritual child. Not otherwise it falls out in Education. A young man is to be educated, and
schools are built, and masters brought together,
and gymnasium erected, and scientific toys and

1 "It is told of Brutus that, when he fell on his sword
after the battle of Philippi, he quoted a line of Euripides, —
'O Virtue! I have followed thee through life and I find thee
at last but a shade.'" — "Heroism," *Essays*, First Series.

monitorial systems and a college endowed with many professorships, and the apparatus is so enormous and unmanageable that the *e-ducation* or *calling out of his faculties* is never accomplished; he graduates a dunce. See how the French Mathematics at Cambridge have quite destroyed the slender chance a boy had before of learning Trigonometry.

Is it otherwise in our philosophic enterprises? They wish to heal the sick, or emancipate the African, or convert the Hindoo, and immediately agents are appointed, and an office established, and Annual Reports printed, — and the least streamlet of the vast contributions of the public trickles down to the healing of the original evil. The Charity becomes a job. Well now, is it otherwise with life itself? We are always getting ready to live, but never living. We have many years of technical education; then many years of earning a livelihood, and we get sick, and take journeys for our health, and compass land and sea for improvement by travelling, but the work of self-improvement, — always under our nose, — nearer than the nearest, is seldom seldom engaged in. A few, few hours in the longest life.

Set out to study a particular truth. Read upon it; walk to think upon it; talk of it; write about it;— the thing itself will not much manifest itself, at least not much in accommodation to your studying arrangements. The gleams you do get out, they will flash as likely at dinner, or in the roar of Faneuil Hall, as in your painfullest abstraction.

Very little life in a lifetime.

M. M. E. writes, that, "the world is full of children, and what in our hearts we take no merit in — blush that it is no more generous — we expose to the weak as justification."

April 20.

A good Inaugural Sermon from Mr. Stearns at Old South this morning; and from Mr. Frothingham this P. M., a good unfolding of the parting of Elijah and Elisha. Elijah said, "Ask what thou wilt." Who could have stood this test? To whom would it not have been a snare? But Elisha said, "Let a double portion of thy spirit be on me." The preacher should have added, I think, that the blessing descended in the asking, the prayer answered itself, as all real prayers do.

Awake, arm of the Lord! Awake, thou Godlike that sleepest! Dear God that sleepest in man, I have served my apprenticeship of bows and blushes, of fears and references, of excessive admiration.

The whole secret of the teacher's force lies in the conviction that men are convertible. And they are. They want awakening. Get the soul out of bed, out of her deep habitual sleep, out into God's universe, to a perception of its beauty, and hearing of its call, and your vulgar man, your prosy, selfish sensualist awakes, a god, and is conscious of force to shake the world.

It seemed to me to-night as if it were no bad topic for the preacher to urge the talent of hearing good sermons upon their congregations. I can hear a good sermon where Surd shall hear none, and Absurd shall hear worse than none. Spend the Sunday morning well, and the hours shall shine with immortal light, shall epitomize history, shall sing heavenly psalms. Your way to church shall be short as the way to the playground is to a child, and something holy and wise shall sit upon all the countenances there and shall inspire the preacher's words with a wisdom not their own. Spend the Sunday morning ill, and you will hardly hear a good sermon anywhere.

Could it be made apparent, what is really true, that the whole future is in the bottom of the heart, that, in proportion as your life is spent

within, in that measure are you invulnerable?
In proportion as you penetrate facts for the law,
and events for the cause, in that measure is your
knowledge real, your condition gradually con-
formed to a stable idea, and the future foreseen.
I have laid my egg, but 't is either old or empty.

It was nobly said by Goethe that he endea-
vored to show his gratitude to all his great contemporaries, Humboldt, Cuvier, Byron, Scott,
or whosoever, by meeting them half way in their
various efforts by the activity and performances
of his own mind. It is like the worthy man whom
I once took up in my chaise as I rode, and who,
on parting, told me he should thank me by ren-
dering the same service to some future traveller.

April 22.

The most original sermon is adopted by each
hearer's self-love as his old Orthodox, or Unitarian, or Quaker, preaching.

April 23.

In desert lands the bird alights on the barrel
of the hunter's gun, and many other facts are
there; but that which I would say is that every
teacher acquires a cumulative inertia; the more
forcible, the more eloquent, have been his inno-

vating doctrines, the more eagerly his school have crowded around him, so much the more difficult is it for him to forfeit their love, to compromise his influence by advancing farther in the same track. Therefore the wise man must be wary of attaching followers. He must feel and teach that the best wisdom cannot be communicated; must be acquired by every soul for itself.

And the prudent world cannot wish that the gifted Channing should advance one step, lest it be left without confidence in its Conductor.

NEWTON, *April* 26.

The Muses love the woods, and I have come hither to court the awful Powers in this sober solitude. Whatsoever is highest, wisest, best, favor me! I will listen and then speak.[1] To be

1 Here follows a passage used in "The Preacher" (*Lectures and Biographical Sketches*, p. 221, Centenary Edition), beginning there: "Unlovely, nay, frightful, is the solitude of the soul which is without God in the world." The sentence in that essay about "this chill, houseless, fatherless, aimless Cain, the man who hears only the sound of his own footsteps in God's resplendent creation," is given in the journal version (omitted here) thus: "This chill, houseless, fatherless baboon, with the image, but not the soul of man." Mr. Cabot, in the preface to *Letters and Social Aims*, explains the diversity of date often found in the posthumously printed

without God in the world — who devised that pregnant expression? . . .

There is no longer distinction between the value of thoughts. To be sweet as sugar is sweet, strong as iron is strong, wise as a miser, happy as a drunkard, is the whole compass of his speculation. And he is left in how terrible a solitude. The hopes that cheered him, the glorious affections that made a sky over all he knew, the unseen powers that watched with tenderness his education, that knit his yet imperfect endeavors to the great Cause of goodness and to the universe that labors for it, the fellowship of all great men working earnestly in the world, the smiles and auspices of departed heroes, yea, and the right and power to rejoice in anything that is won or done — all, all depart from him, he is alone in a barren and mean solitude. He bitterly feels that he must yield the palm of real dignity to the meanest worm or fly, for they are not tormented with a consciousness of total worthlessness as he is.[1] . . .

papers by his account of his arranging these for publication with Mr. Emerson's sanction, in his later days.

1 Here follows, also in "The Preacher," the passage beginning, — "How gloomy is the day," and ending, "is gone forever."

Do you not see that wherever the wise, the good man goes, light springs up in his path — he carries meaning to every dead symbol; the Creator is in his heart, and illustrates and affects his world, through the hands of his servant. But the evil man, that is, the Atheist, goes up and down, and all is dark and pernicious.

Rain, rain. The good rain, like a bad preacher, does not know when to leave off.

God is promoted by the worst. Don't despise even the Kneelands¹ and Andrew Jacksons. In the great cycle they find their place, and like the insect that fertilizes the soil with worm casts, or

1 Abner Kneeland, editor of the *Boston Investigator*, who had just been sent to jail in Boston, convicted of Blasphemy in articles written and published by him expressing disbelief in God, in Christ, in miracles and in immortality (*Pickering's Reports*, vol. xx). Four years later, the young James Russell Lowell, in his Class Poem, thus commented on Mr. Emerson's Divinity School Address : —

> " Woe for Religion, too, when men, who claim
> To place a Reverend before their name,
> Ascend the Lord's own holy place to preach
> In strains that Kneeland had been proud to reach,
> And which, if measured by Judge Thacher's scale,
> Had doomed their author to the county jail,'' etc.
>
> (See Scudder's Biography of Lowell.)

the scavenger bustard ' that removes carrion, they perform a beneficence they know not of, and cannot hinder if they would.

I saw a hawk to-day wheeling up to heaven in a spiral flight, and every circle becoming less to the eye till he vanished into the atmosphere. What could be more in unison with all pure and brilliant images. Yet is the creature an unclean greedy eater, and all his geography from that grand observatory was a watching of barn-yards, or an inspection of moles and field-mice. So with the pelican, crane, and the tribes of sea-fowl — disgusting gluttons all. Yet observe how finely in nature all these disagreeable individuals integrate themselves into a cleanly and pleasing whole.

April 27.

Here is a *Mytilus margaritiferus* as large as a moon and of the same color, and a *Tellina radiata* which reminds the beholder of the rising sun. I think they should call one of those shells, Moon, and the other, Morn. To-day I found also the *Andromeda calyculata*, *Houstonia*, *Potentilla sarmentosa*.² This *Empetrum* and *Smilax* and

1 *Buzzard* was meant.
2 *Chamædaphne calyculata*, *Houstonia cerulea*, *Potentilla pumila* (Gray).

Kalmia[1] and privet, I have wondered oft to what
end they grew. How ridiculous! Ask wrens and
crows and bluebirds. As soon as you have done
wondering and have left the plant, the bird and
the insect return to it as to their daily table. And
so it renews its race for a thousand, thousand
summers.

Natural History gives *body* to our knowledge.
No man can spare a fact he knows. The knowledge of nature is *most permanent*; clouds and
grass are older antiquities than pyramids or Ath-
ens; then they are *most perfect*. Goethe's plant,
a genuine creation. Then they bear strange but
well-established affinities to us. Nobody can
look on a *Cistus* or a *Brentus* without sighing at
his ignorance. It is an unknown America. Linnæus is already read as the Plato who described
Atlantis. A classification is nothing but a cabinet.
The whole remains to be done thereafter.

A religion of forms is not for me. I honor the
Methodists who find, like St. John, all Christianity in one word, Love. To the parishes in
my neighborhood Milton would seem a free-
thinker when he says, "They [the Jews] thought

1 *Corema Conradii, Smilax rotundifolia, Kalmia angusti-
folia* (Gray).

it too much license to follow the charming pipe
of him who founded and proclaimed liberty and
relief to all distresses."

April 28.

Vaccinium tenellum, Pyrus ovalis,[1] *Anemone ne-
morosa, Fragaria virginiana :* the day is as good
for these as for oaks and corn. The air vibrates
with equal facility to the thunder and to the
squeak of a mouse; invites man with provoking
indifference to total indolence and to immortal
actions. You may even shun the occasions of
excitement by withdrawing from a profession
and from society, and then the vast Eternity of
capacity, of freedom, opens before you, but
without a single impulse. A day is a rich abyss
of means, yet mute and void. It demands something godlike in him who has cast off the common yokes and motives of humanity, and has
ventured to trust himself for a taskmaster.
High be his heart, faithful his will, vast his contemplations, that he may truly be a world, society, law to himself; that a simple purpose may
be to him as strong as iron necessity is to others.
It is a faithful saying worthy of all acceptation,
that a reasoning Man, conscious of his powers
and duties, annihilates all distinction of circum-

1   *Amelanchier oblongifolia* (Gray).

stances. What is Rome? what is royalty? what is wealth? His place is the true place, and superior therefore in dignity to all other places. Linnæus at Copenhagen, Oberlin on the high Alps, White at Selborne, Roger Bacon at Oxford, Rammohun Roy in India, and Heber at Bombay, Washington in the Jerseys — these are the Romes, the Empires, the Wealth of these men. The place which I have not sought, but in which my duty places me, is a sort of royal palace. If I am faithful in it, I move in it with a pleasing awe at the immensity of the chain of which I hold the last link in my hand and am led by it. I perceive my commission to be coeval with the antiquity of the eldest causes.

Literature is the conversion of action into thought for the delight of the Intellect. It is the turning into thought what was done without thought.

It aims at ideal truth. But it is only approximation. The word can never cover the thing. You don't expect to describe a sunrise.

Art actualizes thought.
Literature idealizes action.
Mission of the intellect.

The vulgar man seems to himself unmoored the moment he has changed his scene and associates. He misses his chair and his hat-peg. The wise man carries his spring and his regulator within, and is at home in untrodden wilds.

April 29.

Fontenelle said, if men should see the principles of nature laid bare, they would cry, "What! is this all?" How simple they are. How is the wonder perpetually lessened by showing the disproportionate effect upon the eye of simple combination! The shell is a marvel until we see that it was not one effort, but each knot and spine has been in turn the lip of the structure. Shakspeare how inconceivable, until we have heard what Italian Novels and Plutarch's Lives and old English Dramas he had, also what contemporary fund of poetic diction. A Webster's speech is a marvel until we have learned that a part of it he has carried in his head for years, and a part of it was collected for him by young lawyers, and that Mr. Appleton furnished the facts, and a letter from Mr. Swain turned the paragraph. St. Peter's did not leap full grown out of the head of the architect; the part that was builded instructed the eye of the next generation how to build the rest. Mirabeau has his Dumont. The tree did not come from the acorn, but is an annual deposit of vegetation in a form determined by the existing disposition of the parts. Every leaf contains the eyes which are sufficient to originate a forest. The magnet is a marvel when we simply see it spontaneously wheel to the north, and cling to iron like one alive. The wonder diminishes when it is shown to be only one instance of a general law that affects all bodies and all phenomena, light, heat, electricity, animal life. A ship, a locomotive, a cotton factory is a wonder until we see how these Romes were not built in a day, but part suggested part, and complexity became simplicity. The poem, the oration, the book are superhuman, but the wonder is out when you see the manuscript. Homer how wonderful, until the German erudition discovered a cyclus of Homeric poems. It is all one; a trick of cards, a juggler's sleight, an astronomical result, an algebraic formula, amazing when we see only the result, cheap when we are shown the means. This it is to conceive of acts and works, to throw myself into the object so that its history shall naturally evolve itself before me. Well, so does the Universe, Time, History evolve itself, so simply, so unmiraculously from the all-perceiving mind.

G. P. B. tells a ridiculous story about the boy learning his alphabet. "That letter is A," says the teacher. "A," drawls the boy. "That is B," says the teacher. "B," drawls the boy, and so on. "That letter is W," says the teacher. "The Devil! Is that W?" enquires the pupil. Now I say that this story hath an alarming sound. It is the essence of Radicalism. It is Jack Cade himself. Or is it not exquisite ridicule upon our learned Linnæan classifications? "What shell is this?" "It is a *strombus*." "The devil! is that a *strombus*?" would be the appropriate reply.

The fly strikes against the window-pane until at last he learns that, though invisible, there is an obstacle there. The soul of man by a thousand offences learns at last that there is an invisible Law which —

April 30.

There are more purposes in Education than to keep the man at work. Self-questioning is one; a very important end. The disturbance, the self-discord which young men feel is a most important crisis, indispensable to a free, improvable race creature. Give me the eye to see a navy in an acorn.

If I could write like the wonderful bard whose sonnets I read this afternoon, I would leave all, and sing songs to the human race. Poetry with him is no verbal affair; the thought is poetical, and Nature is put under contribution to give analogies and semblances that she has never yielded before. Whether the same or an equal tone of natural verse is now possible? Whether we are not two ages too late? But how remarkable every way are Shakspear's sonnets. Those addressed to a beautiful young man seem to show some singular friendship amounting almost to a passion which probably excited his youthful imagination. They are invaluable for the hints they contain respecting his unknown self. He knew his powers; he loved Spenser; he deplored his own way of living, etc., etc. What said C. C. E. the other day touching a common impression left by Jesus of Nazareth and this poet?

The war of the telescope and the microscope; the mass and the particular. Science ever subdivides. It separates one star into two, a nebula into a constellation, a class into genera, a genus

into species; and ever the most interesting facts
arise from ascertaining habits of an individual.
We should find the individual traits of a robin
or a bee probably far more interesting than their
generic habits when once we arrive to know
them, as much as the traits of one dog affect us
more than, though interesting, the canine character. Newton and Webster charm us more than
accounts of the character of the Saxon Race. It
occurred also in the forest, that there is no need
to fear that the immense accumulation of scientific facts should ever encumber us, since as fast
as they multiply they resolve themselves into
a formula which carries the world in a phial.
Every commonplace we utter is a formula in
which is packed up an uncounted list of particular observations. And every man's mind at
this moment is a formula condensing the result
of all his conclusions.

May 1.

In this still Newton we have seven Sabbaths
in a week. The day is as calm as Eternity —
quite a Chaldean time.

The philosophy of the Wave. The wave
moves onward, but the water of which it is
composed does not. The same particle does not
rise from the valley to the ridge. Its unity is

only phenomenal. So it is with men. There is a revolution in this country now, is there? Well I am glad of it. But it don't convert nor punish the Jackson men, nor reward the others. The Jackson men have made their fortunes; grow old; die. It is the new comers who form this undulation. The party we wish to convince, condemn, loses its identity. Elect Webster President, — and find the Jackson party if you can. All gone, dead, scattered, Webstermen, Southerners, Masons, any and everything. Judicial or even moral sentence seems no longer capable of being inflicted. France, we say, suffered and learned; but the red Revolutionists did not. France to-day is a new-born race that had no more to do with that regicide France than the Sandwich Islanders.

May 3.

The Idea according to which the Universe is made is wholly wanting to us; is it not? Yet it may or will be found to be constructed on as harmonious and perfect a thought, self-explaining, as a problem in geometry. The classification of all natural science is arbitrary, I believe; no method philosophical in any one. And yet in all the permutations and combinations supposable, might not a cabinet of shells or a Flora be thrown into one which should flash on us the very thought? We take them out of composition, and so lose their greatest beauty. The moon is an unsatisfactory sight if the eye be exclusively directed to it, and a shell retains but a small part of its beauty when examined separately.[1] All our classifications are introductory and very convenient, but must be looked on as temporary, and the eye always watching for the glimmering of that pure, plastic Idea. If Swammerdam forgets that he is a man, and when you make any speculative suggestion as to the habits or origin or relation of insects, rebukes you, with civil submission that you may think what you please, he is only concerned for the facts, — he loses all that for which his science is of any worth. He is a mere insect-hunter, and no whit more respectable than the nuthatch or titmouse who are peeping and darting about after the same prey.

This was what Goethe sought in his Metamorphosis of plants. The Pythagorean doctrine of transmigration is an Idea; the Swedenborgian of Affections Clothed, is one also. Let the

1 Compare in *Nature* (Centenary Edition, p. 19) the paragraph in the division "Beauty," beginning, "But this beauty of Nature."

mind of the student be in a natural, healthful and progressive state, let him, in the midst of his most minute dissection, not lose sight of the place and relations of the subject; shun giving it a disproportionate importance, but speedily adjust himself and study to see the thing (though with added acquaintance of its intimate structure) under the sun and in the landscape as he did before. Let it be a point as before. Integrate the particulars. We have no theory of animated nature. When we have, it will be itself the true Classification. Perhaps a study of the cattle on the mountain-side as they graze is more suggestive of truth than the inspection of their parts in the dissection-room. The way they classify is by counting stamens, or filaments, or teeth and hoofs and shells. A true argument, what we call the unfolding an idea, as is continually done in Plato's Dialogues, in Carlyle's *Characteristics*, or in a thousand acknowledged applications of familiar ethical truths, — these are natural classifications containing their own reason in themselves, and making known facts continually. They are themselves the formula, the largest generalization of the facts, and if thousands on thousands more should be discovered, this idea hath predicted already their place and fate. When

shall such a classification be obtained in botany?
This is evidently what Goethe aimed to do, in
seeking the arch-plant, which, being known,
would give, not only all actual, but all possible
vegetable forms. Thus to study would be to
hold the bottle under water instead of filling it
drop by drop.

Monday, *May* 3.

The parliamentary people say, We must not
blink the question. There is an intellectual duty
as imperative and as burdensome as that moral
one. I come, *e. g.*, to the present subject of
classification. At the centre it is a black spot —
no line, no handle, no character; I am tempted
to stray to the accessible lanes on the left hand
and right, which lead round it — all outside of
it. Intellectual courage, intellectual duty says
we must not blink the question, we must march
up to it and sit down before it and watch there,
incessantly getting as close as we can to the
black wall, and watch and watch, until slowly
lines and handles and characters shall appear on
its surface and we shall learn to open the gate
and enter the fortress, unroof it and lay bare its
ground-plan to the day.

Mr. Coleridge has written well on this matter of Theory in his *Friend*. A lecture may be

given upon insects or plants, that, when it is closed, irresistibly suggests the question, "Well, what of that?" An enumeration of facts without method. A true method has no more need of firstly, secondly, etc., than a perfect sentence has of punctuation. It tells its own story, makes its own feet, creates its own form. It is its own apology. The best argument of the lawyer is a skilful telling of the story. The true classification will not present itself to us in a catalogue of a hundred classes, but as an idea of which the flying wasp and the grazing ox are developments. Natural History is to be studied, not with any pretension that its theory is attained, that its classification is permanent, but merely as full of tendency.

May 6.

Well, my friend, are you not yet convinced that you should study plants and animals?[1] To be sure the reasons are not very mighty : but words.

1 It should be remembered that Mr. Emerson, having left his pulpit, was earnestly searching for the highest truth as revealed in Nature by the informing Spirit. Two days after this entry he gave a lecture called "The Naturalist," before the Boston Natural History Society at their annual meeting. A synopsis of this lecture is given in Cabot's Memoir, in the Appendix, vol. ii, p. 712.

To it again. Say then that I will study Natural History to provide me a resource when business, friends, and my country fail me, that I may never lose my temper, nor be without soothing, uplifting occupation. It will yet cheer me in solitude, or, I think, in madness, that the mellow voice of the robin is not a stranger to me, that the flowers are reflections to me of earlier, happier and yet thoughtful hours. Or again, say that I am ever haunted by the conviction that I have an interest in all that goes on around me, that I would overhear the powers — what they say. No knowledge can be spared, or any advantage we can give ourselves, and this is the knowledge of the laws by which I live; but finally say frankly, that all the reasons seem to me to fall far short of my faith upon the subject. Therefore, boldly press the cause as its own evidence; say that you love Nature, and would know her mysteries, and that you believe in your power by patient contemplation and docile experiment to learn them.

May 8.

The men of this world say ever of the Thinker, "How knoweth this man these things, having never learned?" Ho! every one that thirsteth! come ye to the waters, and he that hath no money, come buy wine and milk without money.

The recluse hermit ofttimes more doth see, etc.
A few wise instincts, etc.

WORDSWORTH.

May 16.

I remember when I was a boy going upon the beach and being charmed with the colors and forms of the shells. I picked up many and put them in my pocket. When I got home I could find nothing that I gathered — nothing but some dry, ugly mussel and snail shells. Thence I learned that composition was more important than the beauty of individual forms to effect. On the shore they lay wet and social by the sea and under the sky.[1]

The sun illuminates the eye of the man, but the eye and the heart of the child. His heart is in the right place.

Many eyes go through the meadow, but few see the flowers in it.

May 21.

I will thank God of myself and for that I have. I will not manufacture remorse of the pattern of others, nor feign their joys. I am

[1] The origin of the poem "Each and All."

born tranquil, not a stern economist of Time, but
never a keen sufferer. I will not affect to suffer.
Be my life then a long gratitude. I will trust
my instincts. For always a reason halts after
an instinct, and when I have deviated from
the instinct, comes somebody with a profound
theory teaching that I ought to have followed it:
some Goethe, Swedenborg, or Carlyle. I stick at
scolding the boy, yet conformably to rule, I
scold him. By and by, the reprimand is a proven
error. "Our first and third thought coincide."
I was the true philosopher in college, and Mr.
Farrar and Mr. Hedge and Dr. Ware the false,
yet what seemed then to me less probable?
"There are three things," said my worthy friend
W. W. to me, "that make the gentleman, —
the hat, the collar, and the boots." Ah, that
Professor Teufelsdrock[1] had heard the word!

May 29.

Dr. Darwin's work has lost all its consequence
in the literary world.[2] Why? not from Currie,

1 Mr. Emerson never mastered the spelling of Teufels-
dröckh.

2 Evidently one of the works of the elder Darwin (Dr.
Erasmus). He wrote "The Botanic Garden," a poem, and
later "Zoönomia, or Laws of Organic Life;" later still,
"Phytologia, or Philosophy of Agriculture and Gardening."

nor from Brown. No. A dim, venerable public decides upon every work. When it offers itself, a sort of perplexity, an uneasy waiting for judgment appears in the living literary judges ; but the work presently takes its true place, by no effort, friendly or hostile, but by the real importance of its principles to the constant mind of man. And this in a way that no individual can much affect by blame or praise. It is the specific gravity of the atom. An aspiring young man readily distinguishes in the first circles those who are there by sufferance, and those who constitute them first circles, and attaches himself to the fountains of honor, not to the conduits. The true aspirant goes one step further and discerns in himself the Fountain of these fountainlets, and so becomes the giver of all fine and high influences. In him is the source of all the romance, the lustre, the dignity, that fascinates him in some saloons with an inexpressible charm; for, truth, honor, learning, perseverance, are the Jove and Apollo who bewitched him.

May 30.

Languages as discipline, much reading as an additional atmosphere or two, to gird the loins and make the muscles more tense. It seems time lost for a grown man to be turning the leaves of a dictionary, like a boy, to learn German, but I believe he will gain tension and creative power by so doing. Good books have always a prolific atmosphere about them and brood upon the spirit.

[Newton was still the temporary abiding-place. On May 31 Emerson wrote to his brother Edward in Porto Rico: "Here sit Mother and I among the pine-trees, still almost as we shall lie by and by under them;" and telling Edward of the accession of property that had come to him from his late wife's estate, urged him to come home and join him, saying: "If you will come, we will retreat into Berkshire and make a little world of other stuff."]

June 2.

The life of women is unfortunately so much for exhibition that every the minutest trait pleases which is wholly natural, even to a girl's crying because it thundered, *et ce que disent les femmes l'une de l'autre.*

What more sensible than what they say of Mr. ——, that he sells his splendid Chinese house and goes to live at Watertown because he cannot make a bow and pleasantly entertain the crowd of company that visit him. C. C. E. says he should build a large room.

Preached at Waltham yesterday. Expect every day when some trenchant Iarno [1] will come across me and read me such a lesson. Is the preacher one to make a fool of himself for the entertainment of other people? would he say, When there is any difference of level felt in the footboard of the pulpit and the floor of the parlor, you have not said that which you should say? The best sermon would be a quiet, conversational analysis of these felt difficulties, discords; to show the chain under the leather; to show the true, within the supposed advantage of Christian institutions. There are several worthy people making themselves less because they would act the police officer, and keep the factory people at church. I say, "Be genuine." They answer, "If we should, our society, which has no real virtue, would go to pot." And so the yoke, it is confessed, is only borne out of fear. Suppose they should let the societies go down, and form new and genuine ones. Let such as felt the advantage of a sermon and social worship meet voluntarily and compel nobody.

---

1 A character in Goethe's *Wilhelm Meister*.

June 3.

The lower tone you take, the more flexible your voice is.

June 5.

What perpetual working and counterworking in us, so that many good actions spring from bad motives, and many bad actions from good motives. Verily. Then how slovenly and despite ourselves we are continually jostled into knowledge of truth. D. P. commends peace to the boys, the boys debate the matter and give such cogent reasons to the contrary, that D. P. in anger and fear to be put down, wades out beyond his depth in the other direction, and gets unawares a knowledge of the infinite reason of love. Highest praise and happiness is it to go forward one step of our own seeing and find ourselves in a position whose advantages we foresaw.

Fatal tendency to hang on to the letter and let the spirit go. We will debate the precept about "turning the cheek to the smiter," the "coat and cloke," the "not taking thought what ye shall speak," etc., and question whether it is now practicable, and is now obligatory. Yet every one of us has had his hours of illumination by the same spirit, when he fully understood those commands and saw that he did not need them. He

had the Commander, giving fresh precepts fit
for the moment and the act. Yet it is well that
Christ's are recorded. They show how high the
waters flowed when the spirit brooded upon them,
and are a measure of our deficiency. The wonder
that is felt at these precepts is a measure of our
unreason.

ANTAGONISMS

There are persons both of superior character
and intellect whose superiority quite disappears
when they are put together. They neutralize,
anticipate, puzzle, and belittle each other.

June 8.

The solitary bird that sung in the pine tree
reminded me of one talker who has nothing to
say alone, but when friends come, and the conversation grows loud, is forthwith set into intense activity, mechanically echoing and strength-
ening everything that is said, without any regard
to the subject or to truth.

The soul has its diurnal, annual and secular
periodic motions like the needle. You may doubt
for a day, but you will believe before the week's
end; you may abandon your friendships and
your designs, as you think, on good advice, for

these months, but by and by it will come back as with thunder from all heaven, that God crowns him who persists in his purposes — no fair-weather friend, — that the very armory of heroes and sages is in obscurity, conflict, high heart which sustained itself Alone.

You are there in that place to testify. There was a man in Sais who was very good to all people, but he could not be trusted alone. When he was left alone, all the devils associated themselves to him, and he robbed, murdered, committed adultery, blasphemed, lied, cringed.

June 10.

One has dim foresight of hitherto uncomputed mechanical advantages who rides on the railroad, and moreover a practical confirmation of the ideal philosopher that matter is phenomenal, whilst men and trees and barns whiz by you as fast as the leaves of a dictionary. As our tea-kettle hissed along through a field of mayflowers, we could judge of the sensations of a swallow who skims by trees and bushes with about the same speed. The very permanence of matter seems compromised, and oaks, fields, hills, hitherto esteemed symbols of stability, do absolutely dance by you. The countryman called it "Hell in harness." [1]

What habits of observation has my friend, what keen senses. It would seem as if nothing, though under your nose, was permitted to be visible to you until he had seen it. Thereafter, all the world may see it, and it never leaves your eyes.

Washington wanted a fit public. Aristides, Phocion, Regulus, Hampden had worthy observers. But there is yet a dearth of American genius.

I went to the menagerie Tuesday and saw 14 pelicans, a sacred ibis, a gazelle, zebras, a capibara, ichneumon, hyena, etc. It seems to me like "visiting the spirits in prison." Yet not to "*preach*." There was the mystery. No word could pass from me to them. Animals have been called by some German "the dreams of Nature." I think we go to our own dreams for a conception of their consciousness. In a dream I have the same instinc-

1 It would seem that Mr. Emerson had taken a ride on the portion of the new railroad between Boston and Worcester which was opened in April, 1834, when the locomotive engine had been for the first time introduced in New England.

tive obedience, the same torpidity of the highest
power, the same unsurprised assent to the monstrous, as these metamorphosed men exhibit.
The pelicans remind one of Nick Bottom. One
has a kind of compassionate fear lest they should
have a glimpse of their forlorn condition. What
a horrible calamity would be to them one moment's endowment of reason! Yet sometimes
the negro excites the same feeling, and sometimes
the sharp-witted, prosperous white man. You
think, if he could overlook his own condition,
he could not be kept from suicide. But to the
contemplations of the Reason is there never
penitence.

The scholar seeks the ingenuous boy to ap-
prize him of the treasures within his reach, to
show him poetry, religion, philosophy, and con-
gratulate him on being born into the universe.
The boy's parents immediately call to thank him
for his interest in their son, and ask him to procure him a schoolmaster's situation.

June 18.

Everything teaches, even dilettantism. The
dilettante does not, to be sure, learn anything
of botany by playing with his microscope, and

with the terminology of plants, but he learns what dilettantism is; he distinguishes between what he knows and what he affects to know, and through some pain and self-accusation he is attaining to things themselves.

Webster's speeches seem to be the utmost that the unpoetic West has accomplished or can. We all lean on England; scarce a verse, a page, a newspaper, but is writ in imitation of English forms; our very manners and conversation are traditional, and sometimes the life seems dying out of all literature, and this enormous paper currency of Words is accepted instead. I suppose the evil may be cured by this rank rabble party, the Jacksonism of the country, heedless of English and of all literature — a stone cut out of the ground without hands; — they may root out the hollow dilettantism of our cultivation in the coarsest way, and the new-born may begin again to frame their own world with greater advantage. Meantime Webster is no imitator, but a true genius for his work, if that is not the highest. But every true man stands on the top of the world. He has a majestic understanding, which is in its right place, the servant of the reason, and employed ever to bridge over the gulf between the revelations of his Reason, his Vision, and the Facts within, in the microscopic optics of the calculators that surround him. Long may he live.

It is singular that every natural object, how wearisome soever in daily observation, is always agreeable in description, and doubly so in illustration.

June 20.

What a charm does *Wilhelm Meister* spread over society, which we were just getting to think odious. And yet, as I read the book to-day and thought of Goethe as the *Tag und Jahres Hefte* describes him, he seemed to me, — all-sided, gifted, indefatigable student as he is, — to be only another poor monad, after the fashion of his little race bestirring himself immensely to hide his nothingness, spinning his surface directly before the eye to conceal the universe of his ignorance. The finest poems of the world have been expedients to get bread, or else expedients to keep the writer from the mad-house and amuse him and his fellow men with the illusion that he knew; but the greatest passages they have writ, the infinite conclusions to which they owe their fame, are only confessions. Throughout Goethe prevails the undersong of confession and amazement; the apothegm of Socrates; the recantation of Man. The first questions are always to be asked, and we fend them off by much speaking and many books, so that scarcely can I blame the man who affects to philosophize as some sensualists do, and says his fun is profound calculation. And yet it is best in the poorest view to keep the powers healthy and supple by appropriate action.

" All things," complained the philosopher, " hasten back to unity."

The bells in America toll because Lafayette has died in France. The bells in all the earth, in church, monastery, castle, and pagoda might well toll for the departure of so pure, faithful, heroic, secular a spirit out of the earth to which it has been salt and spikenard. Go in, great heart! to the Invisible, to the kingdom of love and faith. He has

> " Lingered among the last of those bright clouds
> Which on the steady breeze of Honour sail
> In long procession, calm and beautiful."

It occurred that the gestures of the Reason are graceful and majestic, those of the Understanding quick and mean. The uplifted eye of Memory, the solemn pace, perfect repose, and simple attitudes of Meditation inspire respect, but the moment the senses call us back, and the Understanding directs us, we run, start, look askance, or turn and look behind us, we skulk, fumble, exceed in manner and voice, and suffer. Live by reason, and you will not make the foul mouths, nor utter the foul breath nor drag disgracefully sleepy days that convince Alexander that he is mortal. When Minerva, they say, saw her distorted face in a brook, she threw away her hautboy.

June 26.

If friendship were perfect, there would be no false prayers. But what could Wilhelm have done at the Crabs house?

The rare women that charm us are those happily constituted persons who take possession of society wherever they go, and give it its form, its tone. If they sit, as we sit, to wait for what shall be said, we shall have no Olympus. To their genius elegance is essential. It is enough that we men stammer and mince words and play the clown and pedant alternately. They must speak as clearly and simply as a song. I say all this is a happiness, not a merit, and few there be that find it. Society cannot give it, nor the want of society withhold it. Aunt Mary and S. A. R.[1] never wait for the condescending influences of society, but seek it out, scrutinize it, amuse themselves with the little, sympathize with and venerate the great. And Ellen, in a life of solitude, was incapable of an inelegance.

Yesterday the attentions of the poor girl with flowers made me think how elegant is kindness. Kindness is never vulgar. Genius and strong Will may be only phenomena in the chain of causes, and most men and women may grow up to be what they are, as the cows and horses grow in the pastures, but kindness from a perfect stranger — a sudden will to benefit me and everybody — is a salient spring, it is a hint of the presence of the living God. The condition of young women, even the most favored, excites sometimes a profound pity. . . . But kindness, native courtesy, redeems them at once out of your pity; they are happy and the objects of your joy and your respect.

> " Happy, happier far than thou,
>   With the laurel on thy brow,
>   She who makes the humblest hearth
>   Lovely but to one on earth." [2]

1 Mrs. Ripley.   2 [Mrs. Hemans.]

Next door to us lives a young man who is learning to drum. He studies hard at his science every night. I should like to reward his music with a wreath of *Smilax peduncularis*.[1]

Goethe and Carlyle, and perhaps Novalis, have an undisguised dislike or contempt for common virtue standing on common principles. Meantime they are dear lovers, steadfast maintainers of the pure ideal morality. But they worship it as the highest beauty; their love is artistic. Praise Socrates to them, or Fénelon, much more any inferior contemporary good man, and they freeze at once into silence. It is to them sheer prose.

The *Tag und Jahres Hefte* is a book unparalleled in America, an account of all events, persons, studies, taken from one point of view. The problem to be solved is, How shall this soul called *Goethe* be educated? And whatever he does or whatever befalls him is viewed solely in relation to its effect upon the development of his mind. Even in the arms of his mistress at Rome he says he studied sculpture and poetry. To husband our admiration is an intellectual temperance indispensable to health. But Goethe

1 Probably the older name for *S. rotundifolia*, the common catbriar.

was a person who hated words that did not stand for things, and had a sympathy with everything that existed, and therefore never writes without saying something. He will be artist, and look at God and man, and the Future, and the infinite, as a self-possessed spectator, who believed that what he saw he could delineate. Herder wisely questioned whether a man had a right thus to affect the god, instead of working with all his heart in his place. Self-cultivation is yet the moral of all that Goethe has writ, and in indolence, intolerance and perversion I think we can spare an olive and a laurel for him. No man has drawn his materials of fiction from so wide a circuit. Very properly he introduces into the machinery of his romance whatever feeling or impulse the most rapt enthusiast has trusted in. Coincidences, dreams, omens, spiritual impressions, and a habitual religious faith — all these are the materials which, as a wise artist, he avails himself of.

Nevertheless there is a difference between thought and thought, and it is as real a defect in a man not to perceive the right of his moral sentiments to his allegiance, as it is not to be conscious of moral sentiments. Yet Goethe, with all his fine things about *Entsagen*, can write and print too like Rochester and Béranger.

As to Carlyle, he is an exemplification of Novalis's maxim concerning the union of Poetry and Philosophy. He has married them, and both are the gainers. Who has done so before as truly and as well? *Sartor Resartus* is a philosophical poem.

[Added here, *November* 30.]

Goethe is praised as μυριόνους, or all-sided. And, if I understand it, this is the apology that is made for his Epicurean life compared with his religious perceptions. To praise a man for such quality is like praising an observatory for being very low and massive, and a very good fort. It is not more the office of man to receive all impressions, than it is to distinguish sharply between them. He that has once pronounced intelligently the word "Self - renouncement," "Invisible Leader," "Powers of Sorrow," and the like, is forever bound to the service of the superhuman.

We are wonderfully protected. We have scarce a misfortune, a hindrance, an infirmity, an enemy, but it is somehow productive of singular advantage to us. After groaning through years

of poverty and hard labor, the mind perceives
that really it has come the shortest road to a
valuable position, that, though the rough climate
was not good for leaves and flowers, it was good
for timber. It has been saved from what associations. It has been introduced to what thoughts
and feelings. "He knows you not, ye mighty
powers! who knows not sorrow." God brings
us by ways we know not and like not into Paradise.

July 12.

> "Lincoln bell flings o'er the fen
>   His far renowned alarum."

I read this and straight regret that I did not
visit Lincoln Cathedral and hear the far renowned
alarum; such superstitious preference do we give
to other men's senses. Undoubtedly something
in my own sphere or spherule takes the place
to me of that particular gratification. I have
some "Lincoln bell," heard with joy in my ordinary movements. Yet I long to hear this other,
simply out of deference to my fellows in England
who have exalted it by their love. Better believe
in the perfection of thine own lot. Retreat upon
your own spontaneous emotions. Mark the occasions of them, and cheerfully believe that what

has excited true and deep pleasure in one man is fitted to excite the same emotions in all men. So will I find my Lincolnshire in the next pasture, and the "bell" in the first thrush that sings. Napoleon sat back on his horse in the midst of the march to catch the fine tone of a bell.[1] With myself I shall always dwell, but Lincoln and Niagara and Cairo are less accessible. And yet, and yet, can aught approach the effect of the Sabbath morn in quietest retreats? And yet is its sacredness derivative and alien. Some thoughts are superficial, others have their root in your being. Always discriminate, when you would write, between them, and never choose the first for a topic. Diogenes moved his tub in winter into the sun, and in summer into the shade, and compared himself to the Persian King who spent the one season at Susa and the other at Ecbatana.

"As many languages as a man knows," said Charles V, "so many times is he a man." Our eagerness to possess this gift of foreign speech rather hinders than helps us to it. I stand in a company where circulates how much wit and information, yet not one thought can pass from them to me, — I do not understand their speech.

1 This anecdote was later used in the poem "Each and All."

My countryman enters who understands it, and the communication between them and him is perfect. Stung with desire, I devote myself to the task of learning the language, but this perpetual poetic vision before me, which is quite foreign from their experience, and which I shall lose as soon as I master the speech, affords me so much entertainment as to embarrass every particular effort at dialogue, and dispirits me and unfits me for that simple effort to know the thing said to me, and to convey my thought in return, which is the best instructor. Ralph Emerson said to me in Paris, that the Americans think there is some magic in speaking and writing French. He who has mastered the tongue sees nothing behind him but simple addition of particulars, and this new knowledge blends harmoniously with all his experience; and, moreover, it has lost all its anticipated value.

When the wrong handle is grasped of comparative anatomy, the tresses of beauty remind us of a mane. How much is an assembly of men restrained! It seems often like a collection of angels, and a collection of demons in disguise.

Come dal fuoco il caldo, esser diviso non può'l bel dall' eterno.   MICHEL ANGELO.

BANGOR,[1] *July* 15.

The thoughtful man laments perhaps the unpliancy of his organization, which draws down the corners of his mouth to ludicrous longitude, whilst all the company chat and titter around him. What matters it? He actually sympathizes with each of the company more truly than the liveliest chatterbox; for they are all going back from this smiling time to discipline, to silence, labor and anxiety, and then they recall the melancholy man with a fraternal remembrance.

In our plans of life an apparent confusion. We seem not to know what we want. Why, it is plain we can do best something which in the present form of society will be misconstrued and taken for another thing. I wish to be a true and free man, and therefore would not be a woman, or a king, or a clergyman, each of which classes,

---

1 Mr. Emerson had been invited to preach in Bangor for one or more Sundays. Possibly there was a vacancy in the pulpit, for he wrote to Dr. Hedge : "I am almost persuaded to sit down on the banks of this pleasant stream, and, if I could persuade a small number of persons to join my colony, we would have a settlement thirty miles up the river, at once." Evidently he had still the hope of establishing a home with his brothers.

in the present order of things, is a slave. Mr.
Canning judged right in preferring the title of
Mister, in the company of Alexander and Napoleon, to *My Lord*. The simple, untitled, unof-
ficed citizen possessing manners, power, cultivation, is more formidable and more pleasing than
any dignitary whose condition and etiquette only
makes him more vulnerable and more helpless.

Noble strain of the revolutionary papers. See
Williamson, [History of Maine,] volume ii,
pp. 408–411.

And when the port of Boston had been closed
(in June, 1774), sixteen days they tolled the bells
in the town of Falmouth all day, and addressed
an affectionate letter to the inhabitants of Boston.
"We look upon you," they say, "as sufferers
for the common cause of American liberty. We
highly appreciate your courage to endure priva-
tion and distress, sensibly aware that the season
puts to severest trial the virtues of magnanimity, patience, and fortitude, which your example
will honorably exemplify. We beg leave to tender you all the encouragements which the considerations of friendship and respect can inspire,
and all the assurances of succor which full hearts
and feeble abilities can render."

July 18.

The abomination of desolation is not a burned town, nor a country wasted by war, but the discovery that the man who has moved you is an enthusiast upon calculation.

" Indeed all that class of the severe and restrictive virtues are at a market almost too high for humanity." May be so. That gives them their worth. It is that we ourselves, the observers, have been imposed upon and led to condemn the actor before, and the far-sighted heroism of the sufferer has felt the condemnation, and yet persisted in his own judgment and kept up his courage — it is that conviction that adds eagerness to our commendation now.

What is there of the divine in a load of bricks? What is there of the divine in a barber's shop? . . . Much. All.

George A. Sampson died Wednesday evening, 23 July, 1834.

NEWTON, *August* 9.

Carlyle says Society is extinct. Be it so. Society existed in a clan; existed in Alaric and Attila's time, in the Crusades, in the Puritan Conventicles. Very well. I had rather be soli-

tary as now, than social as then. Society exists
now where there is love and faithful fellow-
working, only the persons composing it are
fewer — societies of two or three, instead of nations. Societies, parties, are only incipient stages,
tadpole states of men, as caterpillars are social,
but the butterfly not. The true and finished
man is ever alone. Men cannot satisfy him; he
needs God, and his intercourse with his brother
is ever condescending, and in a degree hypo-
critical.

"He charged them that they should tell no
man." "Hold thy tongue for one day; to-
morrow thy purpose will be clearer." Why, yea,
and it would be good if the minister put off his
black clothes and so affirmed the reality of spiritual distinctions. When I was at the ordination
at Bangor the other day, the men in the pulpit
seemed woodsawyers dressed up, as they stood
up and spoke in succession. It would not out
of my head. By and by a true priest spoke.
. . . Renounce. Work hard. In the great heats
why should you leave your labor for a little
sweat, since the haymaker does not? He *cannot ;* therefore, if you are noble, you will not.
Renounce. When I was in the pasture and
stopped to eat, the familiar cried, Eat not. Tut,

replied I, does Nemesis care for a whortleberry? I looked at the world, and it replied,
Yea. But the clock struck two and the table
was covered with fishes and fowls and confec-
tions. They are very good and my appetite is
keen; and I could not see any good in refusing
the pleasure of a hearty meal that was as great
as the pleasure. Look back, cried the familiar,
at years of good meat in Boston. Do you miss
anything that you forebore to eat? Nothing,
replied I.

First thoughts are from God; but not the
numerically first; allow what space you may for
the mind to grasp the facts, then the thoughts
that are first in place are divine and the second
earthly.

Sunday, *August* 10.

At Mr. Grafton's church this P. M. and heard
the eloquent old man preach his Jewish sermon
dry-eyed. Indeed I felt as a much worse spirit
might feel among worshippers — as if the last
link was severed that bound him to their traditions and he ought to go out hence. Strange
that such fatuity as Calvinism is now, should
be able to stand yet — mere shell as it is — in
the face of day. At every close of a paragraph
it almost seemed as if this devout old man

looked intelligence and questioned the whole thing. What a revival, if St. Paul should come and replace these threadbare rags with the inexhaustible resources of sound Ethics. Yet they are so befooled as to call this sucked eggshell high-toned orthodoxy, and to talk of anything true as *mere morality*. Is it not time to present this matter of Christianity exactly as it is, to take away all false reverence from Jesus, and not mistake the stream for the source? "It is no more according to Plato than according to me." God is in every man. God is in Jesus, but let us not magnify any of the vehicles, as we magnify the Infinite Law itself. We have defrauded him of his claim of love on all noble hearts by our superstitious mouth-honor. We love Socrates, but give Jesus the Unitarian Association.

See two sincere men conversing together. They deport themselves as if self-existent. Are they not for the time two gods? For every true man is as if he should say, I speak for the Universe; I am here to maintain the truth against all comers; I am in this place to testify.

August 11.

Is not man in our day described by the very attributes which once he gave his God? Is not

the sea his minister; the clouds his chariot; the
flame his wheels; and the winds his wings?

August 13.

Blessed is the child; the unconscious is ever
the act of God himself. Nobody can reflect upon
his *unconscious* period, or any particular word or
act in it, with regret or contempt. Bard or Hero
cannot look down upon the word or gesture of
a child; it is as great as they. Little Albert
Sampson asks when his father will come home,
and insists that *his father can't die.*

August 14.

We look up sometimes with surprise to see
that the tree, the hill, the schoolhouse are still
there, and have not vanished in our mood of
pyrrhonism. If there were many philosophers,
the world would go to pieces presently, all sand,
no lime. *Quam parva sapientia.* All society and
government seems to be *making believe*, when we
see such hollow boys with a grave countenance
taking their places as legislators, presidents, and
so forth. It could not be but that at intervals
throughout society there are real men inter-
mixed, whose natural basis is broad enough to
sustain these paper men in common times, as the

carpenter puts one iron bar in his banister to five or six wooden ones. Yet when at other times I consider the capacities of man and see how near alike they all are, and that [they] always seem to be on the verge of all that is great, and yet invisibly retained in inactivity and unacquaintance with our powers, it seems as if men were like the neuters of the hive, every one of which is capable of transformation into the queen-bee, which is done with some one as soon as the sovereign is removed.

The fourth chapter of my meditation is the observation that the soul, or the day, is a turning wheel which brings every one of its manifold faces for a brief season to the top. Now, this dunghill quality of animal courage, indomitable pluck, seems to be the supreme virtue; anon, patience; then, elegance; then, learning; then, wit; then, eloquence; then, wealth; then, piety; then beauty; each seems in turn the one desirable quality; and thus every dog has his day.

It occurred that the fine verse of " Honorable age," etc., in Wisdom of Solomon is quite Greek in its genius, not Jewish.

August 15.

Natural history by itself has no value; it is like a single sex; but marry it to human history, and it is poetry. Whole Floras, all Linnæus', and Buffon's volumes contain not one line of poetry, but the meanest natural fact, the habit of a plant, the organs, or work, or noise of an insect, applied to the interpretation or even associated to [with] a fact in human nature is beauty, is poetry, is truth at once.[1]

Saturday eve, *August* 16.

King Lear and *Antony and Cleopatra* still fill me with wonder. Every scene is as spirited as if writ by a fresh hand of the first class, and there is never straining; sentiments of the highest elevation are as simply expressed as the stage directions. They praise Scott for taking kings and nobles off their stilts and giving them simple dignity, but Scott's grandees are all turgid compared with Shakspear's. There is more true elevation of character in Prince Hal's sentence about the pleached doublet than in any king in the romances. Another mastership of Shakspear is the immortality of the style, the speeches of passion are writ, for the most part, in a style as fresh now as it was when the play was published. The remarkable sentences of

1 This passage is used in *Nature*, vol. i, p. 28 (Centenary Edition), but in not quite so pleasing a form.

Lear, Hamlet, Othello, Macbeth, might as naturally have been composed in 1834 as in 1600.

> " I tax not you, you elements, with unkindness ;
> I never gave you kingdom, called you children,
> You owe me no subscription," etc.

August 17.

Freedom. A very small part of a man's voluntary acts are such as agree perfectly with his conviction, and it is only at rare intervals that he is apprized of this incongruity — " so difficult is it to read our own consciousness without mistakes." Whose act is this church-going, whose this praying? The man might as well be gone, so he leave a Maelzel[1] machine in his place.

Evening.

On the wisdom of Ignorance. Milton was too learned, though I hate to say it. It wrecked his originality. He was more indebted to the Hebrew than even to the Greek. Wordsworth is a more original poet than he. That seems the poet's garland. He speaks by that right, that he has somewhat yet unsaid to say. Scott and Coleridge and such like are not poets, only professors

[1] Johann Nepomuc Mälzel, an Austrian, inventor of an orchestral panharmonicon, visited Boston in 1826.

of the art. Homer's is the only Epic. He is original, yet he separates before the German tele-
scopes into two, ten or twenty stars. Shakspeare,
by singular similarity of fortune, undeniably an
original and unapproached bard, — first of men,
— is yet enfolded in the same darkness as an individual writer. His best works are of doubted
authenticity, and what was his, and what his nov-
elist's, and what the players', seems yet disputed:
a sharp illustration of that relentless disregard
of the individual in regard for the race which
runs through history. It is not an individual,
but the general mind of man that speaks from
time to time, quite careless and quite forgetful of
what mouth or mouths it makes use of. Go to the
bard or orator that has spoken and ask him if
what he said were his own? No; he got it he
knows not where, but it is none of his. For example, Edward Emerson, whence had you those
thunderous sentences in your Master's Oration? [1]

There is nothing in Wordsworth so vicious
in sentiment as Milton's account of God's chariots, etc., standing harnessed for great days. We
republicans cannot relish Watts' or Milton's
royal imagery.

1 Suggesting that Edward was influenced by Webster, in
whose office he was studying at the time of his college address.

Is it not true that contemplation belongs to us, and therefore outward worship, *because* our reason is at discord with our understanding? And that, whenever we live rightly, thought will express itself in ordinary action so fully as to make a special action, that is, a religious form, impertinent? Is not Solomon's temple built because Solomon is not a temple, but a brothel and a change-house? Is not the meeting-house dedicated because men are not? Is not the church opened and filled on Sunday because the commandments are not kept by the worshippers on Monday? But when he who worships there, speaks the truth, follows the truth, is the truth's; when he awakes by actual communion to the faith that God is in him, will he need any temple, any prayer? The very fact of worship declares that God is not at one with himself, that there are two gods. Now does this sound like high treason and go to lay flat all religion? It does threaten our forms; but does not that very word "form" already sound hollow? It threatens our forms, but it does not touch injuriously Religion. Would there be danger if there were real religion? If the doctrine that God is in man were faithfully taught and received, if I lived to speak the truth and enact it, if I pursued every generous sentiment as one enamoured, if the majesty of goodness were reverenced, would not such a principle serve me by way of police at least as well as a Connecticut Sunday? But the people, the people. You hold up your pasteboard religion for the people who are unfit for a true. So you say. But presently there will arise a race of preachers who will take such hold of the omnipotence of truth that they will blow the old falsehood to shreds with the breath of their mouth. There is no material show so splendid, no poem so musical as the great law of Compensation in our moral nature. When an ardent mind once gets a glimpse of that perfect beauty, and sees how it envelopes him and determines all his being, will he easily slide back to a periodic shouting about "blood atoning"? I apprehend that the religious history of society is to show a pretty rapid abandonment of forms of worship and the renovation and exaltation of preaching into real anxious instruction.

August 18.

The Mussulman is right, by virtue of the law of Compensation, in supposing the scraps of paper he saves will be a carpet under his feet over the bridge of Purgatory. He has learned the lesson of reverence to the name of Allah.

August 19.

Never assume. Be genuine. So wrote I for my own guidance months and years ago; but how vainly! Show me in the world the sincere man. Even the wit, the sentiment that seasons the dinner, is a sort of hypocrisy to hide the coarseness of appetite. The child is sincere, and the man when he is alone, if he be not a writer; but on the entrance of the second person, hypocrisy begins.[1]

What mischief is in this art of writing. An unlettered man considers a fact, to learn what it means; the lettered man does not sooner see it than it occurs to him how it can be told. And this fact of looking at it as an artist blinds him to the better half of the fact. Unhappily he is conscious of the misfortune, which rather makes it worse. As cultivated flowers turn their stamens to petals, so does he turn the practick part to idle show. He has a morbid growth of eyes; he sees with his feet. What an unlucky creature is Dr. Channing. Let him into a room; would not all the company feel that, simple as he looked,

1 This sentence occurs in "Friendship," *Essays*, Second Series.

the cat was not more vigilant, that he had the delirium tremens and its insomnolency, that he heard what dropped from any as if he read it in print?

We sit down with intent to write truly, and end with making a book that contains no thought of ours, but merely the tune of the time. Here am I writing a Φ B K poem, free to say what I choose, and it looks to me now as if it would scarce express thought of mine, but be a sort of *fata morgana* reflecting the images of Byron, Shakspear, and the newspapers. We do what we can, and then make a theory to prove our performance the best.

August 22.

The greatest men have been most thoughtful for the humblest. Socrates, of whom see the fine story told in Plutarch on *Tranquillity*; Alfred, Franklin, Jesus Christ and all the Pauls and Fénelons he has made. It requires no ordinary elevation to go by the social distinctions and feel that interest in humanity itself which is implied in attentions to the obscure. Wordsworth is a philanthropist; Fox; Wilberforce; Howard; Montaigne. Washington introduced the ass into America. And, so keep me heaven, I will love the race in general if I cannot in any particular.

August 30.

Were it not a heroic adventure in me to insist on being a popular speaker, and run full tilt against the Fortune who with such beautiful consistency shows evermore her back? Charles's naïf censure last night provoked me to show him a fact, apparently wholly new to him, that my entire success, such as it is, is composed wholly of particular failures, — every public work of mine of the least importance, having been (probably without exception) noted at the time as a failure. The only success (agreeably to common ideas) has been in the country, and there founded on the false notion that here was a Boston preacher. I will take Mrs. Barbauld's line for my motto

" And the more falls I get, move faster on." [1]

I never was on a coach which went fast enough for me.

It is extremely disagreeable, nay, a little fiendish to laugh amid dreams. In bed I would keep my countenance, if you please.

1 Of a brook.

A poem is made up of thoughts, each of which filled the whole sky of the poet in its turn.

NEWTON, *September* 13.

There are some things which we should do, if we considered only our own capacity and safety, which we stick at doing when we think of the estimates and prejudices of other people. For the freest man society still holds some bribe. He wants of it a living, or a friend, or a wife, or a fit employment, or a reputation correspondent to his self-esteem. Is it not possible to draw in his importunate beggar hands and ask nothing but what he can himself satisfy? In some respects certainly. In this matter of reputation — is it not possible to settle it in one's mind immoveably that merit of the first class cannot, in the nature of things, be readily appreciated; that immortal deeds, over which centuries are to pass as days, are not brought to light and wholly comprehended and decided upon in a few hours? The wise man is to settle it immoveably in his mind, that he only is fit to decide on his best action; he only is fit to praise it; his verdict is praise enough, and as to society, "their hiss is thine applause." It is an ordinary enhancement of our admiration of noble thinking and acting that it was done in wilful defiance of present censure out of a clear foresight of the eternal praise of the just. . . .

Next, as to thoughts of the first class. Do not cease to utter them and make them as pure of all dross as if thou wert to speak to sages and demigods, and be no whit ashamed if not one, yea, not one in the assembly should give sign of intelligence. Make it not worthy of the beggar to receive, but of the emperor to give. Is it not pleasant to you, unexpected wisdom? depth of sentiment in middle life? Iarnos and Abbés that in the thick of the crowd are true kings, and gentlemen without the harness and the envy of the throne? Is it not conceivable that a man or a woman in coarse clothes may have unspeakable comfort in being the only human being privy to a virtuous action which he or she is in the act of consummating? . . .

Perhaps you cannot carry too far the doctrine of self-respect. The story that strikes me; the joke that makes me laugh often; the face that bewitches me; the flower, the picture, the building, that, left to myself, I prefer, these I ought to remember, love, and praise. For there is nothing casual or capricious in the impression they make (provided always that I act naturally,) but they make this strong impression because I am fit for them and they are fit for me. But if I forsake my peculiar tastes, overawed by the popular voice or deferring to Mr. Everett's or Mr. Wordsworth's or Baron Swedenborg's tastes, I am straightway dwarfed of my natural dimensions for want of fit nourishment and fit exercise. It is as if you should fill the stomach of a horse with the food of a fish. Lean without fear on your own tastes. Is there danger in the doctrine as if it permitted self-indulgence? Fool! Every man hath his own conscience as well as his own genius, and if he is faithful to himself he will yield that law implicit obedience. All these doctrines contained in the proposition, Thou art sufficient unto thyself (*Ne te quæsiveris extra*) are perfectly harmless, on the supposition that they are heard as well as spoken in faith. There is no danger in them to him who is really in earnest to know the truth, but like everything else, may be a mere hypocrite's cloak to such as seek offence, or to such as talk for talk's sake.

Sunday, *September* 14.

What is the doctrine of *infallible guidance if one will abdicate choice*, but striving to act uncon-

sciously, to resume the simplicity of childhood?
It is to act on the last impression derived from
a knowledge of all the facts, and not wilfully to
secure a particular advantage. The single-minded
actor insists on the tranquillity of his own mind.[1]

Ne te quæsiveris extra. I would insist so far on
my own tastes as to read those books I fancy and
postpone reading those which offer me no attraction. If Dr. Linberg would have me study Swedenborg because I have respect for his doctrines,
I shall hold it sufficient answer that the *aura* of
those books is not agreeable to my intellectual
state. It is not for nothing that one word makes
such impression, and the other none; it is not
without preëstablished harmony, this sculpture
in the memory. The eye was placed where that
ray should fall, to the end that it might testify
of that particular ray. I will not so far do violence
to myself as to read them against my inclination,
believing that those books which at any time I
crave are the books fittest at that time for me.
This is Carlyle's justification for giving such hu-
morous prominence to such incidents as George
Fox's leather suit of clothes. If I obey my pas-

[1] This seems an attempt to reconcile the Quaker doctrine
of Acquiescence with Self-Reliance. This was later done in
"The Oversoul."

sion, instead of my reason, that is another affair. The appeal is always open from Philip drunk to Philip sober.

September 15.

Heard Mr. Blagden[1] preach yesterday with much interest. What an orator would some extraordinary discipline of events make of him! Could some Socrates win him to the love of the True and the Beautiful; or extreme sorrows arouse the mighty interior reactions; or revolutionary violence call into life the best ambition; could any event acquaint him with himself, he would, with his rare oratorical talents, absolutely command us. His manner is the best I know of, and seems to me unexceptionable. As to his preaching, that was good, too, in the main. The skeleton of his sermon, or, as Charles called it, the frame of his kite, was fallacious, illogical after the most ordinary fashion of the Wisners and Beechers, but his strong genius led him continually to penetrate this husk, and, leaning simply on himself, speak the truth out of this unnecessary mask. The conflict of the tradition and of his own genius is visible throughout. He gets his hands and eyes up in describing Jehovah

1 Dr. George Washington Blagden, pastor of the Old South Church.

exalted as in Calvinistic state, and then saves the whole by ending with — "in the heart's affections." I listen without impatience, because, though the whole is literally false, it is really true; only he speaks parables which I translate as he goes; thus, he says, "The carnal mind hates God continually"; and I say, "It is the instinct of the understanding to contradict the reason." One phrase translates the other.

The charm of Italy is the charm of its names. I have seen as fine days from my own window. Then what Boswellism it is to travel! Illustrate, eternize your own woodhouse. It is much cheaper, and quite possible to any resolute thinker.

What matters it, I said to myself on my journey, as the persons in the coach disputed as to the name of the town, whether this bunch of barberry bushes and birches visible from the coach-window be called Bridgewater or Taunton? So, what matter whether this hill and yon green field be called Garofalo, Terni, or Ipswich and Cape Cod? Let the soul be fully awake, and its thought is so much that the place becomes nothing. Remember the Sunday morning in Naples when I said, "This moment is the truest vision, the best spectacle I have seen amid all the wonders, and this moment, this vision I might have had in my own closet in Boston." Hence learn that it is an unworthy superstition for seers to go to Italy or France and come home and describe houses and things; let them see men and magnify the passages of common life. Let them be so man-wise that they can see through the coat, the rank, the language, and sympathize promptly with that other self that under these thin disguises wholly corresponds to their own. . . .

You do not know any Socrates. Very likely. The philosopher whom you have admired in discourse makes a different impression in private life. Very likely. Most men do; their aims are not distinct enough. As his aim becomes more distinct, it will insensibly pervade and characterize his private action, his manners, his table-talk.

The whole matter of Riches and Poverty is reversed by the act of reflexion, whenever it begins. The intellect at once takes possession of another's wealth, and habits, and performances, as if it were its own. Who is rich in the room where Socrates sits but he? Whilst Webster speaks to the Senate, who is formidable but he? The Intellect, fairly excited, overleaps all bounds with equal ease, and is as easily master of millions as master of one. With each divine impulse it rends the thin rinds of the visible and finite and comes out into Eternity, inspires and expires its air. It converses with truths that have always been spoken in the world, and becomes conscious of a closer sympathy with Phocion and Epictetus than with the persons in the house.

Afternoon.

No art can exceed the mellow beauty of one square rood of ground in the woods this afternoon. The noise of the locust, the bee, and the pine; the light, the insect forms, butterflies, cankerworms hanging, balloon - spiders swinging, devils-needles cruising, chirping grasshoppers; the tints and forms of the leaves and trees, — not a flower but its form seems a type, not a capsule but is an elegant seedbox, — then the myriad asters, polygalas, and golden-rods, and through the bush the far pines, and overhead the eternal sky. All the pleasing forms of art are imitations of these, and yet before the beauty of a right action all this beauty is cold and unaffecting.

Noble scene in *I Promessi Sposi*, the humiliation of Fra Cristoforo. That is what we aim to teach in all our Christian rhetoric about the transforming power of godliness.

Young men, struck with particular observations, begin to make collections of related truths and please themselves, as Burton did, with thinking the wheel, an arc of whose curve they discern, will, by their careful addition of arc to arc as they descry them, by and by come full circle, and be contained in the field of their vision. By and by they learn that the addition of particular facts brings them no nearer to the completion of an infinite orbit.

Shall I say that the use of Natural Science seems merely ancillary to Moral? I would learn the law of the diffraction of a ray because, when I understand it, it will illustrate, perhaps suggest a new truth in ethics.

September 16.

How despicable are the starts, sidelong glances, and lookings back of suspicious men. Go forward and look straight ahead, though you die for it. Abernethy says in his Hunter book, that the eye-sockets are so formed in the gods and heroes of Greek Sculpture that it would be impossible for such eyes to squint and take furtive glances on this side and that. You have looked behind you at the passenger and caught his eye looking behind also. What dastards you both are for that moment! The unconscious forever, which turns the whole head or nothing!

September 17.

How truly has poetry represented the difficulty of reflexion in the story of Proteus or Silenus, and in that of Odin's Prophetess! Any evasion, any digression, anything but sitting down before the gates with immoveable determination that they must open. One of the forms the Proteus takes is that of civil self-depreciation. "You quite mistake, sir; I am not that you took me for, a poor, evanescent topic really not worth your consideration; it was my resemblance to a relation that deceived you. Had you not better seek that?"

The poet writes for readers he little thinks of. Persons whom he could not bear, and who could not bear him, yet find passages in his works which are to them as their own thoughts. So Aunt Mary quotes the verses.

"That which Sir William Pepperell willed, came to pass." [1] There is in some men, as it were, a preëxistent harmony stablished between them and the course of events, so that they will at the precise moment that which God *does*. They are pitched to the tune of the time. Or, shall I say, they are like the fly in the coach?

September 22.

One is daunted by every one of a multitude of rules which we read in books of criticism, but when we speak or write *unconsciously* we are carried through them all safely without offending or perceiving one.

October 6.

In September, the roads and woods were full of crickets, and as fast as one falls by the way, the rest eat him up.

The high prize of eloquence may be mine, the joy of uttering what no other can utter, and what all must receive.

I thought how much, not how little accomplishment in manners, speech, practick, address, an open eye discovers in each passenger. If an

1 Williamson.

equal vitality is dealt out to each man, how strange, if diverging by all that force from your line, your neighbor had not attained a degree of mastery in one sort admirable to you. Insist on yourself [1] .... Adhere to your own and produce it with the meek courage that intimates, This possession is my all; is my inheritance from Almighty God and must have value.

October 14.

Every involuntary repulsion that arises in your mind, give heed unto. It is the surface of a central truth.

In Boston, at Second Church, George Sampson told me after I preached my sermon on Habit, that Mr. Washburn said to him, that he wished he was in the habit of hearing such sermons as that; which speech I found to be good praise and good blame. [2]

New York, *October* 18.

Received the tidings of the death of my dear brother Edward on the first day of this month

1 Here follows a short passage printed in "Self-Reliance."

2 This passage is written in here in Mr. Emerson's handwriting of many years later.

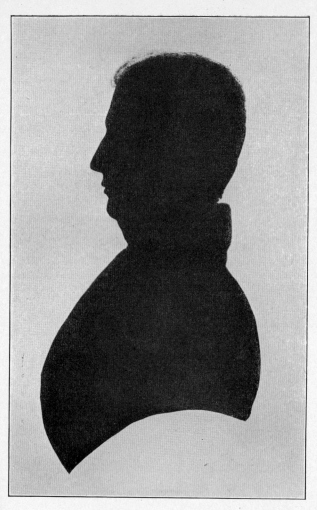

EDWARD BLISS EMERSON

at St. John, Porto Rico. So falls one pile more of hope for this life. I see I am bereaved of a part of myself.

> " Whatever fortunes wait my future life
> The beautiful is vanished and returns not." [1]

October 27.

> " Let them rave !
> Thou art quiet in thy grave." [2]

Even so, how oft saith the spirit, that happier is the lot of the dead than of the living that are yet alive. Who that sees the spirit of the Beast uppermost in the politics and the movements of the time, but only congratulates Washington that he is long already wrapped in his shroud, and forever safe, that he was laid sweet in his grave, the Hope of humanity not yet subju-

1 From Schiller's *Wallenstein*, Coleridge's translation.

For an account of Edward Bliss Emerson, see Cabot's and Holmes's Memoirs of Emerson, also Senator Hoar's *Autobiography*, and Emerson's " In Memoriam E. B. E." in the *Poems* (Centenary and Riverside Editions) before which he placed his brother's " Last Farewell " on leaving home for Porto Rico. See also the " Dirge."

2 Quoted from memory incorrectly from Tennyson's "Dirge."

gated in him.[1] And Edward's fervid heart is also forever still, no more to suffer from the tumults of the natural world. And they who survive and love men have reason to apprehend that, short as their own time may be, they may yet outlive the honor, the religion, yea, the liberty of the country. Yet, yet is

> "Hope the paramount duty which Heaven lays
> For its own honor, on man's suffering heart."

Otherwise one would be oppressed with melancholy and pray to die whenever he heard of the orgies of the Julien Hall or of the outrages of a mob.

The best sign which I can discover in the dark times is the increasing earnestness of the cry which swells from every quarter that a systematic Moral Education is needed. Channing, Coleridge, Wordsworth, Owen, De Gerando, Spurzheim, Bentham. Even Saul is among the Prophets. The gentleman will by and by be found to mean the man of Conscience. Carlyle; also Pestalozzi.

> "Where every man may take liberties there is little Liberty for any man."

1 This sentence appears in the last paragraph of "Heroism" (*Essays*, First Series).

All around us in vulgar daylight are hid (yes, hid in daylight) sublimest laws. De Staël saw them. Ours have not yet been seen. Do not multiply your facts, but seek the meaning of those you have. This eternal superiority belongs to the contemplative man over his more forcible and more honored neighbor, styled the practical man, that the former moves in a real world, the latter in a phenomenal ; that though the seasons of the former's activity may be rare and with intermissions of deepest gloom, yet when he works it is life, properly so called, whilst the latter's endless activity and boundless pretension reminds him too often of the laborer at the poor-house who worked all winter shovelling a ton of coal from the yard to the cellar, and then from the cellar to the yard. Euler's *truth against all experience.*[1]

It is losing time to inquire anxiously respecting the opinions of another speculator. The way his opinions have attained any value is by his forbearing to inquire and merely observing.

Man is great, not in his goals, but in his transition from state to state. Great in act, but instantly dwarfed by self-indulgence.

1 For full quotation, see p. 356.

Not Universal Education, but the *Penny Magazine* has failed. Brougham may have failed, but Pestalozzi has not. Leibnitz said, "I have faith that man may be reformed when I see how much Education may be reformed." Why not a moral Education as well as a discovery of America?

The education of the mind consists of a continual substitution of facts for words, as in petrefaction a particle of stone replaces a particle of wood. But observe that what are called facts are commonly words, as regards the fact-man.

It is rather humiliating to attend a public meeting such as this New York Caucus last evening, and see what words are best received, and what a low, animal hope and fear patriotism is. There is, however, great unity in the audience. What pleases the audience *very much*, pleases every individual in it. What tires me, tires all.

Greatest care is taken instinctively on both sides to represent their own cause as the winning one. The word, "Why then do we despond?" was manifestly a mistake in Mr. Hone's speech. This party-lie aims to secure the votes of that numerous class (whose vote, *weighed*,

would kick the beam) of indifferent, effeminate,
stupid persons, who in the absence of all internal strength, obey whatever seems the voice of
their street, their ward, their town, or whatever
domineering strength will be at the trouble of
civilly dictating to them. But their votes count
like real votes.

Transcribe from *Quarterly Review* the sentences on the progressive influence of the man
of genius. If you kill them, I will write a hymn
to their memory that shall sing itself, might
Luther say.

October 29.

Michel Angelo Buonarotti: John Milton:
Martin Luther: George Fox: Lafayette: Falk-
land, Hampden. Are not these names seeds?
"Men akin unto the Universe." [1]

The sentiment which, like Milton's, comes
down to new generations is that which was no

---

[1] Mr. Emerson was preparing the course of lectures on
Biography which he gave before the Society for the Diffusion
of Useful Knowledge, in Boston, in the following winter.
They were: "Tests of Great Men," "Michel Angelo,"
"Luther," "Milton," "Burke." For short abstracts, see
Cabot's Memoir, vol. ii, Appendix F, p. 712.

sham or half-sentiment to Milton himself, but the utterance of his inmost self, —

>　"plainest taught and easiest learnt
> What makes a nation happy and keeps it so."

Thanks for my sins, my defects; as the stag should have thanked for his feet. As no man thoroughly understands a truth until he has first contended against it, so no man has a thorough acquaintance with the hindrances or the talents of men until he has suffered from the one and seen the triumphs of the other over his own want of the same. I should not be a bard of common life, wants, individualities, in the pulpit, were I not the foolish parlor and table companion that I am.

We always idealize. Hard to find in Paul, Luther, Adams, Lafayette, anything so fine as to bear out our praises. For said not Aristotle, "Action is less near to vital truth than description"? We tinge them with the glories of that Idea in whose light they are seen.

We should hold to the usage until we are clear it is wrong.

How different is one man in two hours! Whilst he sits alone in his studies and opens not his mouth, he is God manifest, in flesh. Put him in a parlor with unfit company, and he shall talk like a fool.

October 31.

It is not to be doubted that the subjectivity (to use the Germanic phrase) of man clothes itself with a different objectivity in every age. Satan, who plays so prominent a part in the theology of the last age, is a hollow word now, but the evil principles which that word designated are no whit abated in virulence. I am bound by all my tastes to a reverence for Luther, yet can I by no means find any but a subjective, that is, essential correspondence in me to his mind. I cannot reanimate and appropriate his difficulties and speculations. Socrates, Bacon. How then Jesus and the apostles? Sometimes it seems nations, ages, were the body of shades of thought. Wrote mother, of Edward, what is true of all, that no words but his *name* can describe the peculiarities of any remarkable person.

But what shall be the action of society? How superficial are our fears and hopes! We meet with a single individual, or read a single newspaper expressing malignant sentiments, and we despond for the republic. By one declaimer of an opposite character our confidence is renewed that all will go well. In these times a ragged coat looks sinister and revolutionary. "Who injures one threatens all."

Luther says, "Pull not by force any one person from the *mass*. Reflect on my conduct in the affair of the indulgences. I had the whole body of the Papists to oppose. I preached, I wrote, I pressed on men's consciences with the greatest earnestness the positive declarations of the Word of God, but I used not a particle of force or constraint. What has been the consequence? This same Word of God has, while I was asleep in my bed, given such a blow to papal despotism as not one of the German princes, not even the Emperor himself, could have done. It is not I, it is the divine Word that has done all." Sublimely is it said in *Natural History of Fanaticism*, of angry persons, "Night does not part the combatants."

At least let the good side of these truths be applied to the true Word which the Poet has uttered whilst he is asleep in his bed, and when he is asleep in the grave it never halts or faints, but prospers in the work whereto it is sent.

I believe in the existence of the material world as the expression of the spiritual or real, and so look with a quite comic and condescending interest upon the show of Broadway with the air of an old gentleman when he says, "Sir, I knew your father." Is it not forever the aim and endeavor of the real to embody itself in the phenomenal? Broadway is Trade and Vanity made flesh. Therein should the philosophers walk as the impersonations of States, as if Massachusetts, Carolina, Ohio, should go out to take an airing.

November 1.

The union of extreme sensitiveness and defiance of opinion is not very uncommon. Every man is bipolar; never a circle; somewhere therefore in each one of never so many million you shall find the contrariety, inconsistency of his nature. And as language translates language, verb, verb, and noun, noun, so, could their surfaces be adjusted to each other, might we find one age corresponding to another age in every minute peculiarity, and every one man to every other man. This makes the interest of biography. I have heard men say they were afraid to read the accounts of suicides in the newspapers last year so remarkable for that crime.

Humboldt's scientific imagination will make the mnemonics of science. I read yesterday his designation of the sudden and violent disturbances of the magnetic equilibrium as "magnetic storms." So before of "volcanic paps."

The speculations of one age do not fit another. The great man of one age is a showing how the great man of this time would have acted in that. Now and then comes a crisis when the contemporaries of one opinion become contemporaries of another, and then the great man becomes the man of two ages, as was Burke. Fault of our mortality, we cannot act in a past age; we compensate ourselves by choosing out of that generation its most human individual and say, "Lo, how man acted!" Some men stand on the solid globe; others have no basis: but some one stands by and puts a shovel under their feet at any moment.

Euler, having demonstrated certain properties of Arches, adds, "All experience is in contradiction to this; but this is no reason for doubting its truth."

November 5.

The elections. Whilst it is notorious that the Jackson party is the *Bad* party in the cities and in general in the country, — except in secluded districts where a single newspaper has deceived a well disposed community, — still, on all the banners, equally of Tory and Whig, good professions are inscribed. The Jackson flags say, "Down with corruption!" "We ask for nothing but our Right." "The Constitution, the Laws," "The Laboring Classes," "Free trade," etc., etc. So that they have not yet come to the depravity that says, "Evil be thou my good." Should the Whig party fail, which God avert! the patriot will still have some confidence in the redeeming force of the latent, i. e., deceived virtue that is contained within the Tory party; and yet more in the remedial, regenerative Nature of Man, which ever reproduces a healthful moral sense even out of stupidity and corruption. Thus the children of the convicts at Botany Bay are found to have sound moral sentiments. Mr. H. says the Tories deserve to succeed, for they turn every stone with an Irishman under, and pick him up.

Surprising tendency of man *in action* to believe in his continuance. If these stormy partisans doubted their immortality in these hours, as in others, it would calm their zeal.

"The moral and intelligent instrumentality from the which the Sovereign Grace refuses to sever itself, is nothing else than the vital force which animates each single believer." *Fanaticism*, p. 8.

Noisy election; flags, boy processions, placards, badges, medals, bannered coaches, everything to get the hurrah on our side. That is the main end. Great anxiety, pale faces are become florid. They count that 1600 minutes are all the time allowed in all three days. Indisposition to business, and great promptness to spend.

The philosophy of the erect position. God made man upright.

The sublime of the ship is that in the pathless sea it carries its own direction in the chart and compass. See Herrick's verses.

'T is as hard to blow a flageolet — it takes so little breath — as to blow a flute, which costs so much; so in writing poetry, to speak simply enough in the abundance of thoughts and images is not easier than to be profound enough in their superficiality.

There is a way of making the biography of Luther as practical and pertinent to-day as the last paragraph from Liverpool upon the price of cotton.

The children of this world are wiser than the children of light. The good cause is always on the defensive, the evil, assailant. Because the unscrupulous can not only avail themselves of innocent means to their ends, but all evil ones likewise. The Whigs can put in their own votes. But the Tories can do this and put them in again in another ward, or bring a gang of forsworn gallows-birds to boot, to elect the officers that are to hunt, try, imprison and execute them. Let the worst come to the worst, and the Whig cause be crushed for a season, and the Constitution be grossly violated, then you should see the weak Whig become irresistible. They would then acquire the gloom and the might of fanaticism, and redeem America as they once redeemed England, and once aforetime planted and emancipated America.

> "How many big events to shake the earth
>   Lie packed in silence waiting for their birth."

Heard Mr. Maxwell at the Masonic Hall, a thoroughly public soul, the mere voice of the occasion and the hour. There are these persons into whom the general feeling enters, and through whom it passes and finds never a hitch or hindrance; they express what is boiling in the bosoms of the whole multitude around them. Plain is it, too, that there are people who justly make the impression of ability upon us, and yet can neither speak nor write nor act well. There is a callus or paralysis somewhere, a slight excess or defect that neutralizes a fine genius.

It is a great step from the thought to the expression of the thought in action. . . . If the wishes of the lowest class that suffer in these long streets should execute themselves, who can doubt that the city would topple in ruins. Do not trust man, great God! with more power until he has learned to use his little power better. Does not our power increase exactly in the measure we learn how to use it?

[Emerson now desired to live close to Nature, and what other spot had the same charm for him as had the low, wooded hills, the old Indian cornfields and the great meadows along the Concord River — Musketaquid — where he and his brothers had taken delight during vacations in boyhood? Doctor Ripley, his step-grandfather, lived in the Manse, built by his predecessor, the young William Emerson, the patriot min-

THE OLD MANSE

ister of the days of the Revolution. He wel-
comed Madam Emerson with her sons, Waldo
and Charles, as boarders, until plans for a more
permanent home could be made.]

CONCORD, *November* 15.

Hail to the quiet fields of my fathers! Not
wholly unattended by supernatural friendship
and favor, let me come hither. Bless my purposes as they are simple and virtuous. Coleridge's fine letter (in London *Literary Gazette*,
September 13, 1834) comes in aid of the very
thoughts I was revolving. And be it so. Hence-
forth I design not to utter any speech, poem or
book that is not entirely and peculiarly my work.
I will say at public lectures, and the like, those
things which I have meditated for their own sake,
and not for the first time with a view to that occasion. If, otherwise, you select a new subject,
and labor to make a good appearance on the
appointed day, it is so much lost time to you,
and lost time to your hearer. It is a parenthesis
in your genuine life. You are your own dupe,
and for the sake of conciliating your audience
you have failed to edify them, and, winning their
ear, you have really lost their love and gratitude.

Respect a man! assuredly, but in general only as the potential God, and therefore richly deserving of your pity and your tears. Now he is only a scrap, an ort, an end, and in his actual being no more worthy of your veneration than the poor lunatic. But the simplest person who, in his integrity, worships God, becomes God: at least no optics of human mind can detect the line where man, the effect, ceases, and God, the Cause, begins.

Unhappy divorce of Religion and Philosophy.

I suppose the materials may now exist for a Portraiture of Man which should be at once history and prophecy. Does it not seem as if a perfect parallelism existed between every great and fully developed man and every other? Take a man of strong nature upon whom events have powerfully acted — Luther or Socrates or Sam Johnson — and I suppose you shall find no trait in him — no fear, no love, no talent, no dream in one that did not translate a similar love, fear, talent, dream, in the other. Luther's Pope and Turk and Devil, and Grace, and Justification, and Catherine de Bore, shall reappear under far other names in George Fox, in John Milton, in

George Washington, in Goethe, or, long before, in Zeno and Socrates. Their circles, to use the language of geometry, would coincide. Here and there, to be sure, are anomalous, unpaired creatures, who are but partially developed, wizzled apples, — as if you should seek to match monsters, one of whom has a leg, another an arm, another two heads.

If one should seek to trace the genealogy of thoughts he would find Goethe's "Open Secret" fathered in Aristotle's answer to Alexander, "that these books were published, and not published." And Mme. de Staël's "Architecture is frozen music," borrowed from Goethe's "Architecture is dumb music," borrowed from Vitruvius, who said, "The architect must not only understand drawing, but also music." [1] And Wordsworth's man "that pleased his childish thought," got from Schiller's "Reverence the dreams of his youth," got from Bacon's *Primæ cogitationes et consilia juventutis plus Divinitatis habent.*

[1] . . . if those great Doctors truly said
That th' Ark to man's proportion was made.
— DONNE. (R. W. E.'s note.)

November 19.

The aged grandsire [1] came out of his chamber last evening into our parlor for the first time since his sickness, in cloak and velvet cap, and attended prayers. In things within his experience he has the most robust, erect common sense, is as youthful, vigorous in his understanding, as a man of thirty; in things without his circle often puerile. He behaved and spoke last evening as Jefferson or Franklin might. His prayer, as usual, with the happiest pertinence. "We have been variously disciplined; bereaved, but not destitute; sick, but thou hast healed, in degree, our diseases; and when there was but a step between us and death, thou hast said, Live." He ever reminds one, both in his wisdom and in the faults of his intellect, of an Indian Sagamore, a sage within the limits of his own observation, a child beyond; his discourse and manners so far fittest, noblest, simplest, the grace and dignity of a child. What could be better than his speech to me after grandmother's death. "Well, the bond that united us is broken, but I hope you

1 Doctor Ripley. Although most of this entry is to be found in Mr. Emerson's sketch "Ezra Ripley" (*Lectures and Biographical Sketches*), it seems appropriate to retain it in its place in the Journal.

and your brothers will not cease to come to this house. You will not like to be excluded, and I shall not like to be neglected." And his conversation with the M —— family after the death of their father, I admired. The son was supposed to be intemperate in his habits. The family and friends were all collected for the funeral when we went in. "Madam, I condole with you; Sir, I condole with you ; and with you all. I remember, Sir, when I came to this town your grandfather was living on this farm, and a most respectable citizen. His father lived here before him. Your father has stood in their place, and lived a useful and respected life. Now, Sir, the name and respectability of your family rests on you. Sir, if you fail — Ichabod — the glory is departed, — and I hope you will not."

History teaches what man can do, and not less what man can suffer and what he can believe. The slowness with which the *stirps generosa, seu historica* in Europe opened their eyes to the monstrous lie of Popery, might startle us as to the possible depth of our own degradation through the sleep of Reason, and prompt a hope of what height we may yet attain.

Is it not an instructive fact in literary history, that of Luther's writing from Wittemberg to Spalatin for the Elector's collection of gems, to assist him in translating the twenty-first chapter of Revelation? They were sent and, after careful examination, returned. (Vide Seckendorf, p. 204.)

And here is another eulogy, a true eulogy of that great man. King Christiern of Denmark, passing through Saxony, sent for Luther. He afterwards declared, "Never have I heard the gospel so well explained as by Luther. So long as I continue to live I shall hold his discourse in remembrance, and shall submit with greater patience to whatever I am destined to endure." Longinus could not improve the sentence, and the last clause should be writ in the diary of every preacher.

The Marseillaise Hymn, and the Ballads of the Reformation, and Watts' Hymnbook, and the *Ranz des Vaches*.

The best cause has been seldom defended on its merits. Men are possessed by the Idea of liberty or right in the matter, but the fewest are able to state in propositions that which makes

the strength and soul of their party. The idea
is deep and pervades the whole mass of men
and institutions involved, but that which makes
the surface is the names of certain men and
other accidents. Even the divine Milton re-
curs with bitterness to tippet and surplice, etc.
These are what, in words, the antagonist party
oppose and revile, and therefore on these (as in
European war, *on the Milanese*) the battle is
fought. Luther has never stated his thought so
well as Mackintosh has done for him; and
dwelleth far more on the bald pates and gray
cloaks of his opponents. Luther was a great
man and, as Coleridge says, acted poems, and
his words, if they will, they may characterize as
half-battles. But the sublime of them, critically
considered, is the material sublime, not the
moral. "If the heavens should pour down
Duke Georges for nine days," etc. "If I don't
burn them, 't is because I can't find fire." "I 'll
go, if all the devils are in the way," etc. It is
like Mahomet's description of the angel whom
he saw in heaven: "It was nine days' journey
from one of his eyes to the other." Mere sublimity of magnitude and number; but Landor
says well, "Where the heart is not moved, the
gods stride and thunder in vain. The pathetic

is the true sublime." I speak of course of the homely monk's sayings as sentences.

The purposes and character which they manifest is quite another Consideration. There is something akin to sublimity. But there is no such force in all his sayings as in " Forgive his virtues too."[1]

Let a man have no presence, no manners. It takes some men so long to get through their preliminaries that everybody avoids them for fear of the trouble. But be a mere word, a mere action; and when parade-days come, then do these long courtesies when there is time and expectation; but spare working-days and working-people.

> O what is Heaven but the fellowship
> Of minds that each can stand against the world
> By its own meek but incorruptible will.[2]

November 21.

Ah, how shone the moon and her little sparklers last eve! There was the light in the self-

---

1 Forgive his crimes; forgive his virtues too,
  Those smaller faults, half converts to the right.
                                    YOUNG.

2 When some friend asked Mr. Emerson to write something in an album, he often wrote these lines.

same vessels which contained it a million years ago.

I perceived in myself this day with a certain degree of terror the prompting to retire. What! is this lone parsonage in this thin village so populous as to crowd you and overtask your benevolence? They who urge you to retire hence would be too many for you in the centre of the desert or on the top of a pillar.[1]

How dear, how soothing to man, arises the Idea of God peopling the lonely place, effacing the scars of our mistakes and disappointments! When we have lost our God of tradition and ceased from our God of rhetoric, then may God fire the heart with his presence.

November 23.

The root and seed of democracy is the doctrine, Judge for yourself. Reverence thyself. It is the inevitable effect of that doctrine, where it has any effect (which is rare), to insulate the par-

[1] Merely social life was always difficult for Mr. Emerson. For this reason he never wished to visit for more than a day. At the Manse, of course, parishioners came to pay their respects to the pastor and his guests. "Urge you to retire" means only *make you want to run away.*

tisan, to make each man a state. At the same time it replaces the dead with a living check in a true, delicate reverence for superior, congenial minds. "How is the king greater than I, if he is not more just?"

How does every institution, every man, every thought embody, clothe itself externally with dress, houses, newspapers, societies. As I sat in the Orthodox Church this day, I thought how brick and laths and lime flew obedient to the master idea that reigns in the minds of many persons, be that idea what it may, Jackson, Antimasonry, Diffusion of Knowledge, Farm School, or Calvinism. Why then should the Swedenborgian doctrine be obnoxious, that in the spiritual world the affections clothe themselves with appropriate garments, dwellings, and other circumstances? . . .

What concerns me more than Orthodoxy, Anti-masonry, Temperance, Workingmen's party, and the other Ideas of the time?

Is the question of Temperance pledges a question whether we will, in a pestilence, go into quarantine?

Wonderful charm in the English elegiac verse

for the expression of amatory sorrow, and the shades of feeling of a mystic; but it is only in newspapers and by second-rate or third-rate poets that I have seen it used. A fine verse of this sort I chanced upon, addressed to Music, in which, after saying that Music links us to higher realities than we see around us, the unknown poet saith

Therefore a current of sadness deep
Through the streams of thy triumph is heard to
sweep.

November 26.

Goethe says of Lavater, that, "it was fearful to live near a man to whom every boundary within which Nature has seen fit to circumscribe us was clear."

"The world in which I exist is another world indeed, but not to come." COLERIDGE.

O what a wailing tragedy is this world, considered in reference to money-matters. Rather melancholy, after asking the opinion of all living, to find no more receivers of your doctrine than your own three or four, and sit down to wait until it shall please God to create some more men before your school can expect increase.

Show a head of Cuvier, Goethe, or Milton to vulgar people, and they see nothing but resemblances to Deacon Gulliver or Mr. Gibbons.

A year ago on November 13, little Ezra Ripley started up in bed and told his father all the stars were falling down. His father bid him sharply go to sleep, but the boy was the better philosopher.[1]

What can be conceived so beautiful as actual nature? I never see the dawn break or the sun set, as last evening, when from every grey or slate-coloured cloud over the whole dome depended a wreath of roses, or look down the river with its tree-planted banks (from the bridge north of the house) absolutely *affecting* an elegancy, without a lively curiosity as to its reality, and a self-recollection that I am not in a dream. Well, is this all superficial, and is the earth itself unsightly? Look at a narcissus, or crocus, or lily, or petal, or stamen, or plumule, — at any process of life, and answer. What can be conceived so

---

[1] This was the night of the most remarkable meteoric shower on record. Ezra Ripley, the child here mentioned, was the grandson of Dr. Ripley. He grew up to a noble manhood, left the profession of law to serve as lieutenant in a Massachusetts regiment in the Civil War, and died in service.

beautiful as an assemblage of bright and opake balls floating in space, covered each with pretty races, and each individual a counterpart and contemplator of the whole. Everything, to be appreciated, must be seen from the point where its rays converge to a focus. This gorgeous landscape, these poetical clouds, what would they be if I should put my eye to the ground? a few pebbles; or into the cloud? a fog. So of human history, and of my own life. We cannot get far enough away from ourselves to integrate our scraps of thought and action, and so judge of our tendency or ascend to our idea. We are in the battle, and cannot judge of its picturesque effect, nor how the day is going, nor at present of its consequences. The shepherd or the beggar in his red cloak little knows what a charm he gives to the wide landscape that charms you on the mountain-top and whereof he makes the most agreeable feature, and I no more the part my individuality plays in the All.[1]

To an idle inquiry whether you are immortal, God maketh no answer. No argument of conviction can be found; but do your duty, and you

---

1 The first note of the opening lines in "Each and All" (*Poems*); evidently a European memory.

are already immortal; the taste, the fear of death
has already vanished. We would study Greek and
Astronomy if life were longer. Study them, and
life is already infinitely long.

December.

Yesterday saw I at Waltham the eclipse of the
Sun, 10.45 digits. The fact that a prediction is
fulfilled is the best part of it; the preternatural
half-night which falls upon the hills, and the
violet shade which touches all the clouds. The
fine fringes of the cloud made the best smoked
glass through which to see the sun, while the
shadow encroached upon his face.

When the young philosopher forgets men's
opinions, nothing seems so worthy employment,
or rather life, as religious teaching. If I could
persuade men to listen to their interior convictions, if I could express, embody their interior convictions, that were indeed life. It were
to cease being a figure, and to act the action of
a man. But for that work he must be free and
true. He must not seek to weld what he believes, to what he does not wish publicly to deny.
Nothing can compensate for want of belief; no
accomplishments, no talents. A believing man, in
a cause worthy of a man, gives the mind a sense

of stability and repose more than mountains. I could not help calling the attention of my venerable neighbor to the different impression made by A[lexander] Everett and James Savage: [1] one, very accomplished, but inspires no confidence; for he is not much of a man; the other, tolerably well equipped, but is himself an upright, single-hearted man, pursuing his path by his own lights and incapable of fear or favor. Columbus did not affect to believe in a new continent and make dinner speeches about it (other than his egg speech), and George Fox and Emanuel Swedenborg never advise people to go to church for the sake of example.

It would give scope for many truths in experimental religion to preach from the text, "There shall be new heavens and a new earth."

1 Alexander Everett, older brother of Edward Everett, a man of wide culture who received honorary degrees from many colleges and learned societies, became President of Jefferson College, Louisiana, and later was sent to Spain as Minister Plenipotentiary. Died 1847. James Savage, a useful, fearless, public-spirited citizen of Boston, founder of the Provident Institution for Savings; a scholar who did valuable work on the history of the early settlers of New England. He was made LL. D. Harvard, and Overseer, Fellow of the American Academy, and President of the Massachusetts Historical Society.

Sometimes we perceive that God is wholly unknown in the world, that the church and the sermon and the priest and the alms are a profanation.

"We were early cast upon thy care," is a heathen expression.

COMPENSATION

Why should I keep holiday
When other men have none?
Why but because, when these are gay,
I sit and mourn alone?

And why, when Mirth unseals all tongues,
Must I be ever dumb?
Ah, late I spoke to breathless throngs,
And now their hour is come.[1]

CONCORD, *December* 2.

The age of puberty is a crisis in the life of the man worth studying. It is the passage from the Unconscious to the Conscious; from the sleep of the Passions to their rage; from careless receiving to cunning providing; from beauty to use; from omnivorous curiosity to anxious stew-

1 These verses, which, slightly altered, Mr. Emerson published in the *Poems* years later, are written in pencil under the above entries in ink, and evidently belong to this period.

ardship; from faith to doubt; from maternal Reason to hard, short-sighted Understanding; from unity to disunion; the progressive influences of poetry, eloquence, love, regeneration, character, truth, sorrow, and of search for an Aim, and the contest for property.

I look upon every sect as a Claude Lorraine glass through which I see the same sun and the same world and in the same relative places as through my own eyes, but one makes them small, another large; one, green; another, blue; another, pink. I suppose that an Orthodox preacher's cry, " The natural man is an enemy of God," only translates the philosopher's that "the instinct of the Understanding is to contradict the Reason"; so Luther's Law and Gospel (also St. Paul's); Swedenborg's love of self and love of the Lord; William Penn's World and Spirit; the Court of Honor's Gentleman and Knave. The dualism is ever present, though variously denominated.

I have not so near access to Luther's mind through his works as through my own mind when I meditate upon his historical position.

When they jeered at the devil, Luther says,

he went away "*Quia est superbus spiritus et non potest ferre contemptum sui.*"

My own picture was ugly enough to me. I read that when his own picture was shown to Erasmus, he said, "Look I like this picture? So am I the greatest knave that liveth," which Luther relates with sharpness.

Francis comes to Doctor Ripley at breakfast to know if he shall drive the cow into the battle-field.[1]

Blessed are the woods. In summer they shade the traveller from the sun; in winter, from the tooth of the wind; when there is snow, it falls level; when it rains, it does not blow in his face. There is no dust, and a pleasing fear reigns in their shade. Blessed are the woods!

I think the most devout persons be the freest of their tongues in speaking of the Deity, as

1 The Old Manse, which had come to Dr. Ripley through his wife, widow of Rev. William Emerson, was close by the battle-ground; and as the original North Bridge had been taken down some forty years before this time, and the new monument had not been erected, the field where the British stood and fired was the Doctor's pasture.

Luther, Fuller, Herbert, Milton, whose words are an offence to the pursed mouths which make formal prayers; and beyond the word, they are free-thinkers also. "Melancthon discoursed with Luther touching the prophets who continually do boast in this sort and with these words, 'Thus saith the Lord,' etc., — whether God spake in person with them or no? Then Luther said, They were very holy, spiritual people, which seriously did contemplate on holy and divine causes: therefore God spake with them in their consciences, which the prophets held for sure Revelations." — *Table-Talk*, p. 362, folio edition. So Saint James he frankly called "*epistola straminea.*"

Bring men near one another, and love will follow.

Once the men of distant countries were painted as of monstrous *bodies* without necks, with tails, etc. But Commerce contradicted the report. Then they were described as having monstrous *minds*, thieves, sottish, promiscuously mixed, destitute of moral sentiments. But Commerce has exposed that slander too, and shown that as face answereth to face in water, so the heart of man to man.

A man is a very vulnerable creature. His manners and dignity are conventional. Leave him alone and he is a sorry sight.

[Here follows the passage on apologies; see "Heroism," *Essays*, First Series, page 260, Centenary Edition.]

How sad, how disgusting, to see this *niedrig* air on the face, a man whose words take hold on the upper world, whilst one eye is eternally down cellar, so that the best conversation has ever a slight savor of sausages and soap-barrels. Basest when the snout of this influence touches the education of young women, and withers the blessed affection and hope of human nature by teaching that marriage is nothing but house-keeping, and that woman's life has no other aim.

Even G. was capable of saying "the worst marriage is better than none," and S. made a similar stab at the sanity of his daughter.

CONCORD, *December* 3.

The poor Irishman, a wheelbarrow is his country.[1]

1 The building of the railroads in New England at this time brought the first important immigration of Irishmen with their families.

When I remember the twofold cord, then fourfold, and, go a little back, a thousand and a millionfold cord of which my being and every man's being consists; that I am an aggregate of infinitesimal parts, and that every minutest streamlet that has flowed to me is represented in that man which I am, so that, if every one should claim his part in me, I should be instantaneously diffused through the creation and individually decease, then I say, If I am but an alms of all, and live but by the charity of innumerable others, there is no peculiar propriety in wrapping my cloak about me and hiding the ray that my taper may emit. What is a man but a congress of nations. Just suppose for one moment to appear before him the whole host of his ancestors. All have vanished; he — the insulated result of all that character, activity, sympathy, antagonism, working for ages in all corners of the earth — alone remains. Such is his origin; well, was his nurture less compound? Who and what has not contributed something to make him that he is? Art, science, institutions, black men, white men, the vices and the virtues of all people, the gallows, the church, the shop, poets, nature, joy, and fear, all help, all teach him. Every fairy brings a gift.

Deliver us from that intensity of character which makes all its crows swans. So soon as I hear that my friend is engaged, I perceive at once that a very ordinary person is henceforward adopted into that rose-colored atmosphere which exhales from his self-love, and every trait, every trifle, every nothing about the new person is canonized by identifying the same with the positive virtue to which it is related, just as children refer the moon to the same region of heaven with the stars. Talent becomes genius; inoffensiveness, benevolence; wilfulness, character; and even stupidity, simplicity. Poor, dear human nature; leave magnifying and caricaturing her; it frets and confuses us. More winning, more sociable and society-making is she as she stands, faults and virtues unpainted, confessed; then the fault even becomes piquant, and is seen to prop and underpin some excellent virtue, Let us deal so with ourselves and call a spade a spade.

December 6.

Do you imagine that because I do not say Luther's creed, all his works are an offence to me? Far otherwise. I can animate them all that they shall live to me. I can worship in that temple as well as in any other. I have only to translate a few of the leading phrases into their equivalent verities, to adjust his almanack to my meridian, and all the conclusions, all the predictions shall be strictly true. Such is the everlasting advantage of truth. Let a man work after a pattern he really sees, and every man shall be able to find a correspondence between these works and his own and to turn them to some account in Rome, London, or Japan, from the first to the hundredth Century.

On reading yesterday afternoon, to Aunt Mary, Coleridge's defence of prayer against the author of *Natural History of Enthusiasm*, she replied, "Yes, for our reason was so distinct from the Universal Reason that we could pray to it, and so united with it, that we could have assurance we were heard."

December 8.

The world looks poor and mean so long as I think only of its great men; most of them of spotted reputation. But when I remember how many obscure persons I myself have seen possessing gifts that excited wonder, speculation and delight in me; when I remember that the very greatness of Homer, of Shakspeare, of Webster and Channing, is the truth with which they reflect the mind of all mankind; when I consider that each fine genius that appears is already predicted in our constitution, inasmuch as he only makes apparent shades of thought in us of which we hitherto knew not (or actualizes an idea); and when I consider the absolute boundlessness of our capacity — no one of us but has the whole untried world of geometry, fluxions, natural philosophy, ethics, wide open before him. When I recollect the charms of certain women, what poems are many private lives, each of which can fill our eye, if we so will, (as the swan, the eagle, the cedar-bird, the canary, each seems the type of bird-kind whilst we gaze at it alone,) and then remember how many millions I know not; then I feel the riches of my inheritance in being set down in this world, gifted with organs of communication with this accomplished company.

Pray heaven that you may have a sympathy with all sorts of excellence, even with those antipodal to your own. If any eye rest on this page, let him know that he who blotted it could not go into conversation with any person of good understanding without being presently gravelled. The slightest question of his most familiar proposition disconcerted him, eyes, face and understanding, beyond recovery. Yet did he, not the less, respect and rejoice in this daily gift of vivacious common sense, which was so formidable to him. May it last as long as the world.

The application of Goethe's definition of genius; "That power which by working and doing gives laws and rules," to common life, to the art of living, is obvious. Deacon Warren, Mr. Turner, Mr. Crafts, and every new, simple heart give us a new image of possible virtues and powers.

If you ask me whether I will be so good as to abstain from all use of ardent spirits for the sake of diminishing by my pint *per annum* the demand, and so stopping the distiller's pernicious pump, I answer, Yes, with all my heart. But will I signify the same fact by putting my name to your paper? No. Be assured, I shall always be found on your side in discouraging this use and traffic. But I shall not deprive my example of all its value by abdicating my freedom on that point. It shall be always my example, the spectacle to all whom it may concern of my spontaneous action at the time.

Why, O diffusers of Useful Knowledge, do you not offer to deliver a course of lectures on Aristotle and Plato, or on Plato alone, or on him and Bacon and Coleridge? Why not strengthen the hearts of the waiting lovers of the primal philosophy by an account of that fragmentary highest teaching which comes from the half fabulous personages Heraclitus, Hermes Trismegistus, and Giordano Bruno, and Vyasa, and Plotinus, and Swedenborg. Curious, now that first I collect their names, they should look all so mythological.

I rejoice in Time. I do not cross the common without a wild poetic delight, notwithstanding the prose of my demeanour. Thank God I live in the country. Well said Bell, that no hour, no state of the atmosphere but corresponded to some state of the mind; brightest day, grimmest night.

December 9.

The dear old Plutarch assures me that the lamp of Demosthenes never went out; that King Philip called his orations *soldiers*, and in a moment of enthusiasm, on hearing the report of one of his speeches, exclaimed, "Had I been there, I too should have declared war against myself." Flying before Antipater, he wrote his own epitaph at Calauria ; ——

Εἴπερ ἴσην ῥώμην γνώμῃ, Δημοσθένες, ἔσχες,
Οὔποτ᾽ ἂν Ἑλλήνων ἦρξεν Ἄρης Μακεδών.

When Epicles twitted him upon his exact preparation, he said, "I should be ashamed to speak what comes uppermost to so great an assembly."

One day his voice failing him, he was hissed, and he cried unto the people, "Ye are to judge of players indeed by the clearness and tuneableness of their voice, but of orators by the gravity and excellency of their sentences." Despising other orators, when Phocion arose, Demosthenes was wont to say, "Pruning-knife of my orations, arise!"

Last night, abed, I recollected four names for four lectures : Luther, Michel Angelo, Milton, George Fox; then comes question of Epaminondas, esteemed by the ancients greatest of the Greeks; Demosthenes for the sake of his oratory and the related topics; Alfred for his human character; Sam. Johnson for his genuineness; Phocion, More, and Socrates, for their three renowned deaths; Hampden for his Saxon soul;

Muley Moloch;[1] Reynolds. But it seemed to me that a fit question to handle in a public lecture is the one involved in the claims and apologies made by people and orators in this New England raft of ours every day. It is said that the people can look after their own interests; that "common sense, though no science, is fairly worth the seven"; that a plain, practical man is better to the state than a scholar, etc.

He were a benefactor to his countrymen who would expose and pillory this state sophism. We hold indeed that those reasons for a public action which are presented to us should be of that simple, humane character as to be fully comprehensible by every citizen of good capacity, as well the uneducated as the educated. That is a good test and condition of such reasons. They should not be addressed to the imagination, or to our literary associations, but to the ear of plain men. Therefore are they such as plain men, farmers, mechanics, teamsters, seamen or soldiers might offer, if they would gravely, patiently, humbly reflect upon the matter. There

1 Abd el Malek, Sultan of Morocco in the sixteenth century. His heroic death in battle is mentioned in the *Spectator*, no. 349. He is there called Muly Moluc. Muley means *My Lord*. See, also, Dryden's *Don Sebastian*.

is nothing in their want of book-learning to hinder. This doctrine affirms that there is imparted to every man the Divine light of reason, sufficient not only to plant corn and grind wheat by, but also to illuminate all his life, his social, political, religious actions. Sufficient according to its faithful use. Sufficient, if faithfully used. The propositions are true to the end of the world, with this inseparable condition; Every man's Reason is sufficient for his guidance, *if used*. But does it mean that because a farmer, acting on deep conviction, shall give a reason as good as Bacon could have given, that therefore the ordinary arguments of farmers are to be preferred to those of statesmen? that whatever crude remarks a circle of people talking in a barroom throw out, are entitled to equal weight with the sifted and chosen conclusions of experienced public men? And because God has made you capable of Reason, therefore must I hear and accept all your selfish railing, your proven falsehoods, your unconsidered guesses as truth? No; I appeal from you to your Reason, which, with me, condemns you. . . . It amounts to this; "Every man's Reason can show him what is right. Therefore every man says what is right, whether he use his Reason or no." I hate this fallacy the more that it is, beside being dire nonsense, a profanation of the dearest truths. Democracy, Freedom, has its root in the sacred truth that every man hath in him the divine Reason, or that, though few men since the creation of the world live according to the dictates of Reason, yet all men are created capable of so doing. That is the equality and the only equality of all men. To this truth we look when we say, Reverence thyself; Be true to thyself. Because every man has within him somewhat really divine, therefore is slavery the unpardonable outrage it is.

There is great delight in learning a new language. When the day comes in the scholar's progress unawares, when he reads pages without recurrence to the dictionary, he shuts up his book with that sort of fearful delight with which the bridegroom sits down in his own house with the bride saying, "I shall now live with you always."

December 11.

When the sick man came out of doors, the stars seemed to shine through his eyes into his heart, and the blessed air that he inhaled seemed to lighten his frame from head to feet.

A little above I referred to one of my characters.[1]   It might be added that if he made his
forms a strait-jacket to others, he wore the same
himself all his years, and so reanimated for his
beholders the order of La Trappe. . . . One
who showed ever, in his fireside discourse, traits
of that pertinency and judgment, softening ever
and anon into elegancy, which make the distinction of the scholar, and which, under better discipline, might have ripened into a Salmasius or
Hedericus. Sage and savage strove harder in
him than in any of my acquaintance, each getting the mastery by turns, and pretty sudden
turns. "Save us," he said in his prayer, " from
the extremity of cold, and violent sudden
changes." — " The society will meet after the
Lyceum, as it is difficult to bring the people
together in the evening, — and no moon," etc.
" Mr. N. F. is dead, and I expect to hear the
death of Mr. B. It is cruel to separate old people from their wives in this cold weather."
Thus is one reminded of the children's prayer,
who in confessing their sins, say, " Yes, I did
take the jump-rope from Mary." Pleasantly

1 Rev. Dr. Ezra Ripley of Concord. A portion of what
follows is included in Mr. Emerson's Memoir of Dr. Ripley,
in *Lectures and Biographical Sketches*.

said he at supper, that his "last cup was not potent in any way, neither in sugar, nor cream, nor
souchong; it was so equally and universally defective, that he thought it easier to make another
than to mend that."

The counsellor's fine simplicity and sweetness
of character saved his speech, the other evening,
from being distressful to the hearers. Charles is
reminded by him of Edward. There are some
points of resemblance. This for one, that neither
was ever put out of countenance.

CONCORD, *December* 14.

Yesterday, I sealed and despatched my letter
to Carlyle. To-day, riding to East Sudbury, I
pleased myself with the beauties and terrors of
the snow; the oak leaf hurrying over the banks
is fit ornament. Nature in the woods is very
companionable. There, my Reason and my
Understanding are sufficient company for each
other. I have my glees as well as my glooms
alone. Confirm my faith (and when I write the
word, Faith looks indignant), pledge me the
word of the Highest that I shall have my dead
and my absent again, and I could be content
and cheerful alone for a thousand years.

I know no aisle so stately as the roads through

the pine woods in Maine. Cold is the snow-drift, topping itself with sand. How intense are our affinities: acids and alkalis. The moment we indulge our affections, the earth is metamorphosed: all its tragedies and ennuis vanish, all duties even; nothing remains to fill eternity with but two or three persons.[1] But then a person is a *cause*. What is Luther but Protestantism? or Columbus but Columbia? And were I assured of meeting Ellen tomorrow, would it be less than a world, a personal world? Death has no bitterness in the light of that thought.

In Boston, Hedge[2] read me good things out of Schleiermacher concerning the twofold divisions of study; 1. Physics, or that which is; 2. Ethics, or that which should be. Also his definition of *Sciences* and *Art*; the one, *all things brought into the mind*; the other, *the mind going into things*. Then the Ascetic, or the discipline of life produced by the opinions. Every man's system should appear in his ascetic. Scarce one man's does.

1 This last sentence occurs in "Friendship," *Essays*, First Series.

2 Dr. Frederic Henry Hedge, clergyman and student of German metaphysics.

December 17.

If it has so pleased God, it is very easy for you to surpass your fellows in genius; but surpass them in generosity of sentiment; see not their meanness, whilst your eyes are fixed on everlasting virtues; being royal, being divine, in your sentiment: "this shall be another morn risen on mid-noon." This shall be your own, — O no; God forbid! not your own, but a vast accession of the Divinity into your trembling clay.

God has made nothing without a crack, except Reason. What can be better than this? "*Quanto era proprio per far tutta la pompa del suo profundo sapere.*" Note in VASARI's *Life of Michel Angelo.*

Poets and painters ever walk abreast.

December 18.

I am writing my lecture of Michel Angelo, clothed with a coat which was made for me in Florence: I would I were clothed with the spirit of beauty which breathed life into Italian art.

Quello ch' apporta mane e lascia sera. — DANTE.

Solon said, "Such as the speech, such is the life of the man."

Loathsome lecture last evening on precocity, and the dissection of the brain, and the distortion of the body, and genius, etc. A grim compost of blood and mud. Blessed, thought I, were those who, lost in their pursuits, never knew that they had a body or a mind.

December 19.

He who makes a good sentence or a good verse exercises a power very strictly analogous to his who makes a fine statue, a beautiful cornice, a staircase like that in Oxford, or a noble head in painting. One writes on air, if he speaks; but no, he writes on mind more durable than marble, and is like him who begets a son, that is, originates a begetter of nations.

The maker of a sentence, like the other artist, launches out into the infinite and builds a road into Chaos and old Night, and is followed by those who hear him with something of wild, creative delight.

December 20.

I like well the doctrine " that every great man, Napoleon himself, is an Idealist, a Poet with different degrees of utterance." As the love of flowers contains the Science of Botany, so the innate love of novelty, — enterprise like that which delighted me when a boy in Atkinson Street with climbing by help of a small ladder and touching for the first time the shingles of the shed; yes, and makes every boy a poet when a fine morning in Spring seducingly shows him the uplands in the neighboring towns on his way to school, — this same desire of the untried, leads the young farmer in Maine to load his little wagon and rattle down the long hills on his way to Illinois.

A strictest correspondence ties all the arts. And it is as lawful and as becoming for the poet to seize upon felicitous expressions and lay them up for use as for Michel Angelo to store his sketch-book with hands, arms, triglyphs, and capitals to enrich his future compositions. The wary artist in both kinds will tear down the scaffolding when the work is finished, and himself supply no clue to the curiosity that would know how he did the wonder.

The chickadees are very busy and happy in Cæsar's Woods[1] between the spots of snow. I

1 On the bluffs over the Great Meadows, near the Manse.

met them yesterday. What is the green leaf under the snow resembling a potentilla?

Spiritual religion is one that cannot be harmed by the vices of its defenders. Unitarianism and all the rest are judged by the standing or falling of their professors. I refuse that test to this. It is true. I see this to be true, though I see it condemns my life, and no man liveth by it. They [spiritual laws] are truth itself; they are the measure of truth; and can no more be affected by my falling away, or all men's denial, than the law of gravity is changed by my acting as if it were not. Yet is it dangerous. It is very far from a system of negatives; it lowly, earnestly sees and declares how its laws advance their reign for evermore into the Infinitude on all sides of us.

Jesus was a setter up more than a puller down. Socrates was also. Both were spiritualists. George Fox, William Penn were urgent doers, hard livers. But they were of wrath. I see the world and its Maker from another side. It seems to me beauty. He seems to me Love.

Spiritual religion has no other evidence than its own intrinsic probability. It is probable because the mind is so constituted as that they [its laws] appear likely so to be. It simply de-

scribes the laws of moral nature as the naturalist
does physical [laws] and shows the surprising
beauties and terrors of human life. It never
scolds and never sneers. It is opposed to Calvinism in this respect, that all spiritual truths
are self-evident, but the doctrines of Calvin are
not, and are not pretended to be by their understanding defenders;—mystery. This is the only
live religion; all others are dead or formal.
This cannot be but in the new conviction of
the mind. Others may. This produces instant
and infinite abuses. It is a two-edged sword,
because it condemns forms, but supplies a better law only to the living. It leaves the dead
to bury their dead. The popular religion is an
excellent constable; the true religion is God himself to the believer and maketh him a perfect
lover of the whole world; but it is only a cloak
of licentiousness to the rest. It would dismiss all
bad preachers and do great harm to society by
taking off restraints.

My Reason is well enough convinced of its
immortality. It knows itself immortal. But it
cannot persuade its down-looking brother, the
Understanding, of the same. That fears for the
cord that ties them, lest it break. Hence Miss

Rotch affirms undoubtedly, "I shall live forever," and, on the other hand, does not much believe in her retaining Personality.

December 21.

Who says we are not chained? He lies. See how greedily you accept the verse of Homer or Shakspear; the outline of Michel Angelo; the strain of Handel; the word of Webster; how thoroughly you understand and make them your own; and are well assured, too, that they are only units from an infinite store of the same kinds; well, now put out your own hands and take one more unit thence. I say you are chained.

Michel Angelo was the Homer of painting. Titian the Moore, or better, the Spenser. The difference is the same betwixt this stern Designer and the beautiful colorists that followed him, as between the severe Aristotle and the ornate Cicero.

Blessed is the day when the youth discovers that Within and Above are synonyms.

Actio agentis nihil aliud est quam extrahere rem de potentia ad actum. ARISTOTLE.

We can all put out our hands towards the desired truth, but few can bring their hands to meet around it. He alone is an artist whose hands can perfectly execute what his mind has perfectly conceived; —

> *Solo a quello arriva*
> *La man che obbedisce all' intelletto.*
>   MICHEL ANGELO.[1]

The domestic man loves no music so well as his kitchen clock and the airs which the logs sing to him as they burn in the fireplace.

The best means of mending a bad voice is to utter judicious remarks with it; the second best is to favor it by silence.

Translation of Michel Angelo's Sonnet VII

" I know not if it is the light of its first maker impressed on the imagination, which the soul

1 Mr. Emerson later rendered the sonnet of Michel Angelo of which these words are a part into verse, beginning thus : —

> Never did sculptor's dream unfold
> A form which marble doth not hold
> In its white block ; yet it therein shall find
> Only the hand secure and bold
> Which still obeys the mind.

>   See *Poems*, " Translations."

perceives, or if from the memory, or from the mind, any other beauty shines through into the heart; or if in the soul yet beams and glows the bright ray of its primitive state, leaving of itself I know not what burning, which is perhaps that which leads me to complain. That which I feel, and that which I see, and that which guides me, is not with me, nor know I well where to find it in me; and it seems to me that another shows it to me. This, lady, happened to me when I first saw you, that a bitter-sweet, a Yes and No, moved me; (certainly it must be your eyes)."

December 22.

It is very easy in the world to live by the opinion of the world. It is very easy in solitude to be self-centred. But the finished man is he who in the midst of the crowd keeps with perfect sweetness the independence of solitude. I knew a man of simple habits and earnest character who never put out his hand nor opened his lips to court the public, and having survived several rotten reputations of younger men, Honor came at last and sat down with him upon his private bench from which he had never stirred. I too can see the spark of Titan in that coarse clay; —

Queis arte benigna
Et meliore luto finxit præcordia Titan.[1]

Wherever is life, wherever is God, there the
Universe evolves itself as from a centre to its
boundless irradiation. Whosoever therefore apprehends the infinite, — and every man can, —
brings all worth and significance into that spot
of space where he stands, though it be a ditch,
a potato-field, a work-bench; or, more properly,
into that state of thought in which he is, whether
it be the making a statue or designing a church
like Michel Angelo, or holding silent meetings like George Fox, and Job Scott, or fighting
battles like Leonidas, Washington, Lafayette;
exploring the law of laws like Plotinus; or loving like Socrates, Petrarch and Angelo; or pre-
scribing the ethics of the scholar like Schiller.
Therefore is it in the option of every generous spirit to denominate that place in which
he now is, his Rome, his world; his sunshine
shall be Susa; his shade, Ecbatana; and let him
rest assured, if he invite them, not one deity
will stay away from his feast. And therefore also

1 These lines from Juvenal might be thus rendered: —

Whose hearts the God of Day
Fashioned with loving hand and from a nobler clay.

is it that every good sentence seems to imply all truth.

Truly exists that *Quoddam vinculum commune* between all the arts and knowledges of men. Vitruvius said that to understand architecture needed, not only to draw well, but also to understand music; and Michel Angelo said of architecture that he who did not understand something of the anatomy of the human body could know nothing of that subject.

The philosophy of *Waiting* needs sometimes to be unfolded. Thus he who is qualified to act upon the Public, if he does not act on many, may yet act intensely on a few; if he does not act much upon any, but, from insulated condition and unfit companions, seem quite withdrawn into himself, still, if he know and feel his obligations, he may be (unknown and unconsciously) hiving knowledge and concentrating powers to act well hereafter, and a very remote hereafter.

God is a rich proprietor, who, though he may find use for sprouts and saplings of a year's growth, finds his account also in leaving untouched the timber of a hundred years, which hardens and seasons in the cold and in the sun.

But a more lowly use (and yet with right feelings all parts of duty are alike lowly) is pleasing; that of serving an indirect good to your friends by being much to them, a reserve by which their sallies of virtue are fortified and they cordially cheered by the thoroughness of a mutual understanding. How has Edward served us most in these last years? by his figures and invoices? or through the healthful influence of his perfect moral health? How serves the Aunt Mary? How but by bearing most intelligible testimony which is felt where it is not comprehended.

> In Friendship too, observe my song,
> There is both equal, broad, and long;
> But this thou must not think to find
> With eyes of body but of mind.
>
> EMPEDOCLES.

> Love, idle of himself, takes up his rest
> And harbors only in a slothful breast.

If I were more in love with life and as afraid of dying as you seem to insinuate, I would go to a Jackson Caucus or to the Julien Hall, and I doubt not the unmixed malignity, the withering selfishness, the impudent vulgarity, that mark those meetings would speedily cure me of my appetite for longevity. In the hush of these woods I find no Jackson placards affixed to the trees.

We republicans do libel the monarchist. The monarchist of Europe for so many ages has really been pervaded by an Idea. He intellectually and affectionately views the King as the State. And the monarch is pervaded by a correspondent idea, and the worst of them has yet demeaned himself more or less faithfully as a State. A crown then is by no means "a stripe of velvet with jewels," nor is Louis XVI Mr. Louis Capet, as we chuse to affirm. Certainly there is something that mightily tickles a human ear in being named a nation, as Elizabeth of England, Mary of Scotland, Anne of Austria.

All pomps and ceremonies of courts do only flourish and idealize the simple facts in which that state began, as the orders of architecture do in every ornament refer to some essential part of the building. "The Pope performeth all ecclesiastical jurisdiction, as in consistory among his cardinals, which were originally but the parish priests of Rome," so to the wise eye, an etiquette is a history.

Mr. Coleridge has thrown many new truths into circulation; Mr. Southey never one.

Yet falsehoods, superstitions, are the props, the scaffolding, on which how much of society stands. Look at the relation betwixt the uneducated and educated classes. "One's afraid and the other dares n't," as the boys say. Each supposes much in the other which is not in him, and so the peace and place is kept. Accurately, I suppose the graduate underestimates the grocer, whilst the grocer far overestimates the graduate, and so the strong hand is kept in submission to what should be the wise head. The reason why Mr. Graduate's secret is kept, and never any accident discovers his bankruptcy and produces a permanent revolution, is, that there is a real object in Nature to which the grocer's reverence instinctively turns, viz., the intellectual man, and though the scholar is not that object, he is its representative, and is, with more or less symptoms of distrust, honored for that he ought to be. . . .

It is a manifest interest which comes home to my bosom and every man's bosom, that there should be on every tower Watchers set to observe and report of every new ray of light, in what quarter soever of heaven it should appear, and their report should be eagerly and reverently received. There is no offence done, certainly, to the community in distinctly stating the claims of this office. It is not a coveted office: it is open to all men. All see their interest in it, yet very few feel any inclination to adopt it as their vocation. The blessed God has given to each his calling in his ruling love, . . . has adapted the brain and the body of men to the work that is to be done in the world. Greenough has an invincible *penchant* to carve marble, and John Haskins to fry caoutchouc. A small number of men meantime have a contemplative turn, and voluntarily seek solitude and converse with themselves, a work which to most persons has a jail-smell. This needs a peculiar constitution, a dormancy of some qualities, and a harmonious action in all, that is rare. It has its own immunities, and also its own painful taxes, like the rest of human works. But where it is possessed, let it work free and honoured, in God's name. . . . Every discovery he makes, every conclusion he announces, is tidings to each of us from our own home. His office is to cheer our labor as with a song by highest hopes.

Of the German Nation: — It is the only nation that addresses the Deity with the appellation Dear. *Lieber Gott!*

The sun is the sole inconsumable fire
And God is the sole inexhaustible giver.

December 23.

A good chapter might be writ of *Optical Deceptions*. A sort of disappointment is felt by an ingenious man on hearing opinions and truths congenial to his own announced with effect in conversation. They are so near to his own thought or expression that he thinks he ought to have spoken first. That is an *Optical Deception* of the mind. If they had not been uttered by this other, he would not have uttered them. It is merely under the influence of this magnet that he becomes intensely magnetic. Take it away, and this effect will subside in him. Perhaps I shall never write of Shakspear's sonnets, yet let any critic execute that work, and I should go to law with him for assault and battery.

Bottom, in Shakspear, is a philosopher of this kidney. He fathers each new part the moment it is named. It fills his whole horizon. He would be that alone. He mistakes his omnivolence for omnipotence. The only remedy is to present still a new thought to withdraw him from the last.

It results from the fact that every thought is

one side of Nature, and really has the whole world under it. This exclusive prominence of one thought is that which Bacon indicated by idols of the cave.

"Time and patience change a mulberry leaf into satin."

A good aunt is more to the young poet than a patron. Molière had more happiness the year round from his old woman than from Louis.

Do, dear, when you come to write Lyceum lectures, remember that you are not to say, What must be said in a Lyceum? but, What discoveries or stimulating thoughts have I to impart to a thousand persons? not what they will expect to hear, but what is fit for me to say.

"No matter where you begin. Read anything five hours a day and you will soon be knowing," said Johnson.

Out of these fragmentary, lob-sided mortals shall the heaven unite Phidias, Demosthenes, Shakspear, Newton, Napoleon, Bacon and Saint John in one person.

December 24.

Him I call rich, that soul I call endowed, whether in man or woman, who by poverty or affliction or love has been driven home so far as to make acquaintance with the spiritual dominion of every human mind. Henceforward he is introduced into sublime society, henceforward he can wave the hand of adieu to all the things he coveted most. Henceforward he is above compassion. He may, it is true, seldom look at his treasure; he may, like one who has brought home his bride, go apart and compose himself and only take furtive glances at his good with a fearful joy, from the very assurance of confirmed bliss, but him I leave in his heaven, and all others I call miserably poor.

A singular equality may be observed between the great men of the first and the last ages. The astronomy, the arts, and the history of sixty centuries give Lafayette, Canning, Webster no advantage over Saladin, Scipio, or Agesilaus. The reason is, the arts, the sciences are in man, and the Spartan possessed and used the very talent in his war that Watt used for economical ends, and the pride and self-sufficiency of the ancient was founded on this very consciousness of infinitely versatile resources. The beggars of Sparta and of Rome hurled defiance with as proud a tone as if Lysander's fleet of tubs had been an Armada, or the rude walls of Sparta had been the bastions of Gibraltar. The resources of the mechanic arts are merely costume.[1] If Fabricius had been shown, instead of Pyrrhus's elephants, Napoleon's park of artillery, he would have displayed no more emotion; he would have found a counter-balance in himself: all the finites cannot outweigh one infinite. All the erudition of an university of doctors is not a match for the mother-wit of one Æsop.

Raphael's three manners of painting may be matched in the biography of every genius.

Nature keeps much on her table, but more in her closet.

A few words writ by a trembling hand of old Isaiah or Homer become an immoveable palisado to guard their sense against change or loss through all the storms and revolutions of time.

[1] The opening sentence and also the last one of this paragraph occur in "Self-Reliance."

"Where there is D E F there must be A B C," saith Sancho's aunt.

[Here follows the passage in "Friendship" (the latter half), beginning, "Let me be alone till the end of the world," and the ten lines ending "than be his echo."]

I lament with a contrition too deep for groaning every sacrifice of truth to fat good-nature, and not less those where Custom has insensibly produced a great alteration in a well-founded opinion. I am thankful that I was permitted to write —— in his bereavement, that I lacked sympathy with the character of his wife. If I praise her virtues, he will now believe me.

An obscure and slender thread of truth runs through all mythologies, and this might lead often to highest regions of philosophy. Isis and Osiris. Eros and Anteros. A singular correspondence is also to be remarked in the fables themselves. "Old Knurre Murre is dead," [1] seems only a

1 The peasant, in the tale, going home in the night, hears a voice say : —

"Hie home, Goodman Platt,
Tell thou the gib-cat,
That steals buttermilk out of the buttermilk vat,
That old Knurre Murre is dead."

travestie of " The great god PAN is dead," in Pythian oracles.

A few persons, three or four, perhaps, are to Burns what nations and races and long chronicles of annals are to Gibbon, and often it may be suspected that Shakspeare tacks the name of Rome or France upon traits to which he had more truly given the name of Nicholas Bacon or John Sylvester.

How beautiful are the feet of him that bringeth good tidings, that publisheth Salvation ! Forever graceful in every unperverted eye are the acts of Jesus of Nazareth, the man who believed in moral nature and therefore spake; who came not in his own name.

There is no object in nature which intense light will not make beautiful, and none which loses beauty by being nearer seen.

It is a thin partition that divides the house-breaker and the hero ; him that, in the conventicle, bawls Glory! and the philosopher who muses in amazement.

Only an inventor that knows how to borrow.

Knowledge transfers the censorship from the Statehouse to the reason of every citizen and compels every man to mount guard over himself, and puts Shame and Remorse for sergeants and maces.

December 27.

We say every truth supposes or implies every other truth. Not less true is it that every great man does in all his nature point at and imply the existence and well-being of all the institutions and orders of a state. He is full of reverence. He is by inclination (though far remote in position) the defender of the grammar school, the almshouse, the Christian Sabbath, the priest, the judge, the legislator, and the executive arm. Throughout his being is he loyal. Such was Luther, Milton, Burke; each might be called an aristocrat, though by position the champion of the people.

Bacon never mentions Shakspear nor Spenser, though often very inferior Latin and Greek poets. Milton's praise of Shakspear is most unequal to the subject, and Jonson's much more. Milton, in his turn, was not seen by his contemporaries, and was valued most as a scholar.

Tasso, Dante, Michel Angelo make no figure in Milton's estimate.

Everything may be painted, everything sung, but, to be poetized, its feet must be just lifted from the ground.

Snow and moonlight make all landscapes alike.

I believe the Christian religion to be profoundly true; true to an extent that they who are styled its most orthodox defenders have never, or but in rarest glimpses, once or twice in a lifetime, reached.

I, who seek to be a realist, to deny and put off everything that I do not heartily accept, do yet catch myself continually in a practical unbelief of its deepest teachings.

It taught, it teaches the eternal opposition of the world to the truth, and introduced the absolute authority of the spiritual law. Milton apprehended its nature when he said, " For who is there almost that measures wisdom by simplicity, strength by suffering, dignity by lowliness?" That do I in my sane moments, and feel the ineffable peace, yea and the influx of God, that attend humility and love, — and before the cock crows, I deny him thrice.

" There's nothing good or bad, but thinking makes it so."

A friend once told me that he never spent anything on himself without deserving the praise of disinterested benevolence.

Saturday night.

There is in every man a determination of character to a peculiar end, counteracted often by unfavorable fortune, but more apparent, the more he is left at liberty. This is called his genius, or his nature, or his turn of mind. The object of Education should be to remove all obstructions, and let this natural force have free play and exhibit its peculiar product. It seems to be true that no man in this is deluded. This determination of his character is to something in his nature; something real. This object is called his Idea. It is that which rules his most advised actions, those especially that are most his, and is most distinctly discerned by him in those days or moments when he derives the sincerest satisfaction from his life. It can only be indicated by any action, not defined by anything less than the aggregate of all his genuine actions; perhaps then only approximated. Hence the slowness of the ancients to judge of the life before death. " Expect the end." It is most accurately denoted by the man's name, as when we say the Scipionism of Scipio; [1] or, "There spoke the soul of Cæsar." The ancients seem to have expressed this spiritual superintendence by representing every human being as consigned to the charge of a Genius or Dæmon by whose counsels he was guided in what he did best, but whose counsels he might reject.

" Heathen philosophers taught that whosoever would but use his ear to listen might hear the voice of his guiding Genius ever before him, calling, and, as it were, pointing to that way which is his part to follow."   MILTON, volume i.

December 28.

Whenever I open my eyes, I read that everything has expression, a mouth, a chin, a lock of hair, the lappet of a coat, a cream-pot, a tree, a stone, the crimp or plait of a cap. So much I

---

1 Yet, later, Mr. Emerson used to smile at the poverty-stricken newspaper reporters, who often wrote of his last evening's discourse: " The lecture was — well — Emersonian."

concede to the physiognomist and craniologist. At the same time I see well enough how different is the expression of a pink ribbon upon one and upon another head. But ah! the pink ribbons of clouds that I saw last eve in the sunset, modulated with tints of unspeakable softness, and the air meantime had so much vivacity and sweetness that it was a pain to come indoors. Charles saw the same flecks of cloud and likened them to gold fishes. Had they no expression? Is there no meaning in the live repose which that amphitheatre of a valley behind Ball's Hill reflects to my eye, and which Homer or Shakspeare could not re-form for me in words? The leafless trees become spires of flame in the sunset, with the blue East for their background, and the stars of the dead calices of flowers, and every withered stem and stubble rimed with frost, with all their forms and hues contribute something to the mute music.[1]

Rather let me be " a pagan suckled in a creed outworn " than cowardly deny or conceal one particle of my debt to Greek art, or poetry, or

---

[1] The last half of this paragraph, though printed in *Nature*, is refreshing among the philosophic speculations, and in form more local than in the book.

virtue. Certainly I would my debt were more, but it is my fault, not theirs, if 't is little. But how pitiful if a mind enriched ánd infused with the spirit of their severe yet human Beauty, modulating the words they spake, the acts they did, the forms they sculptured, every gesture, every fold of the robe; especially animating the biography of their men with a wild wisdom and an elegance as wild and handsome as sunshine; the brave anecdotes of Agesilaus, Phocion, and Epaminondas; the death of Socrates, that holy martyr, a death like that of Christ; the purple light of Plato which shines yet into all ages, and is a test of the sublimest intellects — to receive the influences, however partial, of all this, and to speak of it as if it were nothing, or, like a fool, underpraise it in a sermon, because the worshippers are ignorant, and incapable of understanding that there may be degrees and varieties of merit, and that the merit of Paul shall not be less because that of Aristotle is genuine and great, — I call that mean-spirited, if it were Channing or Luther that did it.

Be it remembered of Milton, who drank deeply of these fountains, that, in an age and assembly of fierce fanatics, he drew as freely from these resources and with just acknowledgement, as from those known and honored by his party : —

"His soul was like a star and dwelt apart."

If I were called upon to charge a young minister, I would say Beware of Tradition : Tradition which embarrasses life and falsifies all teaching. The sermons that I hear are all dead of that ail. The preacher is betrayed by his ear. He begins to inveigh against some real evil, and falls unconsciously into formulas of speech which have been said and sung in the church some ages, and have lost all life. They never had any but when freshly and with special conviction applied. But *you* must never lose sight of the purpose of helping a particular person in every word you say. Thus, my preacher summed the deaths of the past year, and then reminded the bereaved that these were admonitions of God to them, etc., etc. Now all these words fell to the ground. They are Hamlet's "many *As*-es of great charge"; mere wind. He ought to have considered whether it were true, as his ear had always heard, to be sure without contradiction, that deaths *were* admonitions. By enumerating in his mind the persons that would be included in this address, he would quickly perceive that there was great disparity in the cases. Many had mourned, but were not now mourners; that some of the deaths were to the survivors desirable; some quite indifferent; that some of the survivors were persons of that habitual elevation of religious view as to have just views of death and so were above this prose. Others were of such manifold business or preoccupation of mind as that any death must occupy but a subordinate place in their thoughts, and if anywhere the words might be spoken with strict propriety, they were yet so general as not likely to strike that ear. I am prolix on this instance, yet the fault is obvious to a discerning ear in almost every sentence of the prayers and the sermons that are ordinarily heard in the church. Not so with Edward Taylor,[1] that living Methodist, the Poet of the church. Not so with the Swedenborgians, if their pulpit resembles their book.

December 29.

A critic pronounced that Wordsworth was a good man, but no poet. "Ah!" said one present, "you know not how much poetry there is in goodness!"

1 "Father" Taylor, the ex-seaman and powerful preacher of the Sailors' Bethel at the North End of Boston.

Charles says he has four stomachs, like a camel, and what law he reads in the morning he puts into the first stomach till evening; then it slides into the second.

Every truth is a full circle.

"He made himself of no reputation." The words have a divine sound.

To the music of the surly storm that thickens the darkness of the night abroad, and rocks the walls and fans my cheek through the chinks and cracks,[1] I would sing my strain, though hoarse and small. Yet, please God, it shall be lowly, affectionate and true. It were worth trial whether the distinction between a spiritual and traditional religion could not be made apparent to an ordinary congregation. There are parts of faith so

---

1 Mr. Emerson occupied the northwest second-story chamber of the Manse. There he worked upon *Nature,* which he had alluded to in his journal at sea (September 5) as a book already begun, but it was not published until September, 1836. Hawthorne, when he temporarily occupied the house some ten years later, wrote the *Mosses from an Old Manse* there. In the south gable of the third story is a little room, known as the Saints' Chamber, which from early days gave hospitality to ministers and scholars.

great, so self-evident, that when the mind rests in them the pretensions of the most illuminated, most pretending sect pass for nothing. When I rest in perfect humility, when I burn with pure love, what can Calvin or Swedenborg say to me?

But to show men the nullity of church-going compared with a real exaltation of their being, I think might even promote parish objects and draw them to church. To show the reality and infinite depth of spiritual laws, that all the maxims of Christ are true to the core of the world; that there is not, can't be, any cheating of nature, might be apprehended.

Every spiritual law, I suppose, would be a contradiction to common sense. Thus I should begin with my old saws, that nothing can be given; everything is sold; love compels love; hatred, hatred; action and reaction always are equal; no evil in society but has its check which coexists; the moral, the physical, the social world is a *plenum*, and any flood in one place produces equal ebb in another; nothing is free but the will of man, and that only to procure his own virtue: on every other side but that one he beats the air with his pompous action; that punishment not follows but accompanies crime.

They have said in churches in this age, "Mere Morality." O God, they know thee not who speak contemptuously of all that is grand. It is the distinction of Christianity, that it is moral. All that is personal in it is nought. When any-one comes who speaks with better insight into moral nature, he will be the new gospel; miracle or not, inspired or uninspired, he will be the Christ; persons are nothing.[1] If I could tell you what you know not; could, by my knowledge of the divine being, put that within your grasp which now you dimly apprehend, and make you feel the moral sublime, you would never think of denying my inspiration. The whole power of Christianity resides in this fact, that it is more agreeable to the constitution of man than any other teaching. But from the constitution of man may be got better teaching still.[2]

Morality requires purity, but purity is not it;

[1] Compare, in "Worship" (*Conduct of Life*): "Men talk of 'mere morality' — which is much as if one should say, 'Poor God with nobody to help him.'" Also in "The Sovereignty of Ethics" (*Lectures and Biographical Sketches*): "'Mere morality' means — not put into a personal master of morals."

[2] Mr. EMERSON, in the Journal, here makes a written reference to the entry, on the 9th August previous, about the "Jewish sermon" that he heard that Sunday.

requires justice, but justice is not that; requires beneficence, but is something better. Indeed there is a kind of descent and accommodation felt when we leave speaking of Moral Nature to urge a virtue it enjoins. For to the soul in her pure action all the virtues are natural, and not painfully acquired. Excite the soul, and it becomes suddenly virtuous. Touch the deep heart, and all these listless, stingy, beef-eating bystanders will see the dignity of a sentiment; will say, This is good, and all I have I will give for that. Excite the soul, and the weather and the town and your condition in the world all disappear; the world itself loses its solidity, nothing remains but the soul and the Divine Presence in which it lives. Youth and age are indifferent in this presence.

"Overturn, overturn, and overturn," said our aged priest, "until he whose right it is to reign, shall come into his kingdom."

The great willow tree over my roof is the trumpet and accompaniment of the storm and gives due importance to every caprice of the gale, and the trees in the avenue announce the same facts with equal din to the front tenants. Hoarse concert: they roar like the rigging of a ship in a tempest.

The Unitarian preacher who sees that his Orthodox hearer may with reason complain that the preaching is not serious, faithful, authoritative enough, is by that admission judged. It is not an excuse that he can with clearness see the speculative error of his neighbor. But when a man speaks from deeper convictions than any party faith, when he declares the simple truth, he finds his relation to the Calvinist or Methodist or Infidel at once changed in the most agreeable manner. He is of their faith, says each.

It is really a spiritual power which stopped the mouths of the regular priests in the presence of the fervent First Quaker and his friends. If the dead-alive never learned before that they do not speak with authority from the Highest, they learn it then, when a commissioned man comes, who speaks because he cannot hold back the message that is in his heart. Certainly I read a similar story respecting Luther; that the preacher's heart, stout enough before, misgave him when he perceived Luther was in the audience.

The height of virtue is only to act in a firm

belief that moral laws hold. Jesus and Saint Paul and Socrates and Phocion believed, in spite of their senses, that moral law existed and reigned, and so believing, could not have acted otherwise. The sinner lets go his perception of these laws, and then acts agreeably to the lower law of the senses. The logic of the sinner and of the saint is perfect. There is no flaw in either Epicureanism or Stoicism.

Does not Aristotle distinguish between Temperance for ends and Temperance for love of temperance? Each of these virtues becomes dowdy in a sermon. They must be practiced for their elegance; the virtuous man must be a poet and not a drudge of his virtues, to have them perfect. If he could *by implication* perform all the virtues, that is, not aim to be temperate, nor aim to be honest, nor aim to be liberal, but in his lofty piety be all three without knowing it, then is he the good moralist. The Ecclesiastical dogma of " Faith, not Works " is based on this truth.

Jesus believed in moral nature, and he did not come in his own name. (When a preacher does not say he comes in his own name, he generally looks it, or speaks it plainer than by words.)

AUTHORS OR BOOKS QUOTED OR REFERRED TO IN JOURNAL FOR 1834

[In this list, and hereafter, those standard authors, Mr. Emerson's favorites, that appear nearly every year, will be omitted in the list of his reading or references, namely : —

Homer, Plato, Plutarch, Virgil, Cicero, Horace, Juvenal, Montaigne, Bacon, Shakespeare, Ben Jonson, Beaumont and Fletcher, Donne, Herrick, Herbert, Milton, Sir Thomas Browne, Jeremy Taylor, Pascal, George Fox, Locke, Newton, Fénelon, Young, Pope, Johnson, Swedenborg, Pitt, Hume, Burke, Gibbon, Stewart, Jeffrey, Mackintosh, De Gérando, De Staël, Wordsworth, Scott, Landor, Coleridge, Byron, Napoleon.]

Empedocles ; Vyasa ; Plotinus'; Hermes Trismegistus ; Sheking (Chinese) ; Arabian Proverbs ;

Dante, *Paradiso ;* Petrarch ; Machiavelli ;

John Barbour, *Bruce ;*

Michel Angelo's Poems, *apud* Signor Radici in *Retrospective Review ;* Vasari's Life of, *apud Library of Useful Knowledge ;*

Luther, *apud* Coleridge, *Table Talk ;*

Earl of Rochester ; Swammerdam ;

Gilbert White, *Natural History of Selborne ;* Linnæus, *Metamorphosis of Plants ;* Oberlin ; Erasmus Darwin ; Friedrich Augustus Wolf ;

Goethe, *Tag und Jahres Hefte, Entsagen ;* Schiller, *Wallenstein, apud* Coleridge ; Novalis (Friedrich von Hardenberg) ; Reginald Heber ;

Brougham, *Practical Observations on the Education of the People ;* Spurzheim, *View of the Elementary Process of Education ;* Robert Dale Owen, *Outline of the System of Education at New Lanark ;*

Dr. Jacob Bigelow, *Plants of the Vicinity of Boston ;* Humboldt ;

Mrs. Barbauld, *The Brook ;* Tennyson, *Dirge ;* Béranger, *Chansons ;*

Carlyle, *Characteristics ;*

Edinburgh and *Retrospective Reviews.*

JOURNAL

THE NEW HOME IN CONCORD
MARRIAGE TO LIDIAN JACKSON
CHARLES EMERSON
COURSE OF LECTURES IN BOSTON
ALCOTT
PREACHING IN EAST LEXINGTON

JOURNAL XXVI

1835

(From Journal B)

"To think is to act"

CONCORD, *January 6, 1835.*

No doubt we owe most valuable knowledge to our conversation, even with the frivolous; yet when I return, as just now, from more than usual opportunities of hearing and seeing, it seems to me that one good day here is worth more than three gadding days in town. Sunday I went for the first time to the Swedenborg Chapel. The sermon was in its style severely simple, and in method and manner had much the style of a problem in geometry, wholly uncoloured and unimpassioned. Yet was it, as I told Sampson Reed, one that, with the exception of a single passage, might have been preached without exciting surprise in any church. At the opposite pole, say rather in another Zone from this hard truist, was Taylor,[1] in the afternoon, wish-

1 Rev. Edward Taylor.

ing his sons a happy new year, praying God for his servants of the brine, to favor commerce, to bless the bleached sail, the white foam, and through commerce to Christianize the universe. "May every deck," he said, "be stamped by the hallowed feet of godly captains, and the first watch and the second watch be watchful for the Divine light." He thanked God he had not been in Heaven for the last twenty-five years, — then indeed had he been a dwarf in grace, but now he had his redeemed souls around him. And so he went on, — this poet of the sailor and of Ann Street, — fusing all the rude hearts of his auditory with the heat of his own love, and making the abstractions of philosophers accessible and effectual to them also. He is a fine study to the metaphysician or the life philosopher. He is profuse of himself; he never remembers the looking-glass. They are foolish who fear that notice will spoil him. They never made him, and such as they cannot unmake him; he is a real man of strong nature, and noblest, richest lines on his countenance. He is a work of the same hand that made Demosthenes and Shakspear and Burns, and is guided by instincts diviner than rules. His whole discourse is a string of audacious felicities harmonized by a spirit of joyful love. Everybody is cheered and exalted by him. He is a living man and explains at once what Whitefield and Fox and Father Moody were to their audiences, by the total infusion of his own soul into his assembly, and consequent absolute dominion over them. How puny, how cowardly, other preachers look by the side of this preaching! He shows us what a man can do. As I sat last Sunday in my country pew, I thought this Sunday I would see two living chapels, the Swedenborg and the Seamen's, and I was not deceived.

January 7.

Bitter cold days, yet I read of that inward fervor which ran as fire from heart to heart through England in George Fox's time. How precisely parallel are the biographies of religious enthusiasts — Swedenborg, Guyon, Fox, Luther, and perhaps Boehmen. Each owes all to the discovery that God must be sought within, not without. That is the discovery of Jesus. Each perceives the worthlessness of all instruction, and the infinity of wisdom that issues from meditation. Each perceives the nullity of all conditions but one, innocence; the absolute submission which attends it. All becomes simple, plain in word and act. Swedenborg and the Quakers have much to say of a new name that shall be given in heaven.

The most original writer feels in every sentence the influence of the great writers who have established the conventions of composition ; and the religious Revolution effected by Jesus Christ insensibly or avowedly models each of these succeeding reforms. The boldest vision of the prophet communing with God only, is confined and coloured and expressed according to the resistless example of the Jewish.

Luther's jocularity and learning give him the most reputation for sanity. The Quaker casts himself down a passive instrument of the Supreme Reason, and will not risque silencing it by venturing the coöperation of his Understanding. He therefore enacts his first thought, however violent or ludicrous, nor stays to consider whether the purport of his vision may not be expressed in more seemly and accustomed forms.

January 8.

There is an elevation of thought from which things venerable become less, because we are in the presence of their Source. When we catch one clear glimpse of the moral harmonies which accomplish themselves throughout the everlasting Now and throughout the omnipresent Here, how impertinent seem the controversies of theologians. God is before us, and they are wrangling about dead gods. What matters it whether the inspiration was plenary or secondary; whether this or that was intended by the prophet; whether Jesus worked a miracle or no; if we have access inwardly to the almighty and all-wise One Inspirer of all prophecy, container of all Truth and Sole Cause of Causes? All the Godhead that was in either of those ages, in either of those men, was the perception of these resplendent laws which, at this very moment, draw me, at the same time that they outrun and overwhelm my faculties. The Teacher that I look for and await shall enunciate with more precision and universality, with piercing poetic insight those beautiful yet severe compensations that give to moral nature an aspect of mathematical science. He will not occupy himself in laboriously reanimating a historical religion, but in bringing men to God by showing them that he is, not was, and speaks, not spoke.

January 9.

The only true economy of time is to rely without interval on your own judgment. Keep the eye and ear open to all impressions, but

deepen no impression by effort, but take the
opinion of the Genius within, what ought to
be retained by you, and what rejected by you.
Keep, that is, the upright position. Resign
yourself to your thoughts, and then every object will make that mark, that modification of
your character which it ought. This were better
advice to a traveller than Sir Henry Wotton's,
"*Il viso sciolto, i pensieri stretti.*" [1] All your time
will be lived; the journey, the dinner, the waiting, will not need to be subtracted.

"The spirit of prophecy is the witness of
Jesus." Madame Guyon's incapability to speak
before the captious is Swedenborg's inability to
utter what is not believed,[2] "though they folded
their lips to indignation." Prayer is—is it not?
— the forcible subjugation for the time of the
Understanding to the Reason.

I wrote in my last blotting book that we need
a theory of interpretation or Mythology. How
true a picture is Prometheus.[3] . . .

1 Open countenance and secret thoughts.
2 Said of the angels.
3 The substance of what follows in the MS. is omitted, as
printed in "History," *Essays I,* p. 31, Centenary Edition.

There are some occult facts in human nature that are natural magic. The chief of these is, the glance (*œillade*). The mysterious communication that is established across a house between two entire strangers, by this means, moves all the springs of wonder. It happened once that a youth and a maid beheld each other in a public assembly for the first time. The youth gazed with great delight upon the beautiful face until he caught the maiden's eye. She presently became aware of his attention, and something like correspondence immediately takes place. The maid depressed her eyes that the man might gaze upon her face. Then the man looked away, that the maiden might gratify her curiosity. Presently their eyes met in a full, searching, front, not to be mistaken glance. It is wonderful how much it made them acquainted. The man thought that they had come nearer together than they could by any other intercourse in months. But he felt that by that glance he had been strangely baulked. The beautiful face was strangely transformed. He felt the stirring of owls and bats and horned hoofs, within him. The face, which was really beautiful, seemed to him to have been usurped by a low devil, and an innocent maiden, for so she still seemed to him, to be possessed. And that glance was the confession of the devil to his inquiry. Very sorry for the poor maiden was the man, and when the assembly separated, and she passed him as a stranger in the crowd, her form and feet had the strangest resemblance to those of some brute animal. It is remarkable too that the spirit that appears at the windows of the house does at once, in a manner, invest itself in a new form of its own to the mind of the beholder.[1]

January 12.

Truth is beautiful. Without doubt; and so are lies. I have no fairer page in my life's album than the delicious memory of some passages at Concord on the Merrimack when affection contrived to give a witchcraft surpassing even the deep attraction of its own truth to a parcel of accidental and insignificant circumstances. Those coach wheels that rolled into the mist and darkness of the July morning. The little piazza, a piece of silk, the almshouse, the D—— girl, and such other things, which were not the charm, have more reality to this groping memory than the charm itself which illuminated them.

1 Two or three sentences of the above paragraph were printed, years later, in the essay " Behaviour " in *Conduct of Life*.

"Passing sweet
Are the remains of tender memory."

Be assured there is as deep a wisdom in embroidered coats and blue and pink ribbons, as
in truth and righteousness.'

Is it not the stupendous riches of man's nature that gives an additional delight to every
new truth? When I read a problem, I would be
a geometer; poetry, a poet; history, a historian;
sermons, a preacher; when I see paintings, I
would paint; sculpture, carve; and so with all
things, the manifold soul in me vindicates its
acquaintance with all these things. Similar delight we have in the admirable artist's, soldier's,
or sailor's life. We individuate ourselves with
him, and judge of his work. What is this but
our first ride round our estate to take possession,
promising ourselves withal, after a few visits
more, to have an insight and give a personal
direction to all the affairs that go on within our
domain, which is the All?

January 13.

"Our very sign-boards show there has been
a Titian in the world." Do you think that Aris-

1 In "Love," *Essays II,* pp. 174, 175, these memories
are expressed in a less personal form.

totle benefits him only who reads the Ethics and the Rhetoric? Or Bacon, or Shakspear, or the Schools, those only who converse in them? Far otherwise; these men acted directly upon the common speech of men and made distinctions which, as they were seen to be just by all who understood them, were rigidly observed as rules in their conversation and writing; and so were diffused gradually as improvements in the vernacular language. Thus the language *thinks* for us, as Coleridge said.

Also Simeon the Stylite is not quite useless to me, nor Danton, nor Robespierre, nor Rabelais, nor Aretin. And the merest speculatists— Plotinus and Dante— act most intensely on me. Fine sketch of the life of Descartes in Cousin.

The student at his first course of philosophical lectures looks wistfully at every knob and ball and glass rod or cylinder, as menacing him with the occult energies which they are about to disclose to their compeller.

I think I will read for a Lyceum lecture the three deaths of Phocion, Socrates and Sir Thomas More. Perhaps the martyrdom of Sir John Cobham in Southey's *Book of the Church* might serve as a fourth.

My friend Mr. —— will be a good minister

> " When it shall please the Lord
> To make his people out of board."

It is a great happiness when two good minds meet, both cultivated and with such difference of learning as to excite each the other's curiosity, and such similarity as to understand each other's allusions in the Touch-and-go of conversation. They make each other strong and confident. . . . The unspoken part of this conversation is the most valuable. How many secrets that have puzzled us for years are then told, and with most unexpected issues. You may find, for example, that the reason of your friend's superiority in power arises, strangely enough, not from a defect, but a superfluity in your constitution. Far, very far from envy is this free communication. A mutual respect rejoices them both. Coöperation, and not exclusiveness is the fruit.

The great value of Biography consists in the perfect sympathy that exists between like minds. Space and time are an absolute nullity to this principle. An action of Luther's that I heartily approve do I adopt also. We are imprisoned in life in the company of persons painfully unlike us, or so little congenial to our highest tendencies, and so congenial to our lowest, that their influence is noxious, and only now and then comes by us some commissioned spirit that speaks as with the word of a prophet to the languishing, nigh dead faith in the bottom of the heart, and passes by, and we forget what manner of men we are. It may be that there are very few persons at any one time in the world who can address with any effect the higher wants of men. This defect is compensated by the recorded teaching and acting of this class of men. Socrates, St. Paul, Antoninus, Luther, Milton have lived for us as much as for their contemporaries, if by books or by tradition their life and words come to my ear. We recognise with delight a strict likeness between their noblest impulses and our own. We are tried in their trial. By our cordial approval we conquer in their victory. We participate in their act by our thorough understanding of it. And thus we become acquainted with a fact which we could not have learned from our fellows, that the faintest sentiments which we have shunned to indulge from the fear of singularity are older than the oldest institutions, — are eternal in man ; that we can find ourselves, our private thoughts, our preferences, and aversions, and our moral judgements perhaps more truly matched in an ancient Lombard, or Saxon, or Greek, than in our own family.

It is a beautiful fact in human nature that the roar of separating oceans, no, nor the roar of rising and falling empires, cannot hinder the ear from hearing the music of the most distant voices ; that the trumpet of Homer's poetry yet shrills in the closet of the retired scholar across three thousand years ; that the reproof of Socrates stings as like the bite of a serpent, as it did Alcibiades. These affinities atone to us for the narrowness of our society, and the prison of our single lot, by making the human race our society, and the vast variety of human fortune the arena of actions on which we, by passing judgement, take part. History, taken together, is as severely moral in its teaching as the straitest religious sect. And thus we are fortified in our moral sentiments by a most intimate presence of sages and heroes.

Pythagoras is said (falsely, I suppose) to have declared that he remembered himself to have existed before, under the name of Euphorbus, at the siege of Troy. Which of us who is much addicted to reading but recognizes his own saying or thinking in his favorite authors?

January 14.

Apollo kept the flocks of Admetus, said the priests; another significant fable. Every man is an angel in disguise, a god playing the fool. It seems as if Heaven had sent its insane angels into our world as an asylum, and here they will break out into rare music and utter at intervals the words they have heard in Heaven, and then the mad fit returns and they mope and wallow like dogs. When the gods come among men they are not known. Jesus was not. Socrates and Shakspear were not.[1]

My thoughts tame me. Proud may the bard be among his fellow men, but when he sits waiting his inspiration he is a child, humble, reverent, watching for the thoughts as they flow to him from their unknown source. The moment of inspiration, — I am its reverent slave. I watch and watch and hail its aurora from afar.[2]

[1] The first sentence in this paragraph and the concluding ones are printed in "History," *Essays I.*

[2] Cf. "The Poet," *Poems*, Centenary Edition, p. 313.

January 15.

Saw the morn rise from the hilltop, but could not wait for the sun. Those long slender bars of cloud swim like fishes in the sea of crimson light.

> Nor am I ashamed to be
> A lover of that silent sea.[1]

My grandfather William Emerson left his parish and joined the Northern army, in the strong hope of having great influence on the men. He was bitterly disappointed in finding that the best men at home became the worst in the camp, vied with each other in profanity, drunkenness and every vice, and degenerated as fast as the days succeeded each other, and instead of much influence, he found he had none.[2] This so affected him that when he became sick with the prevalent distemper, he insisted on taking a dismission, not a furlough, and, as he died on his return, his family lost, it is said, a major's pension.

1 Here follows the passage in *Nature*, " Beauty," " How does Nature deify us," etc.

2 Mr. Emerson did not take into account that his uniformly brave and hopeful grandfather had, when he wrote the letter on which this paragraph is based, the poison of mortal disease already working in his blood; hence his depression.

We are all glad of warm days, they are so economical, and in the country in winter the back
is always cold.[1]

January 16.

The whole of heraldry is in courtesy. A man
of fine manners can pronounce your name in
his conversation with all the charm that ever
" My Lord" or "Your Highness" or "Your
Grace " could have had to your ear.

January 23.

Home again from Plymouth, with most
agreeable recollections.

Some thoughts lost. The C——s and
B——s can finish their sermon, the man of
genius cannot, because they write words and
pages which are finite things and can be numbered and ended at pleasure ; he writes after
nature, which is endless. His work, therefore,
when it is best concluded, he sees to be only
begun. May I say without presumption that,
like Michel Angelo, I only block my statues.

Mr. Hoar, in the coach, said of Judge Marshall " that if his intellects failed, he could lose
as much as would furnish brains to half a dozen

1 The modern reader must remember that open fires were
the sole dependence for warmth.

common men, before common men would find it out."

It is one of the laws of composition that, let the preparation have been how elaborate, how extended soever, the moment of *casting* is yet not less critical, not the less all-important moment on which the whole success depends.

Ichabod Morton at Plymouth said that he did not, in dealing with his brother, look very sharply to his own interest or mind the loss of a few dollars. He wished to treat all men in the same way.

January 30.

I spent at Plymouth with Lydia Jackson.

February 2.

Let Christianity speak ever for the poor and the low. Though the voice of society should demand a defence of slavery, from all its organs, that service can never be expected from me. My opinion is of no worth, but I have not a syllable of all the language I have learned, to utter for the planter. If by opposing slavery I go to undermine institutions, I confess I do not wish to live in a nation where slavery exists. The life of this world has but a limited worth in my eyes, and really is not worth such a price as the toleration of slavery. Therefore — therefore — though I may be so far restrained by unwillingness to cut the planter's throat as that I should refrain from denouncing him, yet I pray God that not even in my dream or in madness may I ever incur the disgrace of articulating one word of apology for the slave-trader or slaveholder.

Yesterday, had I been born and bred a Quaker, I should have risen and protested against the preacher's words. I would have said that in the light of Christianity is no such thing as slavery. The only bondage it recognizes is that of sin.

Clytemnestra, in Sophocles, thinks herself too violently reproved by her daughter. Electra answers, —

> " 'T is that you that say it, not I ; you do the deeds,
>   And your ungodly deeds find me the words."

> The childhood shows the man,
> As morning shows the day.
>
> *Paradise Regained.*

" Nothing great was ever achieved without enthusiasm."

February 11.

It needs to say something, they tell me, of the French Revolution. Why, yes, I believe that it has been advantageous on the whole. I very readily seek and find reasons for any such proposition, because whilst I believe that evil is to be hated and resisted and punished, at least forcibly hindered, yet offences must needs come, and out of them comes good as naturally and inevitably as the beautiful flower and the nourishing fruit out of the dark ground. I believe that the tendency of all thought is to Optimism. Now for the French Revolution. I believe, in the first place, that it would be an advantage, though we were not able to point out a single benefit that had flowed thence, and were able to show many calamities. I should still incline to think that we were too near to judge, like a soldier in the ranks who is quite unable, amid the din and smoke, to judge how goes the day, or guess at the plan of the engagement.

If I could see no direct good which it had occasioned, I should still say, See what great lessons it has taught the governor and the subject. It has taught men how surely the relaxing of the moral bands of society is followed by cruelty. It taught men that there was a limit beyond which the terrors of a standing army and of loyal association could not avail; that there was a limit beyond which the patience, the fears of a down-trodden people could not go.

February 14.

Grand is that word of Milton in his letter to Diodati excusing his friend for not writing to him, "for though you have not written, your probity writes to me in your stead."

Well said the wise aunt to-day, "Elizabeth grows on one; she is capable of humility; her manners to the obscure are without fault."[1]

February 16.

If Milton, if Burns, if Bryant, is in the world, we have more tolerance, and more love for the changing sky, the mist, the rain, the bleak, over-cast day, the indescribable sunrise and the immortal stars. If we believed no poet survived on the planet, nature would be tedious.

February 25.

On visits. If I had anything to say to you, you would find me in your house pretty quick.

1 Miss Elizabeth Hoar, always regarded as a sister by Mr. Emerson because of her engagement to his brother Charles.

I looked upon trades, politics, and domestic life as games to keep men amused and hinder them from asking *cui bono?* until their eyes and minds are grown. Then came Edward's tragic verses,[1] and I thought we give full leave to the poor man and to the parting man to feel bitterness; but not less bitter (though we give them no allowance) are the sad farewells of the realist amidst home, friends, and wealth.

March 17.

Many days give me marine recollections, as to-day. It is because when the wind is loud and the air clear, the great masses of cloud move so fast as to suggest immediately their vicinity to the sea. The wind blowing from the west, they must reach the coast, and shade the sea in an hour. Instantly, therefore, comes up before the eye the cold blue sea gathered up into waves all rippled and scored over with wind-lines, and a few sail scudding on their several tracks, though scarce seen to move over the broad black circle.

But nature is a picture-frame which fits equally well a comic or a mourning piece.

Taylor in the preface to this healthful poem, *Van Artevelde*, says that sense must be the

1 "The Last Farewell," which Mr. Emerson printed with his own poems.

basis of all consummate poetry. It is well and truly said. We have almost a theory of Shakspear, the wonder of Shakspear is almost diminished, when we say, Strong sense is the staple of his verse, because what is to be accounted for, is the extent of the man; that he could create not one or two, but so manifold classes and individuals, and each perfect. But we are quite familiar with the expertness and power of men of sense in every new condition, and this experience supplies us with a just analogy.

March 18.

"Beauty with the ancients was the tongue on the balance of expression," said Winckelmann. What meant he? Answer: —

> Beauty no other thing is than a beam
> Flashed out between the middle and extreme.
>
> HERRICK.

> *Hunc solem et stellas, et decedentia certis*
> *Tempora momentis, sunt qui formidine nulla*
> *Imbuti spectant.*
>
> HORACE.

March 19.

As I walked in the woods I felt what I often feel, that nothing can befal me in life, no calamity, no disgrace (leaving me my eyes) to which Nature will not offer a sweet consolation. Standing on the bare ground with my head bathed by the blithe air, and uplifted into the infinite space, I become happy in my universal relations. The name of the nearest friend sounds then foreign and accidental. I am the heir of uncontained beauty and power. And if then I walk with a companion, he should speak from his Reason to my Reason; that is, both from God. To be brothers, to be acquaintances, master or servant, is then a trifle too insignificant for remembrance.[1] O, keep this humor, (which in your life-time may not come to you twice,) as the apple of your eye. Set a lamp before it in your memory which shall never be extinguished.

I think Taylor's poem[2] is the best light we have ever had upon the genius of Shakspear. We have made a miracle of Shakspear, a haze of light instead of a guiding torch, by accepting unquestioned all the tavern stories about his want of education and total unconsciousness. The internal evidence all the time is irresistible

1 Part of this paragraph occurs in *Nature*, chapter i.
2 *Philip Van Artevelde.*

that he was no such person. He was a man, like
this Taylor, of strong sense and of great cultivation; an excellent Latin scholar, and of extensive and select reading, so as to have formed his
theories of many historical characters with as
much clearness as Gibbon or Niebuhr or Goethe.
He wrote for intelligent persons, and wrote with
intention. He had Taylor's strong good sense,
and added to it his own wonderful facility of
execution which aerates and sublimes all language the moment he uses it, or, more truly,
animates every word.

I ought to have said in my wood-thoughts
just now, that there the mind integrates itself
again. The attention, which had been distracted
into parts, is reunited, reinsphered. The whole
of nature addresses itself to the whole man. We
are reassured. It is more than a medicine. It is
health.

In talking, weeks ago, with M. M. E. I was
ready to say that a severest truth would forbid
me to say that ever I had made a sacrifice. That
which we are in healthy times seems so great
that nothing can be taken from us that seems
much. I loved Ellen, and love her with an affec-

tion that would ask nothing but its indulgence to make me blessed. Yet when she was taken from me, the air was still sweet, the sun was not taken down from my firmament, and however sore was that particular loss, I still felt that it was particular, that the universe remained to us both, that the universe abode in its light and in its power to replenish the heart with hope.

Distress never, trifles never abate my trust. Only this Lethean stream that washed through us, that gives sometimes a film or haze of unreality, a suggestion that, as C. said of Concord society, "we are on the way back to Annihilation,"—only this threatens my trust. But not that would certify me that I had ever suffered. Praise! Praise and Wonder! And oft we feel so wistful and babe-like that we cannot help thinking that a correspondent sentiment of paternal pleasantry must exist over us in the bosom of God.

March 19.

" Spare the poor emmet, rich in hoarded grain ;
    He lives with pleasure, and he dies with pain."

At Waltham they have 11,000 spindles ; at Lowell, 200,000.

"The road that Luxury levels for the coach,
Industry may travel with his cart."

E. B. E.

Through Nature's ample range in thought to stroll,
And start at man, the single mourner there.

YOUNG.

Heaven kindly gives our blood a moral flow.

YOUNG.

Landor writes that "no man ever argued so
fairly as he might have done." And in a reflecting, highly cultivated society it seems as if
no man could ever be in a passion, or act with
a negligent, self-forgetting greatness. Can Webster in the American Senate, for any conceivable
public outrage, scream with real passion? The
reporters say he did the other day. They did
not think so when they wrote it, and nobody
believes it was anything else than a fine, wise,
oratorical scream.

Never utter the truism, but live it among men
and by your fireside.

This rebellious Understanding is the incorri-
gible liar; convict him of perfidy, and he answers
you with a new fib. No man speaks the truth
or lives a true life two minutes together.

March 23.

There is no greater lie than a voluptuous book like Boccaccio. For it represents the pleasures of appetite, which only at rare intervals, a few times in a life-time, are intense, and to whose acme continence is essential, as frequent, habitual, and belonging to the incontinent. . . .

Settle it in your own mind that you must choose between your own suffrage and other people's. I used to think, all men use to think, that you can have both; but you cannot. Secure your own, and you shall be assured of others, twenty years hence, but you must part with them so long. Before this Reason with bright eternal eyes, even merits that seem pure and saint-like compared with practices and reputations of the mob, are seen to be vulgar and vile. There are merits calculated on shorter and longer periods; better than those of the hour are the Benthamite and the Calvinist, who keep the law all their life for pay; but these dwindle before the incalculable eternity which the lover of virtue embraces in the present moment.

The virtue of the intellect consists in preferring work to trade. Brougham, Canning, Everett, convert their genius into a shop, and turn every faculty upside down that they may sell well. Allston, Wordsworth, Carlyle, are smit with the divine desire of creation, and scorn the auctioneers. Now what you do for the shop is so much taken from science.

R.[1] cannot eat sponge cake without a ram-rod.

There is almost no earnest conversation, so much of display enters into it. Put two people of good condition together, the talk on one or both parts will probably be merely defensive; that is, they are not thinking how they may learn something, but how they may come off well. Change your parties, and perhaps you excite the ambition of each speaker to say something brilliant, to leave a good opinion of himself.

Ordinarily men do not exchange thoughts and converse in method, that is, advancing. One goes East, the other West. The preacher goes among his people, the professor among his scholars, and finds an universal admiration of his sermons or lessons; but the first word they speak on the general subject shows him that these dis-courses never penetrated farther than the ears.

[1] Dr. Ripley, who always refused it without this adjunct.

They have a sort of instinctive respect for his train of thought and the profession which belongs to it, but they live in another train of thought that in *particulars* flatly contradicts his. And when he thinks a perfect understanding is obtained, he finds the whole battle remains to be fought. Did you ever take part in a conversation which advanced? Commonly it is merely pastime. They circulate round point-no-point. Each remains fast in his own aura and not once do they communicate.

Dr. H., Mr. B., Mr. S., Mr. I., the most powerful men in our community, have no theory of business that can stand scrutiny, but only bubble built on bubble without end. They skate so fast over a film of ice that it does not break under them. It seems, when you see their dexterity in particulars, as if you could not overestimate the resources of good sense, and when you find how utterly void they are of all remote aims, as if you could not underestimate their philosophy.

Cannot a man contemplate his true good so steadily as to be willing to renounce all thirst for display, and make all his doings tentative, imperfect, because aiming ever at truth and perfection lying out of himself; instead of tricking out what trifles he has picked up and disposing them to advantage in little popular poems or conversations or books? I think he had better live in the country, and see little society, and make himself of no reputation.

Sects fatten on each other's faults. How many people get a living in New England by calling the Unitarians prayerless, or by showing the Calvinists to be bigots. Hallett feeds on the Masons, and McGavin on the Catholics. The poor man that only sees faults in himself will die in his sins. Charles thinks the Unitarians pursue a low, conservative policy. The high, the generous, the self-devoted sect will always instruct and command mankind.

It is because I am such a bigot to my own whims, that I distrust the ability of a man who insists much on the advantage to be derived from literary *conversazione*. Alone is wisdom. Alone is happiness. Society nowadays makes us low spirited, hopeless. Alone is heaven.

March 26.

The wild delight runs through the man, in spite of real sorrows. Nature says, He is my creature, and spite of all his impertinent griefs he shall be glad with me. Almost I fear to think how glad I am.

I went by him in the night. Who can tell the moment when the pine outgrew the whortleberry that shaded its first sprout. It went by in the night.

March 27.

He who writes should seek not to say what may be said, but what has not been said that is yet true. I will read and write. Why not? All the snow is shovelled away, all the corn planted, and the children and the creatures on the planet taken care of without my help. But if I do not read, nobody will. Yet am I not without my own fears. Captain Franklin after six weeks' travelling to the North Pole on the ice, found himself two hundred miles south of the spot he set out from: the ice had floated. And I sometimes start to think I am looking out the same vocables in the Dictionary, spelling out the same sentences, solving the same problems. — My ice may float also.

March 28.

If life were long enough, among my thousand and one works should be a book of nature whereof Howitt's *Seasons* should be not so much the model as the parody. It should contain the natural history of the woods around my shifting camp for every month in the year. It should tie their astronomy, botany, physiology, meteorology, picturesque, and poetry together. No bird, no bug, no bud, should be forgotten on his day and hour. To-day the chickadees, the robins, bluebirds and song-sparrows sang to me. I dissected the buds of the birch and the oak; in every one of the last is a star. The crow sat above as idle as I below. The river flowed brimful, and I philosophised upon this composite, collective beauty which refuses to be analysed. Nothing is beautiful alone. Nothing but is beautiful in the whole. Learn the history of a craneberry. Mark the day when the pine cones and acorns fall.

A wonderful sight is the inverted landscape. Look at the prospect from a high hill through your legs, and it gives the world a most pictorial appearance.

Saturn, they say, devoured his children, thereby presignifying the man who thought, and instantly turned round to see how his thoughts were made : the hen that eats the egg.

March 29.

Certainly a man would be glad to do his country service, but he cannot cram his service down its throat. It is time enough if he come when he is called. It is enough for him if he has eyes to see, that he is infinite spectator, without hurrying, uncalled, to be infinite doer. Let him brood on his immortality, —

> " For every gift of noble origin
> Is breathed upon by Hope's perpetual breath."

He cannot look to work directly on men, but obliquely. Few men bring more than one or two points into contact with society at once; they must be content to influence it thereby. Hereafter they may find more purchase.

We live and grow by use. If you sit down to write, with weak eyes, and awaken your imagination to the topic, you will find your eyes strong.

March 31.

The tree is a congeries of living vegetables; so it often seems as if man was a congeries of living spirits, according to Goethe's monadism. One of them looks to see what another does. Many dissimilar things are done with like earnestness.

The robin hops about in the field as if he was waiting for somebody — hop, hop, hop — and then stops again.

The dreams of an idealist have a poetic integrity and truth. Their extravagance from nature is yet within a higher nature, and terrible hints are thrown to him out of a quite unknown intelligence. I have been startled two or three times by the justice as well as the significance of the intimations of this phantasmagoria. Once or twice the conscious fetters of the Spirit have been unlocked and a freer utterance seemed attained.

April 10.

I fretted the other night at the hotel at the stranger who broke into my chamber after midnight, claiming to share it. But after his lamp had smoked the chamber full and I had turned round to the wall in despair, the man blew out his lamp, knelt down at his bedside, and made in low whisper a long earnest prayer. Then was the relation entirely changed between us. I fretted no more, but respected and liked him.

Coleridge said it was no decisive mark of poetic genius that a man should write well concerning himself. Is it not because the true genius, the Shakspeare and Goethe, sees the tree and sky and man as they are, enters into them; whilst the inferior writer dwells evermore with himself, "twinkling restlessly"?

A man is seldom in the upright position two moments together, but when he is, let him record his observations and they shall be fit for "the Spiritual Inquirer."

Le Baron Russell has visited me and shown me the stars. Hither came G.,[1] as usual appearing as if bestridden by a restless and invisible rider.

April 11.

Glad to hear music in the village last evening under the fine yellow moon: it sounds like cultivation, domestication. In America, where all are on wheels, one is glad to meet with a sign of adorning our own town. It is a consecration, a beautifying of our place. A bugle, clarionet and flute are to us a momentary Homer and Milton. Music is sensuous poetry.

1 Dr. Le Baron Russell of Plymouth, later of Boston, a friend of Mr. Emerson's through life. G. is Mr. George P. Bradford.

April 12.

The gods make those men very bad who talk much about them, says Landor's Cyrus. It must be owned that the Idea of God in the human mind is a very changing luminary. Sometimes seen; never quite unremembered; often quite hidden, to the degree that the Spirit asks, Is there any? But the moral sentiments are immutable. Was there ever a moment in your life when you doubted the existence of the Divine Person? Yes. Was there ever a moment in your life when you doubted the duty of speaking the truth? No. Then is one mutable, the other immutable.

[Here follows the passage on the dark hours of life, found in the opening paragraph of "The Tragic," first printed in the *Dial* (see *Natural History of Intellect*).]

A man feels that his time is too precious, the objects within reach of his spirit too beautiful, than that his attention should stoop to such disfigurements, as Antimasonry, or Convent Riots, or General Jackson and the Globe. Yet welcome would be to him the principle out of which these proceed, for all the laws of his being are beautiful. This Translation the wise is ever making.

"Already my opinion has gained infinitely in force when another has adopted it." This is the reason why a writer appears ever to so much more advantage in the pages of another man's book than in his own. Coleridge, Wordsworth, Schelling are conclusive, when Channing or Carlyle or Everett quotes them, but if you take up their own books, then instantly they become, not lawgivers, but modest, peccable candidates for your approbation.

LANGUAGE OF NATURE

No man ever grew so learned as to exhaust the significance of any part of nature. Nature never became a toy to a wise spirit. The flowers, the animals, the mountains reflected all the wisdom of his best hour as much as they had delighted the simplicity of his childhood.

April 14.

"*Ne te*,"[1] *etc.* Every man is a wonder until you learn his studies, his associates, his early acts and the floating opinions of his times, and then he developes himself as naturally from a point as a river is made from rills. Burke's orations are but the combination of the *Annual*

---

1 *Ne te quæsiveris extra.*

Register, which he edited, with the "Inquiry on the Sublime and Beautiful," which he wrote at the same time. Swedenborg is unriddled by learning the theology and philosophy of Continental Europe in his youth. Each great doctrine is then received by the mind as a tally of an Idea in its own reason, and not as news.

Rev. Dr. F. consoled my father on his deathbed by telling him he had not outlived his teeth, etc., and bid my mother expect now to be neglected by society.

April 16.

This "snow in summer," which falls so fast to-day, is like a wound from a friend. Dr. Ripley calls it "robin-snow."

Why must always the philosopher mince his words and fatigue us with explanation? He speaks from the Reason, and being, of course, contradicted word for word by the Understanding, he stops like a cog-wheel at every notch to explain. Let him say, *I idealize*, and let that be once for all; or, *I sensualize*, and then the Rationalist may stop his ears. Empedocles said bravely, " I am God; I am immortal; I contemn human affairs "; and all men hated him.

Yet every one of the same men had had his religious hour when he said the same thing.

Fable avoids the difficulty, is at once exoteric and esoteric, and is clapped by both sides. Plato and Jesus used it. And History is such a fable.

Plato had a secret doctrine, — had he? What secret can he conceal from the eyes of Montaigne, of Bacon, of Kant?

Let the imaginative man deny himself and stick by facts. As a man must not bring his children into company naked, and must not bring more children into the world than he can clothe, so the idealist must retain his thoughts until they embody themselves in fit outward illustrations.

A court house is a good place to learn the limits of man. The best counsel are not orators, but very slovenly speakers; to use Mr. Warren's fine apology for Baylies, "they spread their ability over the whole argument, and have not strong points." The interminable sentences of Mr. H., clause growing out of clause "like the prickly pear," as Charles said, reminded me of nothing so much as certain vestry prælections. But in the court house the worth of a man is gauged.[1]

An advantage shines on the Abolition side, that these philanthropists really feel no clog, no check from authority — no discord, no sore place in their own body which they must keep out of sight or tenderly touch. People just out of the village, or the shop, reason and plead like practised orators, such scope the subject gives them, and such stimulus to their affections. The Reason is glad to find a question which is not, like Religion or Politics, bound around with so many traditions and usages that every man is forced to argue unfairly, but one on which he may exhaust his whole love of truth, — his heart and his mind. This is one of those causes which will make a man. Never is a good cause in facts long at loss for an ideal equipment.[2]

1 Concord was a shire-town until 1858, when the courts were transferred to Lowell, and the sessions of the Supreme Court once a year, and of the Court of Common Pleas three times a year, drew a large attendance from the neighborhood to hear the leaders of the Bar.

2 Mr. Emerson used to say (or quote), " Eloquence is dog-cheap at an Antislavery Chapel."

It was alarming to see the lines of sloth in so many faces in the court house; the flame of life burns very dim. The most active lives have so much routine as to preclude progress almost equally with the most inactive.

" Je défie un cœur comme le vôtre d'oser mal penser du mien," writes Rousseau to Diderot.

April 19.

It is a happy talent to know how to play. Some men must always work if they would be respectable; for the moment they trifle, they are silly. Others show most talent when they trifle. Be it said of W. that his excess of reverence made it impossible for him to realize ever that he was a man; he never assumed equality with strangers, but still esteemed them older than himself, though they were of his own age or younger. He went through life postponing his maturity and died in his error.[1]

April 22.

I have made no record of Everett's fine Eulogy at Lexington on the 20th, but he is all art, and I find in him nowadays, maugre all his gifts

1 This passage seems to be a veiled allusion to himself.

and great merits, more to blame than praise. He is not content to be Edward Everett, but would be Daniel Webster. This is his mortal distemper. Why should such a genius waste itself? Have we any to spare? . . . Daniel Webster, Nature's own child, sat there all day and drew all eyes. Poor Everett! for this was it that you left your own work, your exceeding great and peculiar vocation, the desire of all eyes, the gratitude of all ingenuous scholars — to stray away hither and mimic this Man, that here and everywhere in your best and (for work) unsurpassed exertions, you might still be mere secondary and satellite to him, and for him hold a candle?

Webster spoke at the table few and simple words, but from the old immoveable basis of simplicity and common natural emotion to which he instinctively and consciously adheres.

"We only row; we 're steered by fate."

The involuntary education is all. See how we are mastered. With the desire of dogmatising, here we sit chatting. With desire of poetic reputation, we still prose. We would be Teachers, but in spite of us we are kept out of the pulpit, and thrust into the pew. Who doth it? No

man : only Lethe, only Time ; only negatives ;
indisposition ; delay ; nothing.

On the same auspicious morning I received a
letter from Carlyle the wise, the brave, and his
intimations of a visit to America, which purpose
may God prosper and consummate !

Better a great deal have friends full grown
before they are made acquainted, like Moody
and Webster; they have the pleasant surprise of
the bare result ; a man meets a man. What fact
is more valuable than the difference of our
power alone and with others.[1]

April 23.

The order of things consents to virtue. Such
scenes as luxurious poets and novelists often
paint, where temptation has a quite overcom-
ing force, never or very rarely occur in real
life.

It is very hard to know what to do if you
have great desires for benefitting mankind ; but
a very plain thing is your duty. It may be suspected then that the depth of wisdom and the
height of glory is there. Self-Union, — never
risk that. Neither lie, nor steal, nor betray,

1 Here follows the passage on the happy flow of a letter to
a friend. See first page of "Friendship," *Essay I.*

for you violate consciousness. Nothing is self-evident but the commandments of consciousness.

"The limbs of my buried ones," etc. I dislike the bad taste of almost everything I have read of Jean Paul; this scrap for instance: Shakspear never said these hard artificial things.

We think we are approaching a star. I fear it is a nebula. At least individual aims are very nebulous.

May 1.

Cloudy and cold: is not May morning sure to be?

May 9.

Spin out your web to the end of your yarn. Ten rivers stream from your finger ends.

A frost this morn.

If what you have read in newspapers you had read in good books, how much would you know?

May 11.

A foolish German fairy tale, *The Short Mantle*, which I read in English long years ago, made my cheeks glow again and almost the gracious drops fall at the triumph of the chaste and gentle Genelas.[1] Very docile we are to such pretty tales, but to verify them in our own chaste life and simple spiritual excellence very slow indeed.

It is a fine flattery to tell your friend he is a singular mind, an incalculable person.

I am disqualified by hearing this strife concerning Goethe from judging truly of his genius. He is that which the intelligent hermit supposes him to be, and can neither be talked up nor talked down.

We are all wise for other people, none for himself. That wise Fessenden told me never to have two related ideas without putting them on paper.

Genius seems to consist merely in trueness of sight, in using such words as show that the man was an eye-witness, and not a repeater of what was told. Thus, the girl who said "the

1 This story is found in many forms. In the *Fabliau du Mantel Mal Taillé*, the hero's name is Venelas. See also "The Boy and the Mantle" in *Percy's Reliques* and Child's collection of Ballads.

earth was a-gee;" Lord Bacon when he speaks of exploding gunpowder as "a fiery wind blowing with that expansive force," etc.—these are poets.

Hard Times. In this contradictory world of truth the hard times come when the good times are in the world of commerce; namely, sleep, full eating, plenty of money, care of it, and leisure; these are the hard times. Nothing is doing, and we lose every day.

The young preacher is discouraged by learning the motives that brought his great congregation to church. Scarcely ten came to hear his sermon. But singing, or a new pelisse, or Cousin William, or the Sunday School, or a proprietors' meeting after church, or the merest anility in Hanover Street, were the beadles that brought and the bolts that hold his silent assembly in the church. Never mind how they came, my friend, never mind who or what brought them, any more than you do who or what set you down in Boston in 1835. Here they are, real men and women,—fools, I grant, but potentially divine, every one of them convertible. Every ear is yours to gain. Every heart will be glad and proud and thankful for a master.

There where you are, serve them and they must serve you. They care nothing for you, but be to them a Plato; be to them a Christ, and they shall all be Platos, and all be Christs.

May 13.

Do believe so far in your doctrine of Compensation as to trust that greatness cannot be cheaply procured. Self-denial and persisting self-respect can alone secure their proper fruits. Act naturally, act from within, not once or twice, but from month to month, without misgiving, without deviation, from year to year, and you shall reap the costly advantages of moral accomplishments. Make haste to reconcile you to yourself, and the whole world shall leap and run to be of your opinion. Imprison that stammering tongue within its white fence until you have a necessary sentiment or a useful fact to utter, and that said, be dumb again. Then your words will weigh something, — two tons, like St. John's.

What a benefit if a rule could be given whereby the mind could at any moment *East* itself, and find the sun. But long after we have thought we were recovered and sane, light breaks in upon us and we find we have yet had no sane moment. Another morn rises on mid-noon.

Who is capable of a manly friendship? Very few. Charles thinks he can count five persons of *character;* and that Shakspear and the other writers of the first class infused their character into their works and hence their rank. We feel an interest in a robust healthful mind, an Alfred, Chaucer, Dante, which Goethe never inspires.

The truest state of mind, rested in, becomes false. Thought is the manna which cannot be stored. It will be sour if kept, and to-morrow must be gathered anew. Perpetually must we *East* ourselves, or we get into irrecoverable error, starting from the plainest truth and keeping as we think the straightest road of logic. It is by magnifying God, that men become Pantheists; it is by piously personifying him, that they become idolaters.

As the world signified with the Greek, Beauty, so skepticism, alas! signifies sight. Not in his goals but in his transition man is great.

See the second aphorism of the *Novum Organum*, that neither the hand nor the mind of man can accomplish much without tools, etc., etc.: "nec intellectus sibi permissus, multum valet." This is the defence of written or premeditated preaching, of the written book, of the composed poem. No human wit unaided is equal to the production at one time of such a result as the *Hamlet* or *Lear*, but by a multitude of trials and a thousand rejections and the using and perusing of what was already written, one of those tragedies is at last completed — a poem made that shall thrill the world by the mere juxtaposition and interaction of lines and sentences that singly would have been of little worth and short date. Rightly is this art named Composition, and the composition has manifold the effect of the component parts. The orator is nowise equal to the evoking on a new subject of this brilliant chain of sentiments, facts, illustrations, whereby he now fires himself and you. Every link in this living chain he found separate; one, ten years ago; one, last week; some of them he found in his father's house, or at school when a boy; some of them by his losses; some of them by his sickness; some by his sins. The Webster with whom you talk admires the oration almost as much as you do, and knows himself to be nowise equal, unarmed, that is, without this tool of Synthesis, to the splendid effect which he is yet well pleased you should impute to him.

No hands could make a watch. The hands brought dry sticks together, and struck the flint with iron, or rubbed sticks for fire, and melted the ore, and with stones made crowbar and hammer; these again helped to make chisel and file, rasp and saw, piston and boiler, and so the watch and the steam-engine are made, which the hands could never have produced, and these again are new tools to make still more recondite and prolific instruments. So do the collated thoughts beget more, and the artificially combined individuals have in addition to their own a quite new collective power. The main is made up of many islands, the state of many men, the poem of many thoughts, each of which, in its turn, filled the whole sky of the poet, was day and Being to him.

May 14.

There is hardly a surer way to incur the censure of infidelity and irreligion than sincere faith and an entire devotion. For to the common eye, pews, vestries, family prayer, sanctimonious looks and words constitute religion, which the devout man would find hindrances. And so we go, trying always to weld the finite and infinite, the absolute and the seeming, together. On the contrary, the manner in which religion is most positively affirmed by men of the world is bare-faced skepticism. When I write a book on spiritual things I think I will advertise the reader that I am a very wicked man, and that consistency is nowise to be expected of me.

When will you mend Montaigne? When will you take the hint of nature? Where are your Essays? Can you not express your one conviction that moral laws hold? Have you not thoughts and illustrations that are your own; the parable of geometry and matter; the reason why the atmosphere is transparent; the power of composition in nature and in man's thought; the uses and uselessness of travelling; the law of Compensation; the transcendent excellence of truth in character, in rhetoric, in things; the sublimity of self-reliance; and the rewards of perseverance in the best opinion? Have you not a testimony to give for Shakspear, for Milton? one sentence of real praise of Jesus, is worth a century of legendary Christianity. Can you not write as though you wrote to yourself, and drop the token, assured that a wise hand will pick it up?

I recorded worse things in my Italian Journal than one I omitted; that a lady in Palermo

invited me to come and ride out with her in her
barouche, which I did, though the day was rainy
and so the coach was covered. She did not invite me to dine, so I made my obeisance, when
on our return I had waited upon her into the
house; then I *walked* home through a drench-
ing rain in a city where I was an entire stranger, but not until I had paid her coachman my
half dollar who waylaid me on the stairs. To as
fat an understanding as mine I cannot but think
it might have occurred, that, to send the guest
home or to pay one's servants, would really be
a finer compliment. But it is a good specimen
of the misery of finery.

Address your rede to the young American,
and know that you hook to you all like minds
far or near, whether you shall know them or
not. And remember Brutus.

"*Pherecydes Syrus primus dixit animos hominum
esse sempiternos.*" CICERO, *Tusc. Quest.* lib. 1, c. 16.

The chapter on Optical Delusions in our life-
time is very large. How many times have we
resolved not to be again deceived by one and
the same!

Commerce, which vulgarises great things, will never quite degrade for the poet the miracle of the letter which floats round the globe in a pine ship and comes safe to the eye for which it was writ.[1]

Good story Squire Adams told here of countryman travelling between day and sunrise, and seeing the locomotive and its train of cars on the railroad. He saw the smoke and the wheels, his horse was frightened, ran, turned over the wagon, and broke it; and he crawled to a house for help. They asked him what had happened. He could not well tell what, but that it looked like hell in harness.

Trifles move us more than laws. Why am I more curious to know the reason why the star form is so oft repeated in botany, why the number five is such a favorite with Nature, than to understand the circulation of the sap and the formation of buds?[2] Those two wonders of electro-magnetism and the polarisation of light have also a peculiar interest.

1 See "Prudence" in *Essays I,* p. 236, Centenary Ed.
2 Why Nature loves the number five
    And why the star-form she repeats.
        Poems, "Woodnotes I."

May 16.

Robert Herrick delights in praising Ben Jonson, and has many panegyrical pieces to others, and in one copy of verses praising many, Beaumont and Fletcher and others, yet never drops the name of Shakspear. 'Tis like the want of the statues of Cassius and Brutus in the funeral of Junia, " *Eo ipso præfulgebant, quod non visebantur.*" Herrick's merit is the simplicity and manliness of his utterance, and only rarely the weight of his sentences. He has, and is conscious of having, a noble idiomatic use of his English, a perfect plain-style from which he can at any time soar to a fine lyric delicacy, or descend to the coarsest sarcasms without losing his firm footing. But this power of speech was accompanied by an assurance of fame. A similar merit is that of the American Hillhouse, though no approach to Herrick's wealth.

Landor thinks that a knowledge of poetry is reserved for some purer state of sensation and existence.

The observation of a mere observer is more unsuspicious than that of a theorist. I ought to have no shame in publishing the records of one who aimed only at the upright position, more anxious that the thing should be truly seen than careful what thing it was. As we exercise little election in our landscape, but see for the most part what God sets before us, I cannot but think mere enumeration of the objects would be found to be more than a catalogue, — would be a symmetrical picture, not designed by us, but by our Maker, as when we first perceive the meaning of a sentence which we have carried in the memory for years.

May 24.

Coincidences, dreams, animal magnetism, omens, sacred lots, have great interest for some minds.[1] . . .

May 29.

In your Rhetoric, notice that only once or twice in history can the words "dire" and "tremendous" fit.

He weakens who means to confirm his speech by vehemence, feminine vehemence.

"A tremendous faculty, that of thinking on one's legs" is a newspaper description of elo-

1 Here follows the long paragraph, beginning thus, in "Demonology," originally printed in the *Dial.* See *Lectures and Biographical Sketches.*

quence; and this is a tolerable use of the word noticed above.

At the Sunday School meeting, G. P. B. remarked that his measure of a good speech was the desire it imparted to himself to speak, and open the suggestions of the man on the floor. Mr. L—— spoke, and the eminent propriety of his manner answered to the audience the same purpose as if he had said something. All people agreed it was a good speech. Yet is not nature cheated, for these men accomplish nothing. Their effect is as merely phenomenal as their work.

Add to G. P. B.'s remark just now, our frequent experience of receiving intellectual activity from an acting mind. I read, two days since, verses of Eliot, the poet, which filled me with desire to write, with faith in the art.

Now he will render a service to his countrymen who in these days will patiently collect the experiences of this kind and so write rules for the discipline of the intellect. Could you show me how in every torpid hour I could wake to full belief and earnest labor, O give me the recipe. Better yet : could you point me to the divine page of Cudworth, Plato, Bacon, Herbert,

Carlyle, Michel Angelo, or of Paul, or of God in nature, where I could find a timely restoration of my reason under the insanity of passion, do that, and the joy of a Saviour shall be yours.

> Happy the wit or dunce; but hard
> Is it to be half a bard.

May 30.

The ideal philosophy is much more akin to virtue than to vice. When the mountains begin to look unreal, the soul is in a high state, yet in an action of justice or charity things look solid again.

I am convinced that we are very much indebted to each other for stimulus, and for such confirmation to our own thoughts that we venture to try them in practice, a step we should have long postponed but for that seconding.

June 1.

In this age of seeming, nothing can be more important than the opening and promulgation of the gospel of Compensations to save the land. The men who put manner for matter at our public meetings should learn that they have lost their time. The man who mistakes his profession, the Scholar who takes his subject from dictation and not from his heart, should know that he has lost as much as he seems to have gained. And when the vain speaker has sat down, and the people say "what a good speech!" it still takes an ounce to balance an ounce. Societies as well as individuals are bubbles. But nature cannot be cheated. That only profits which is profitable. Life alone can impart life, and though we burst, we can only be valued as we make ourselves valuable.

The irresistible conclusion of your chapter on Compensation should be, Therefore, the Devil is an Ass.

Levi Woodbury occupies the position once filled by Alexander Hamilton; Jackson that of Washington; Isaac Hill is a member of the Senate as much as Daniel Webster. But does any one living imagine that this equal *nominal* standing makes the standing of these men *identical?* It is perfectly well known both to Washington and to Jackson the gulf that is between them; and likewise to Hamilton and to Woodbury; and likewise to Webster and to Hill.

Mr. Allston would build a very plain house and have plain furniture, because he would hold

out no bribe to any to visit him who had not
similar tastes to his own — a good ascetic.

Sir Henry Wotton said of Sidney that " his
wit was the measure of congruity."

June 4.

It seems as if every sentence should be pre-
fixed with the word *True*, or *Apparent*, to indicate the writer's intention of speaking after that
which is, or that which seems. Thus, *truly*, our
power increases exactly in the measure that we
know how to use it, but *apparently*, Andrew
Jackson is more powerful than John Marshall.

In Heaven, utterance is place enough. Heaven
is the name we give to the True State, the world
of Reason, not of the Understanding; of the
Real, not the Apparent. It exists always, whether
it is ever to be separated from the Hell or not.
It is, as Coleridge said, another world, but not to
come. The world I describe is that, where only
the laws of mind are known; the only economy of
time is saying and doing nothing untrue to self.[1]

Knowledge is hard to get and unsatisfying
when gained. Knowledge is a pleasing provoca-

1 The passage about being the Devil's child, in " Self-
Reliance" (*Essays I*) follows this.

tion to the mind beforehand, and not cumbersome afterwards.

Am I true to myself? then nations and ages do guide my pen, then I perceive my commission to be coeval with the oldest causes.

June 10.

Aristotle Platonizes. Cudworth is like a cow in June which breathes of nothing but clover and scent-grass. He has fed so entirely on ancient bards and sages that all his diction is redolent of their books. He is a stream of Corinthian brass in which gold and silver and iron are molten together out of ancient temples.

I endeavor to announce the laws of the First Philosophy. It is the mark of these that their enunciation awakens the feeling of the moral sublime, and great men are they who believe in them. Every one of these propositions resembles a great circle in astronomy. No matter in what direction it be drawn, it contains the whole sphere. So each of these seems to imply all truth. Compare a page of Bacon with Swift, Chesterfield, *Lacon*,[1] and see the difference of great and

1 A book of maxims, by Charles Caleb Colton, 1820.

less circles. These are gleams of a world in which we do not live: they astonish the understanding.

June 16.

Books. Blessed art and blessed instruments of pen, ink and paper that hold fast the representatives of the related thoughts. Here logic holds, and between the major and minor of a syllogism cannot the mind whisk away because a thrush flies out of a bush, or a smart Golden Senecio catches the eye, or an elegant lupine lifts its blue spires in the path.

June 20.

The advantage in Education is always with those children who slip up into life without being objects of notice. Happy then those who are members of large families.

Literature. I asked in the woods, What I would know of Homer, if the Œdipus were ready to reply. We would know whether in the mind of his age were any radical differences from ours? Whether they had an equivalent for our organized *morale* ? Whether we have lost by Civilization any force, by Christianity any virtue? Machinery encumbers. Homer is to us nothing personal, merely the representative of

his time. I believe that to be his sincerest use
and worth. The most abstract questions are
really operating actively on men, though they
know it not, and the real interest that effervesces
in this love of literary gossip is a wise curiosity
in the human soul to know if our fellow is our
counterpart. I suppose we would most anxiously
know what is his moral sentiment, and not so
curiously inquire, whether he managed better
than we, with our fellow-beings — the sea, and
the land, the plants, the animals, fire, and light.

When we read a book in a foreign language,
we suppose that an English version of it would
be a transfusion of it into our own consciousness.
But take Coleridge or Bacon, or many an English
book besides, and you immediately feel that the
English is a language also, and that a book writ
in that tongue is yet very far from you, — [from]
being transfused into your own consciousness.
There is every degree of remoteness from the
line of things in the line of words. By and by
comes a word true and closely embracing the
thing. That is not Latin, nor English, nor any
language but *thought*. The aim of the author
is not to tell truth — that he cannot do, but to
suggest it. He has only approximated it himself

and hence his cumbrous, embarrassed speech: he uses many words, hoping that one, if not another, will bring you as near to the fact as he is. For language itself is young and unformed. In heaven it will be, as Sampson Reed said, "one with things." Now, there are many things that refuse to be recorded,—perhaps the larger half. The unsaid part is the best of every discourse.

The good of publishing one's thoughts is that of hooking to you like-minded men, and of giving to men whom you value, such as Wordsworth or Landor, one hour of stimulated thought. Yet, how few! Who in Concord cares for the first philosophy in a book? The woman whose child is to be suckled? The man at Nine-acre-Corner who is to cart sixty loads of gravel on his meadow? the stageman? the gunsmith? Oh, no! Who then?

June 21.

Poetry preceded prose, as the form of sustained thought, as Reason, whose vehicle poetry is, precedes the Understanding. When you assume the rhythm of verse and the analogy of nature, it is making proclamation, "I am now freed from the trammels of the Apparent; I speak from the Mind."

June 22.

It is unpleasing to meet with those anomalous wits who say brilliant things and yet have no proportioned strength of mind; Chalmers, Edward Irving, Brougham, Randolph, or, more frequently, talkers who impose upon us by the vivacity or weight of single remarks, and when you better know the speaker,

"You wonder how the devil they got there."

The more genius, usually, the more conformity there is to the general model. But these seem hybrids.

I wrote L.[1] that this speechmaking seems to turn the man out of doors, to turn his timber into flowers, and make him like unto Apicius who sold his house, but kept the balcony to see and be seen in.

Aunt saith, "The finest wits have their sediment."

Some persons in Rhode Island saying to George Fox, that, if they had money enough, they would hire him to be their minister, he

[1] Miss Jackson, to whom he was now engaged.

said, "Then it was time for him to be gone, for
if their eye was to him, or to any of them, then
would they never come to their own teacher."

June 24.

"Three silent revolutions in England; first,
when the professions fell from the church.
2. When literature fell from the professions.
3. When the press fell from literature." COLE-
RIDGE.

I remembered to Charles to-night the English gentleman whom I saw in the cold hostelrie
at Simplon at the top of the mountain, and whose
manners so satisfied my eye. He met there un-
expectedly an acquaintance, and conversed with
him with great ease and affectionateness, and as
if totally unconscious of the presence of any other
company, yet with highbred air.

The self-existency of the gentleman is his best
mark. He is to be a man first, with original perceptions of the true and the beautiful, and thence
should grow his grace and dignity. Then he is
God's gentleman and a new argument to the stoic.

"When I am purified by the light of heaven
my soul will become the mirror of the world, in

which I shall discern all abstruse secrets." Warton quotes this, he says, from an ancient Turkish poet. — *History of English Poetry*.

Books are not writ in the style of conversation. One might say they are not addressed to the same beings as gossip and cheat in the street. Neither are speeches, orations, sermons, academic discourse, on the same key of thought, or addressed to the same beings. The man that just now chatted at your side of trifles, rises in the assembly to speak, and speaks to them collectively in a tone and with a series of thoughts he would never think of assuming to any one of them alone. Because man's universal nature is his inmost nature.

Idealism is not so much prejudiced by danger as by inconvenience. In our speculative habits we sometimes expect that the too solid earth will melt. Then we cross the ocean sweltering, seasick, reeling, week after week, with tar, harness-tub, and bilge, and, as an ingenious friend says, it is carrying the joke too far.

June 26.

If you would know what nobody knows, read what everybody reads, just one year afterwards, and you shall be a fund of new and unheard-of speculations.

The mystery of Humility is treated of by Jesus, by Dante, by Chaucer in his Griselda, by Milton and by Sampson Reed; or listen to the discourse of a wise man to a crowd in a perfect conviction that nobody hears it but you.

June 27.

I wrote Hedge that good society seemed an optical illusion that ought to be classed with Bacon's Idols of the Cave. Carlyle affirms it has ceased to exist. C. C. E. affirms that it has just begun — Greek and Roman knew it not. To me it seems that it is so steadily and universally thwarted by death, sickness, removal, unfitness, ceremony, or what not, that a design to hinder it must be suspected. Every person is indulged with an opportunity or two of equal and hearty communication enough to show him his potential heaven. But between cultivated minds the first interview is the best, and it is surprising in how few hours the results of years are exhausted. Besides, though it seem ungrateful to friends whom the heart knoweth by name, yet the value of the conversation is not measured according to the wisdom of the company, but by quite other and indefinable causes, the fortunate moods. I think we owe the most recreation and most memorable thoughts to very unpromising gossips.

(I copied the above from memory.)

June 29.

George Fox's chosen expression for the God manifest in the mind is the Seed. He means that seed of which the Beauty of the world is the Flower, and Goodness is the Fruit.

I replied this morning to the Committee that I would do what I could to prepare a Historical Discourse for the Town Anniversary.[1] Yet why notice it? Centuries pass unnoticed. The Saxon king was told that man's life was like the swallow that flew in at one window, fluttered around, and flew out at another. So is this population of the spot of God's earth called Concord. For a moment they fish in this river, plow furrows in the banks, build houses on the fields, mow the grass. But hold on to hill or tree never so fast, they must disappear in a trice.[2]

1 The occasion was the celebration of the two hundredth birthday of Concord, September 12, 1835.

2 Compare "Hamatreya" in *Poems*. The paragraph in

The contemplation of Nature is all that is fine. Who can tell me how many thousand years, every day, the clouds have shaded these fields with their purple awning. The little river by whose banks most of us were born, every winter for ages has spread its crust of ice over the great meadows which in ages it has formed. The countless families that follow or precede man, keep no jubilee, mark no era; the fly and the moth in burnished armor, these little emigrants travel fast, they have no baggage-wagon, all night they creep; the ant has no provision for sleep. The trees that surround us grew up in the days of Peter Bulkeley. This first celebration from that everlasting Past. The oaks that were then acorns wave their branches in this morning's wind. The little flower that at this season stars the woods and roadsides with its profuse blooms won the eye of the stern pilgrim with its humble beauty. The maple grew red in the early frost over those houseless men burrowing in the sand.

the journal which immediately follows occurs in the opening passage of the "Historical Address," but it is given here for its beauty, and because the Discourse, though printed as a pamphlet for the use of the citizens that year, was not included in the Works until after Mr. Emerson's death. It is found in the *Miscellanies*, Riverside and Centenary Editions.

The mighty pine, yet untouched, towered into the frosty air. And yet another kind of permanence has also been permitted. Here are still the names of the first fifty years. Here is Blood, Willard, Flint, Wood, Barrett, Heywood, Hunt, Wheeler, Jones, Buttrick. And if the name of Bulkeley is wanting, the honor you have done me this day shows your kindness for his blood.[1]

July 1.

A windmill, so soon as it is far enough in the landscape to look like a toy, is picturesque; nearer it is disagreeable. The robin, like the geranium family, wears sober colors. Charles says that painting the vans red is adding insult to injury.[2]

"There is scarce truth enough alive to make societies secure," says Shakspear in *Measure for Measure*.

In the memory of the disembodied soul the

1 Rev. Joseph Emerson, minister of Milton and afterwards of Mendon, married Elizabeth, granddaughter of Peter Bulkeley.

2 There was a windmill on the hill behind the Court House on the road to the Manse.

days or hours of pure Reason will shine with a
steady light as the life of life, and all the other
days and weeks will appear but as hyphens which
served to join these.

July 2.

The distinction of science objective and subjective I find in Norris's *Ideal World*.

Admirable passages quoted from St. Augustine's *De Libero Arbitrio*, lib. ii : " And yet as
rich as thy furniture is, O City of God, thy
gates stand always open, free to all comers. For
thy immoveable wealth needs no guard, the
Exchequer of Light and Truth is secure against
all thievish attempts, and the treasures of wisdom, though common to all, can yet be rifled
or carried away by none."

Norris's first volume was an unexpected delight this afternoon. He fights the battles and
affirms the facts I had proposed to myself to do.
But he falls, I so think, into the common error
of the first philosophers, that of attempting to
fight for Reason with the weapons of the Understanding. All this polemics and syllogism
and definition is so much waste paper, and Montaigne is almost the only man who has never
lost sight of this fact.

July 4.

Talked last eve. with George Bradford of Locke, who, I maintained, had given me little. I am much more indebted to persons of far less name. I believe his service was to popularize metaphysics, allure men of the world to its study, if that indeed be a service. George gave a good account of his friend Alcott, who is a consistent spiritualist, and so expects the influence of Christianity into trade, government and arts.[1]

The arts languish now because all their scope is exhibition; when they originated, it was *to serve* the gods. . . . The Catholic Religion has turned them to continual account in its service. Now they are mere flourishes. Is it strange they perish? Poetry, to be sterling, must be more than a show; must have, or be, an earnest meaning. Chaucer, Wordsworth; *per contra* Moore and Byron.

I study the art of solitude: I yield me as gracefully as I can to my destiny. Why cannot one get the good of his doom, and since it is from eternity a settled thing that he and society shall be nothing to each other, why need he blush

1 The first mention of this valued friend.

so, and make wry faces and labor to keep up a poor beginner's place, a freshman's seat in the fine world?

One of the good effects of hearing the man of genius is that he shows the world of thought to be infinite again, which you had supposed exhausted.

July 15.

Why do I still go to pasture where I never find grass; to these actors without a purpose, unless a poor mechanical one, these talkers without method, and reasoners without an idea? At the Divinity School this morning I heard what was called the best performance, but it was founded on nothing and led to nothing, and I wondered at the patience of the people. This afternoon the king of the House of Seem spoke, and made as if he was in earnest with pathetic tones and gesture, and the most approved expressions, — and all about nothing ; and he was answered by others with equal apparent earnestness, and still it was all nothing. The building seemed to grudge its rent, if the assembly did not their time. Stetson,[1] who jokes, seems the only wise man. It is a pity three hundred men

1 Rev. Caleb Stetson, a classmate of Emerson's.

should meet to make believe or play Debate.
They are all so solemn and vehement, that I
listen with all my ears, and for my life can't find
any idea at the foundation of their zeal.

I forgive desultoriness, trifling, vice even, in
a young man, so long as I believe that he has
a closet of secret thoughts to which he retires as
to his home, and which have a sort of parents'
interest in him wherever he is. At sight of them
he bows. But if he is not in earnest about anything, if all his interest is good breeding and
imitation, I had as lief not be as be him.

Great pudder make my philanthropic friends
about the children. I should be glad to be convinced they have taught one child one thing.
G—— and B——, no doubt, teach them just
as much as the minister did before, not a jot
more; for the children don't understand anything they say.

QUOTATION

Coleridge loses by De Quincey, but more by
his own concealing, uncandid acknowledgment
of debt to Schelling. Why could not he have
said generously, like Goethe, I owe all? As soon
as one gets so far above pride, as to say all truth
that might come from him, and that now does

come from him, as truth and not as his truth, as soon as he acknowledges that all is suggestion, then he may be indebted without shame, to all.

I see that the young men like to speak at public meetings just as they would take exhilarating gas, 'tis so pretty an intoxication. Oh, for the days of the Locrian halters again.[1]

The wit of man is more elastic than the air our bodies breathe. A whole nation will subsist for centuries on one thought, and then every individual man will be oppressed by the rush of his conceptions, and always a *plenum* with one grain or sixty atmospheres.

Let not the voluptuary dare to judge of literary, far less of philosophical questions. Let him wait until the blindness that belongs to pollution has passed from his eyes.

We all have an instinct that a good man, good and wise, shall be able to say intuitively, i. e., from God, what is true and great and beautiful.

1 A story of Plutarch's. The Locrians had halters around the necks of the speakers so that they could shut off their discourse.

Never numbers, but the simple and wise shall judge. Not the Wartons and Drakes, but some divine savage, like Webster, Wordsworth, and Reed, whom neither the town or the college ever made, shall say that we shall all believe. How we thirst for a natural thinker!

I find good things in this manuscript of Oegger,[1] and I am taken with the design of his work. But it seems as if everybody was insane on one side, and the Bible makes them as crazy as Bentham or Spurzheim or politics. The ethical doctrines of these theosophists are true and exalting, but straightway they run upon their Divine Transformation, the Death of God, etc., and become horn-mad. To that point they speak reason, then they begin to babble, and so this man cries out, Wo to them that do not believe, etc., etc. This obstinate Orientalism that God is a petty Asiatic king and will be very angry

---

1 Guillaume Caspar Lencroy Oegger, professor of philosophy, and vicar of Notre Dame in Paris. The work referred to is *The True Messiah, or The Old and New Testaments examined according to the Principles of the Language of Nature.* A translation of a part of it was published later in Boston, by Miss Elizabeth P. Peabody. It may have been her manuscript that Mr. Emerson had.

if you do not prostrate yourself, they cannot get rid of.

But now and then outbreaks the sublimity of truth. . . .

"We shall pass to the future existence as we enter into an agreeable dream: all nature will accompany us there."

Much that is best is hid by being next to us. Who in Christendom knows the beauty and grandeur of the Lord's Prayer?

July 24.

"In the first age of the world, by reason of the number of their days, their memories served instead of books." (HOOKER.) There is no book like a memory, and none that hath such a perfect index and that of every kind, alphabetical, systematic, and arranged by names of persons and all manner of associations.

"I say three persons," ingenuously confessed St. Augustine (on the Trinity: v. 9), "not that I may say something, but that I may not say nothing." (*Apud* OEGGER.)

Most persons exist to us merely or chiefly in relations of time and space. Those whom we love, whom we venerate, or whom we serve, exist to us independently of their relations.

O Thou who drawest good out of the fury of devils, save me.

Yesterday I visited Jonas Buttrick [1] and Abel Davis; the former aged seventy, the latter seventy-nine years. Both were present at Concord fight. Davis was one of the militia under command of——. Jonas Buttrick remembers Major Hosmer and Captain Davis [2] going back and forward often, and said of Captain Davis that "his face was red as a piece of broadcloth — red as a beet. He looked very much worried." I asked, "Worried with fear?" "No." Both agree that Captain Davis had the right of the companies, but know not why. Jonas Buttrick thinks

1 Son of Major John Buttrick, who led the attack on the British at the North Bridge. Jonas was then eleven years old, and so, of course, was only an eager spectator of the action, which took place partly on his father's farm.

2 Joseph Hosmer, whose spirited question to his superiors, "Are you going to let them burn the town?" seems to have influenced the attack, was at that time lieutenant acting as adjutant. Mr. Emerson's informants call him by his later title of Major. Captain Isaac Davis of Acton, who with his company led the column by Buttrick's side, fell dead at the first volley.

that he did not come up from Acton until after the consultation of the officers and the conclusion to fight, and that he took the right because that was the side on which he most conveniently joined the troops. Abel Davis thinks that Major [Buttrick] having given up his company to ———, Captain Davis had the right in virtue of his rank.[1]

Dr. Palfrey remarked at Cambridge, when we talked of the manners of Wordsworth and Coleridge, that there seemed to be no such thing as a conventional manner among the eminent men of England, for these people lived in the best society, yet each indulged the strongest individual peculiarities.

For literature, one is ever struck with the fact that the good once is good always. The average strength is so fixed that among thirty jumpers the longest jump will be likely to be the longest of three hundred, and a very long jump will remain a very long jump a century afterward.

Richard Hooker wrote good prose in 1580. Here it is good prose in 1835. There have not

[1] A probable reason was assigned by other survivors, namely, that the Acton company alone had bayonets.

CONCORD BATTLEGROUND IN 1837

been forty persons of his nation from that time to this who could write better.

The *Quarterly Review* toils to prove that there is no selfish aristocracy in America, but that every man shakes hands heartily with every other man, and the chancellor says, " My brother, the grocer." And to fix this fact will be to stamp us with desired infamy. I earnestly wish it could be proved. I wish it could be shown that no distinctions created by a contemptible pride existed here, and none but the natural ones of talent and virtue. But I fear we do not deserve the praise of this Reviewer's ill opinion. The only ambition which truth allows is to be the servant of all. The last shall be first.

I read with great delight the *Record of a School*.[1] It aims all the time to show the symbolical character of all things to the children, and it is alleged, and I doubt not, truly, that the children take the thought with delight. It is remarkable that all poets, orators and philosophers

1 This remarkable book is the Journal of Mr. Amos Bronson Alcott's private school in Boston, kept by Miss Elizabeth P. Peabody, his assistant, later well known for her philanthropic life.

have been those who could most sharply see and most happily present emblems, parables, figures. Good writing and brilliant conversation are perpetual allegories. " My fortunes are in the moult," says Philip van Artevelde. Webster is such a poet in every speech. " You cannot keep out of politics more than you can keep out of frost," he said to Clifford. " No matter for the baggage, so long as the troop is safe," he said when he lost his trunk. " Waves lash the shore," etc.; Indians' whole speech. " Back of the hand," was Crockett's expression. All the memorable words of the world are these figurative expressions. Light and heat have passed into all speech for knowledge and love. The river is nothing but as it typifies the flux of time. Many of these signs seem very arbitrary and historical. I should gladly know what gave such universal acceptance to Cupid's arrow for the passion of love; and more meanly, the horn for the shame of cuckoldom.

Ephraim Stow, says the newspaper, was born on the last day of the year, which gave occasion to a parish wit to remark that " he came near not being born at all."

" One of those crystal days which are neither hot nor cold."

Mrs. R. cited a well-known character to show that trick and pretension impose on nobody, but that my friend is reverenced for his liberality.

Everybody leads two or three lives, has two or three consciousnesses which he nimbly alternates. Here am I daily lending my voice, and that with heat often, to opinions and practices opposite to my own. Here is M. M. E. always fighting in conversation against the very principles which have governed and govern her.

Very good remark saw I in the very good *Record of a School*, concerning unity reproduced by the mind out of severed parts. Yes, all men have thoughts, images, facts, by thousands and thousands, but only one of many can crystallize these into a symmetrical one by means of the nucleus of an Idea.

Humphrey Heywood showed me his fine toy-cart which his father made for him. I see nothing of the farmer but his plain dealing and hard work; yet there are finer parts which, but for this child, would remain latent; his love and the taste which makes a fanciful child's wagon for its manifestation.

A good example of that *prosopopœia* I wrote of, is Thompson's [1] "Come to nurse our bantling in the Cradle of Liberty. Yet I do not know whether that is right. Methinks he has grown so great that if we should rock him in Faneuil Hall his feet would dangle out the door." . . . One of the best examples of this sort is Burke's "shearing the wolf."

[Here follow many pages of extracts from Oegger's *True Messiah, or The Old and New Testaments examined according to the Principles of the Language of Nature*; a few of these are given.]

"People suppose that when God produced our visible world the choice that he made of forms and colors for animals, plants and minerals was entirely arbitrary on his part. This is false. Man may sometimes act from whim; God never can. The visible creation then cannot, must not (if we may use such expressions), be

1 George Thompson, the English Abolitionist, who faced insult and violence in his crusade, at this time, against slavery in the United States.

anything but the exterior circumference of the invisible and metaphysical world, and material objects are necessarily kinds of *scoriæ* of the substantial thoughts of the Creator.[1] . . . For God to create is only to show. The universe in its minutest details existed for God as really before the creation, as after it; because it existed in him substantially, as when the statue exists in the block of marble from which the sculptor extracts it.

" By the creation, we only have been enabled to perceive a portion of the infinite riches eternally buried in the Divine Essence. The *perfect* especially must have always thus existed in God. The *imperfect* alone can have received a kind of creation by means of man, a free agent, though under the influence of a Providence which never loses sight of him.

" Neither the form nor the color of any object in nature can have been chosen without a reason. Everything that we see, touch, smell, — everything from the sun to a grain of sand, . . . has flowed forth by a supreme reason from that world where all is spirit and life. No fibre in the animal, no blade of grass in the vegetable, no form of crystallization in inanimate matter, is without

1 This sentence is quoted in *Nature*, p. 35, Centenary Edition.

its clear and well-determined correspondence in the moral and metaphysical world. And if this is true of colors and forms, it must, by a still stronger reason, be true of instincts of animals, and the far more astonishing faculties of man. Consequently, the most imperceptible thoughts and affections which we imagine we have conceived by our own power; the compositions which we consider our own in philosophy and literature; the inventions which we believe we have made in the arts and sciences; the monuments that we think we are erecting; the customs that we fancy we establish in the things which men consider great, as in the most insignificant transactions of civil and animal life, — all this existed before us; all this is simply given to us, and given with a supreme reason, according to our different wants. *An infinitely little degree of consent to receive*, which forms our moral liberty, is the only thing that we have for our own. . . . And indeed, but for all these emblems of life which creation offers, there would be no appreciable moral idea or moral sentiment, no possible means — we fear not to say it — for God to communicate a thought, and affection to his creature, any more than for one feeling creature to communicate it to another. . . .

" Had there been no *father*, could you know anything of *tenderness?* Had there never been a *generous man*, could you know what is generosity? Love; maladies; defilements; the persecutions show what is atrocity, etc., etc. The necessity of indicating moral distinctions alone explains monstrosities and disgusting images unworthy of the Creator, which nature offers to the eye of degraded man. The abyss of our being cannot be revealed but by the appreciable phenomena of life. . . . "

" Man and the serpent form the right angle: other animals fill the whole quadrant, and any other kind of beings is geometrically impossible."

" Jehovah addresses himself to all his intelligent creation, and each being finds in his words what is appropriate to himself. The pure spirits who act on the human race must necessarily be always in advance of it in knowledge of the oracles of the most High, the perfect accomplishment of which oracles they concur to produce, spite of the united efforts of all degraded spirits," etc.

Every man must live upon a principle and move according to its will, as in the vehicular state every soul rides upon its ray. I have seen the adoption of a principle transform a proser into an orator. Every transgression that it makes of routine makes man's being something worth.

Humility is a great time-saver. The whole business must wait whenever each individual of the company has some personal recollection, some apology or explanation to make. All sit impatiently deferring till his impertinent vanity is adjusted and then go on. I, who know the supreme folly of the thing, can collect instances, not only from last night's conversation, but from my own sayings two nights ago at Dr. Willard's.

July 30.

It is affecting to see the old man's, Thaddeus Blood's, memory taxed for facts occurring sixty years ago at Concord fight. "It is hard to bring them up," he says; "the truth never will be known." The Doctor [Ripley], like a keen hunter, unrelenting follows him up and down, barricading him with questions; yet cares little for the facts the man can tell, but much for the confirmation of the printed History. "Leave me, leave me to repose."

Every principle is an eye to see with. Facts in thousands of the most interesting character are slipping by me every day unobserved, for I see not their bearing, I see not their connexion. I see not what they prove. By and by I shall mourn in ashes their irreparable loss.

No distinction in principle can be broader than that taken by the abolitionist against Everett. Everett said that in case of a servile war, though a man of peace, he would buckle on his knapsack to defend the planter. The Philanthropist who was here this morning[1] says that he is a man of peace, but, if forced to fight on either side, he should fight for the slave against his tyrant.

I know nothing of the source of my being, but I will not soil my nest. I know much of it after a high, negative way, but nothing after the understanding. God himself contradicts through me and all his creatures the miserable babble of Kneeland[2] and his crew; but if they set me to affirm in propositions his character and provi-

1 Perhaps George Thompson.

2 Abner Kneeland who, a short time before, had been sent to jail for publications held by the Court to be blasphemy.

dence, as I would describe a mountain or an Indian, I am dumb. Oft I have doubted of his person, never that truth is divine.

You affirm that the moral development contains all the intellectual, and that Jesus was the perfect man. I bow in reverence unfeigned before that benign man. I know more, hope more, am more, because he has lived. But, if you tell me that in your opinion he has fulfilled all the conditions of man's existence, carried out to the utmost, at least by implication, all man's powers, I suspend my assent. I do not see in him cheerfulness: I do not see in him the love of natural science: I see in him no kindness for art; I see in him nothing of Socrates, of Laplace, of Shakspear. The perfect man should remind us of all great men. Do you ask me if I would rather resemble Jesus than any other man? If I should say Yes, I should suspect myself of superstition.

Ages hence, books that cannot now be written may be possible. For instance, a cumulative moral and intellectual science. If I would know something of the elements and process of the moral sublime, where shall I now seek the analysis? If I would know the elementary distinction of spiritual and intellectual, where shall I inquire? A sentence showing a tendency is all that a century contributes to psychology. Where shall I find the result of phrenology? of animal magnetism? of extacy? By and by, books of condensed wisdom may be writ by the concentrated lights of thousands [of] centuries which shall cast Bacon and Aristotle into gloom. As the American Encyclopædia said of Astronomy, "How many centuries of observation were necessary to make the motion of the earth suspected!"

July 31.

Every day's doubt is whether to seek for Ideas, or to collect facts; for all successful study is the marriage of thoughts and things. A continual reaction of the thought classifying the facts, and of facts suggesting the thought.

When shall I be tired of reading? When the moon is tired of waxing and waning, when the sea is tired of ebbing and flowing, when the grass is weary of growing, when the planets are tired of going.

The act of duty that might have been omitted, but that was inserted in a past day, pleases, in

remembering the contingency, with a better satisfaction than that with which we see the mail
stage roll off in its cloud of dust, if, breathless
with haste, we have arrived just in time to get
our letter in.

I wrote yesterday that these orators of a principle owed everything to it, and our good friend
Samuel J. May may instruct us in many things.
He goes everywhere and sees the leaders of
society everywhere, his cause being his ticket
of admission, and talks on his topic with no intelligent person who does not furnish some new
light, some unturned side, some happy expression, or strike off some false view or expression,
of the philanthropist. In this way his views are
enlarged and cleared and he is always attaining to the best expressions. As when he said
the question between the Colonization and the
Abolition men was "whether you should remove
them [the negroes] from the prejudice, or the
prejudice from them."

It is, my God, an antidote to every fear, the
conviction twice recently forced on me, that
men reverence virtue never by the appearance,
but accurately according to its weight. Nothing

but an ounce will balance an ounce. Thus alone is the will strong; thus He whose right it is to reign shall reign. Spit at consequences; launch boldly forth into the pure element, and that which you think will down you, shall buoy you up.

[Here follows the last part of the passage on the stars in the first page of *Nature*.]

Men believe that some of their fellows are more happily constituted than themselves after the pattern of themselves. They have in fortunate hours had the eye opened, whereby the world was newly seen, as if then first seen, and which seemed to say that all prior life, however loud and pretending, was but death or sleep. They believe that some men add to this Eye a Tongue to tell their vision, and a certain degree of control over these faculties; that the spirits of the prophets are subject to the prophets; and they wish such men to take the chronicle of their parish, or their age, and in the auspicious hour let the facts pass through their mind and see if they will not take the form of picture and song.

When I cast my look inward and look upon God as mine, I may well defy the future, and looking upon all the rough weather ahead as exercises to try the faith of the combatants, I may merrily predict a victory.

The Reason has her victories. $15,000 were subscribed in a very short time in New York by these Abolitionists, $2,000 at one meeting in Boston, and $5,000 at another, and forthwith paid. So put that against the burning convent and the Julien Hall.

My two facts referred to on the last page were the bountiful E. R. [Ezra Ripley?] and the Christian Sam May, who both pass for that they are in things to praise and things to blame.

> For Christ made no cathedrals
> Ne with him was no Cardinals.
>
> CHAUCER.

Once in a while we meet with poetry which is also music, — "high and passionate thoughts to their own music chaunted." The following lines of John Barbour (1365) remind me of the music I heard lately : —

> This was in the moneth of May
> When birdis singis in ilk spray,
> Melland their notes with seemly soun,
> For softness of the sweet seasoun,

And levis of the branchis spred,
And bloomis bright beside them bred,
And fields are strovit with flowris
Well sawer and of ser colouris.

Me it pleases well to skip the minuter designation of the plants, and to slight also the
chronicles of kings, so that I can learn somewhat of the history of wit in this world of men;
to know what have been the entertainments of
the human spirit from age to age, what are the
best things that it hath said, and who and what
they were who said them. Yet the beauty that
drew us to one or another pursuit, as botany,
medicine, history of poetry, and the like, is
presently lost sight of in the details of the study
itself, and none the less poetical than the herb-
alist, the doctor, the critic.

A system-grinder hates the truth. To make
a step into the world of thought is given to but
few men; to make a second step beyond his
first, only one in a country can do; but to carry
the thought out to three steps marks a great
Teacher. Aladdin's Palace, with its one unfinished window which all the gems in the royal
treasury cannot finish in the style of the meanest of the profusion of jewelled windows that

were built by the genie in a night, is but too true a picture of the efforts of Talent to add a scene to Shakspear's play or a verse to Shakspear's songs.

August 1.

A sparrow or a deer knows much more of Nature's secrets than a man, but is less able to utter them. And those men who know the most can say the least.

Jacob Behme is the best helper to a theory of Isaiah and Jeremiah. You are sure he was in earnest, and, could you get into his point of view, the world would be what he describes. He is all imagination. —"Aurora, i. e. the Dayspring or Dawning of the Day in the Orient, or Morning Redness in the Rising of the Sun; i. e., the Root or Mother of Philosophy, Astrology and Theology from the True Ground," etc., etc., by J. Behme. Written in Gerlitz in Germany, A. D. 1612, ætatis suæ 37. London, 1656.

"O world, where is thy humility, where is thy angelical love? At that very instant when the mouth says 'God save thee,' then, if the heart were seen, it might be said, 'Beware, look to thyself, for it bids the Devil take thee.'" BEHME. "O thou excellent, angelical kingdom, how comely dressed and adorned wert thou once! how

hath the devil turned thee into a murderous den.
Dost thou suppose thou standest now in the
flower of thy beauty and glory? No! Thou
standest in the midst of hell; if thine eyes were
opened, thou wouldst see it. Or dost thou think
that the Spirit is drunken and doth not see
thee?" BEHME.

There sits the Sphinx from age to age, in the
road, Charles says, and every wise man that
comes by has a crack with her.[1] But this Oegger's plan and scope argue great boldness and
manhood, to depart thus widely from all routine
and seek to put his hands, like Atlas, under
Nature, and heave her from her rest. Why the
world exists, and that it exists for a language or
medium whereby God may speak to man, this
is his query, this his answer.

Saturday eve.

The distinction of Fancy and Imagination
seems to me a distinction in kind. The Fancy ag-
gregates; the Imagination animates. The Fancy
takes the world as it stands and selects pleasing
groups by apparent relations. The Imagination
is Vision, regards the world as symbolical, and

[1] See *Nature*, p. 34.

pierces the emblem for the real sense. Sees all external objects as types. A fine example is the [account] of the execution of Lord Russell. (*Anecdotes* [Spence?], p. 11.)

God hides the stars in a deluge of light. That is his chosen curtain. So he hides the great truths in the simplicity of the common consciousness. I am struck with the contrast, which I have repeatedly noted before, between the positiveness with which we can speak of certain laws — an evidence equal to that of consciousness — and the depth of obscurity in which the Person of God is hid. From month to month, from year to year, I come never nearer to definite speaking of him. He hideth himself. I cannot speak of him without faltering. I unsay as fast as I say my words. He is, for I am. Say rather, He is. But in the depth inaccessible of his being he refuses to be defined or personified.

After thirty, a man wakes up sad every morning, excepting perhaps five or six, until the day of his death. It was strange after supposing for years that my respected friend was the heart of the county and blended thoroughly with the people, to find him wholly isolated, more even

than I, walking among them with these "monu-
mental" manners unable to get within gunshot
of any neighbor except professionally. Yet the
fulness of his respect for every man and his self-
respect at the same time have their reward, and
after sitting all these years on his plain wooden
bench with eternal patience, Honor comes and
sits down by him.[1]

August 3.

Charles wonders that I don't become sick at
the stomach over my poor journal. Yet is ob-
durate habit callous even to contempt. I must
scribble on, if it were only to say in confirmation
of Oegger's doctrine that I believe I never take
a step in thought when engaged in conversation
without some material symbol of my proposition figuring itself incipiently at the same time.
My sentence often ends in babble from a vain
effort to represent that picture in words. How
much has a figure, an illustration, availed every
sect. As when the reabsorption of the soul into
God was figured by a phial of water broken in
the sea. This morn, I would have said that a
man sees in the gross of the acts of his life the
domination of his instincts or genius over all
other causes. His Wilfulness may determine the

1 Evidently Hon. Samuel Hoar.

character of moments, but his Will determines that of years.

While I thus talked, I *saw* some crude *symbols* of the thought with the mind's eye, — as it were, a mass of grass or weeds in a stream, of which the spears or blades shot out from the mass in every direction, but were immediately curved round to float all in one direction. When presently the conversation changed to the subject of Thomas à Kempis's popularity, and how Aristotle and Plato come safely down, as if God brought them in his hand (though at no time are there more than five or six men who read them), and of the Natural Academy by which the exact value of every book is determined, maugre all hindrance or furtherance; then saw I, as I spoke, the old pail in the Summer Street kitchen with potatoes swimming in it, some at the top, some in the midst, and some lying at the bottom; and I spoiled my fine thought by saying that books take their place according to their specific gravity "as surely as potatoes in a tub. . . ."

It occurred with regard to à Kempis that it is pleasant to have a book come down to us of which the author has, like Homer, lost his individual distinctness, is almost a fabulous personage, so that the book seems to come rather out of the spirit of humanity and to have the sanction of human nature than to totter on the two legs of any poor Ego.

For language of nature, Ichabod Morton uses no other; Peter Hunt, Crockett, and the Vermont drover. So, in the 17th century, it appeared in every book, "And to put finger in the eye and to renew their repentance, they think this is weakness." THOS. SHEPARD, 1645, *New England's Lamentation.*

I suspect that wit, humor, and jests admit a more accurate classification by the light of the distinction of the Reason and the Understanding. Nothing is so cheap as jests of the sort that fill Byron's "Heaven and Earth." They might be manufactured by the thousand. All the dinner wit that assails Swedenborg and his church is cut off the same piece.

"He shall be as a god to me," said Plato, "who can rightly define and divide."

Who can make a good sentence can make a good book. *Ex ungue leonem.* If you find a good thing in the writing of a mediocre man, be sure he stole it.

Edw. Bagshaw wrote (1662) "an answer to all that Roger L'Estrange intends to write."

We have little control of our thoughts. We are pensioners upon Ideas.[1] . . .

I wrote to Miss Peabody [on Swedenborg] that I should certainly not have denied, awake, that the spiritual contains the intellectual nature, or that the moral is prior, in God's order, to the intellectual; which I believe. The two attributes of wisdom and goodness always face and always approach each other. Each when perfect becomes the other. Yet to the moral nature belongs sovereignty, and so we have an instinctive faith that to it all things shall be added, that the moral nature being righted, the circulations of the universe take effect through the man as a member in its place, and so he learns the sciences after a natural or divine way. A good deed conspires with all nature, as the hand sang with the voice in the angels' concert; but there is a kind of falsehood in the enunciation of a chemical or astronomical law by an unprincipled savant. But whilst all considerate persons incline, I suppose, to this general

1 Here follows a passage on "prisoners of Ideas." (See "Intellect," *Essays I*, pp. 328, 329, Cent. Ed.)

confession, there still stand the uncontested facts that in our experience is almost no proportioned cultivation. The blacksmith has a strong arm, the dancer a strong foot; great proficiency in the mathematics may coexist with extreme moral insensibility, and the splendors of holiness with a contempt for learning; — such lobsided, one-eyed half-men are we now, and such a yawning difference between our *esse* and our *posse*.

I am content to find these differences, I am content to wait long before many refractory facts. A great tendency I like better than a small revelation, and I hate to be imprisoned in premature theories. I have no appetite such as Sir Thomas Browne avows for difficultest mysteries, that my faith may have exercise; but I had rather not understand in God's world than understand through and through in Bentham's and Spurzheim's.

I like what you say of your aversion at being confined to Swedenborg's associations, and I confirm myself with similar declarations whenever my critical acumen, with which you make yourself so merry, is at fault in the great Life. You have studied much the character of Jesus, and I read with pleasure every considered expression of praise of him. But perfect, in the sense of complete man, he seems not to me to be, but a very exclusive and partial development of the moral element, such as the great Compensation that balances the universe provides to repair accumulated depravity. The weight of his ethical sentences deserves more than all the consideration they have, and his life is one original pure beam of truth, but a perfect man should exhibit all the traits of humanity and should expressly recognize intellectual nature. Socrates I call a complete, universal man, fulfilling all the conditions of man's existence. Sublime as he is, I compare him not as an ethical teacher to Christ, but his life is more humane.

Ah, Homer! Ah, Chaucer! Ah, Shakspear! But we live in the age of propriety. Their elegance is intrinsic, ours super-added; their cleanness is sunshine, ours painting and gilding.[1]

Classification. A thought comes single, like a foreign traveller, but if you can find out its name, you shall find it related to a powerful and numerous family.

1 Mr. Emerson during this month gave an address before the American Institute of Education "On the Best Mode of Inspiring a Correct Taste in English Literature." (See Cabot's Memoir, vol. ii, Appendix F.)

August 5.

Our summer, Charles says, is a galloping consumption, and the hectic rises as the year approaches its end.

Wordsworth's "Ode to Duty" singeth, —

> There are who ask not if thine eye
> Be on them; who in love and truth,
> Where no misgiving is, rely
> Upon the genial sense of youth;
> Glad hearts! without reproach or blot,
> Who do thy work and know it not.

Happy they and their counterparts in the intellectual kingdom, who sit down to write and lend themselves to the first thought and are carried whithersoever it takes them, and solve the problem proposed in a way they could not have predicted, and are not now conscious of their own action. Merely they held the pen. The problem, whilst they pondered it, confounded them.

The birds fly from us, and we do not understand their music. The squirrel, the musquash, the insect have no significance to our blind eyes; such is now the discord betwixt man and nature. Yet it is strange that all our life is accompanied by Dreams on one side, and by the Animals on the other, as monuments of our ignorance, or Hints to set us on the right road of inquiry.

The life of a contemplator is that of a reporter. He has three or four books before him and now writes in this, now in that other, what is incontinuously said by one or the other of his classes of thought.

It is a good trait of the manners of the times that Thaddeus Blood told me this morning that he (then twenty years old) and Mr. Ball (fifty) were set out to guard Lieutenant Potter, the British Officer taken at Lexington, 19 April, '75; and, whilst staying at Reuben Brown's, Potter invited them both to dine with him. He, Lieutenant Potter, asked a blessing, and after dinner asked Mr. Ball to dismiss the table, " which he did very well for an old farmer." Lieutenant Potter then poured out a glass of wine to each and they left the table. Presently came by a company from Groton, and Lieutenant Potter was alarmed for his own safety. They bolted the doors, etc., etc.

Bateman, he thinks, could not have made the deposition in Dr. R's History. A ball passed through his cap and he cried, "A miss is as good as a mile." Immediately another ball struck his ear and passed out at the side of his mouth, knocking out two teeth. He lived about three weeks, and his wounds stunk intolerably. It was probably Carr's or Starr's deposition.[1]

The powers of the poetical genius seem quite local, and to give no felicity in any other work transcending the strait limits of that vein. Wordsworth writes the verses of a great, original bard, but he writes ill, weakly, concerning his poetry, talks ill of it, and even writes other poetry that is very poor.

True love watched every word and gesture of her shepherd and believed in her heart that things he did and thought not of were beautiful. Faint love talked of her affection, but cared

1 The depositions of many participants in the action of the 19th of April were taken by order of the Provincial Congress shortly afterwards, and published also by their order in a pamphlet entitled *Narrative of the Excursion and Ravages of the King's Troops under the Command of General Gage, on the Nineteenth of April, 1775, together with the Depositions taken by Congress to Support the Truth of it*. Dr. Ripley, however, irritated by a pamphlet published in Lexington in 1825, wrote, in 1827, *A History of the Fight at Concord*, etc., containing the depositions.

only for those words and deeds of the swain that respected herself. What else, though it were more wise and good, she noted never.

If you read much at a time, you have a better sight of the plan and connexion of the book, but you have less lively attention. If you read little, fine things catch your eye and you read accurately, but all proportion and ulterior purpose are at an end.

Charles doubts whether all truth is not occasional; not designed to be stored for contemplation, but alive only in action.

Make much of your own place. The stars and celestial awning that overhang our simple Concord walks and discourses are as brave as those that were visible to Coleridge as he talked, or Dryden, or Ben Jonson and Shakspear, or Chaucer and Petrarch and Boccaccio when they met.

For the history of Psalm - singing in our churches, see Warton, *History of English Poetry*, volume iii, p. 447.

Hurra when next it rains (in the private sky) for Miss Fanny Kemble's Journal, and Lyell's Geology !

The human mind seems a lens formed to concentrate the rays of the Divine laws to a focus, which shall be the personality of God. But that focus falls so far into the infinite that the form or person of God is not within the ken of the mind. Yet must that ever be the effort of a good mind, because the avowal of our sincere doubts leaves us in a less favorable mood for action, and the statement of our best thoughts, or those of our convictions that make most for theism, induces new courage and force.

August 6.

I think I may undertake, one of these days, to write a chapter on Literary Ethics, or the Duty and Discipline of a Scholar. The camel and his four stomachs shall be one of his emblems.

In Dunbar of Saltoun's *Golden Targe* (Warton, *History of English Poetry*, volume iii, p. 102) one of the *dramatis personæ* is New-Acquaintance, who " embraces him a while, but soon takes her leave and is never seen afterwards."

I suppose a reason why one man apprehends physical science better than another is that his fancy is stronger, so that he can comply with the prescribed conditions of the problem long enough for the full apprehension of the law; as in learning the Precession of the Equinoxes he can keep the picture of the sun where he ought in his mind, and figure to himself the nutation of the axis of the earth, etc., etc. But I, alas, write my diagrams in water.

In 1542 Robert Wyer printed the *Scole Howse*, in which the writer is thus merciless to women. His name is unknown. I fear it was a private revenge.

> Trewely some men there be
> That live alway in great horroure,
> And say it goeth by destinye
> To hang or wed, both hath one hour;
> And whether it be, I am well sure
> Hanging is better of the twayne,
> Sooner done and shorter payne.
>
> WARTON, *History of English Poetry*,
> volume iii, p. 426.

August 8.

Yesterday I delighted myself with Michel de Montaigne. With all my heart I embrace the grand old sloven. He pricks and stings the sense of virtue in me — the wild Gentile stock,

I mean, for he has no Grace. But his panegyric of Cato, and of Socrates in his essay of Cruelty (volume ii) do wind up again for us the spent springs and make virtue possible without the discipline of Christianity, or rather do shame her of her eye-service and put her upon her honor. I read the Essays in Defence of Seneca and Plutarch; on Books; on Drunkenness; and on Cruelty. And at some fortunate line which I cannot now recal, the spirit of some Plutarch hero or sage touched mine with such thrill as the war-trump makes in Talbot's ear and blood.

I know no truer poetry in modern verse than Scott's line,

"And sun himself in Ellen's eyes."

Every fact studied by the Understanding is not only solitary but desart. But if the iron lids of Reason's eye can be once raised, the fact is classified immediately and seen to be related to our nursery reading and our profoundest science.

August 13.

Add to what was said August 6 concerning Literary Ethics, that no doubt another age will have such sermons duly preached, and immortality will be proved from the implication of the

intellect. For who can read an analysis of the
faculties by any acute psychologist like Coleridge, without becoming aware that this is proper study for him and that he must live ages to
learn anything of so secular a science?

August 14.

We would call up him who left half told
The story of Cambuscan bold,

but the great contemporary just now laid in the
dust no man remembers; no man asks for him
who broke off in the first sentences the Analysis
of the Imagination, on the warning of a friend
that the public would not read the chapter. No
man asks, Where is the Chapter?[1]

August 15.

I bought my house and two acres six rods of
land of John T. Coolidge for 3,500 dollars.

[Mr. J. T. Coolidge of Boston had the house
built for his son, about 1825. It faced on the Cambridge Turnpike just where it leaves the "Great
Road" where the stages passed to and from
Boston. The main house was of an L shape, but
Mr. Emerson soon had the square completed
by a parlor behind his study, with a chamber

1 Coleridge died in July, 1834.

THE EMERSON HOME

above. The prolongation towards the flower-garden and brook beyond was part of the original house and contained kitchen, servants' chambers, and wood-shed. Although on low land in a river-town, these disadvantages were met by the sandy soil and the mile-long southward slope of the opposite tableland, which gave the region a different climate in cold weather from the rest of Concord Plain, shutting off the north, and storing sun-heat by day to neutralize the night damp. The excellent cellar was always dry and light.

Both Mr. and Mrs. Emerson had had threatenings in their lungs before they came there, but both lived well beyond threescore and ten. The trees did not overshadow the house, and the southeast yard and orchard, and garden on the south, were sunny and sheltered.

The fire in 1872 only burned off the roof of the main house and part of the top of the walls, though smoke and water did great damage below.

The general appearance of the house when Mr. Emerson brought his wife thither was about as shown in the illustration (made about 1852), except that some trees were smaller and others not yet planted. The study faced north and west, and its windows only show in perspective towards the right in the picture.

In a letter telling his brothers of the purchase, Mr. Emerson said of the house, "It is in a mean place and cannot be fine until trees and flowers give it a character of its own. But we shall crowd so many books and papers and, if possible, wise friends into it, that it shall have as much wit as it can carry."]

August 25.

Visited Miss Harriet Martineau at Cambridge to-day;[1] a pleasant, unpretending lady whom it would be agreeable to talk with when [not?] tired and at ease; but she is too weary of society to shine, if ever she does. She betrayed by her facile admiration of books and friends her speedy limits. The ear-trumpet acts as chain as well as medium, making Siameses of the two interlocutors. Henry Reeve, Henry Taylor of Manchester, John S. Mill, and W. J. Fox, she regarded as the ablest young men in England. What pleased me most of her communications was that W. J. Fox, though of no nerve, timid as a woman, yet had the greatest moral courage.

1 Miss Martineau visited Mr. and Mrs. Emerson later, and in her *Retrospect of American Travel* gives a pleasant account of the visit. Mr. Cabot quotes in his Memoir (vol. i, p. 296) her sketch of Mr. Emerson.

As Charles said at my commentary, "Go and be hanged, but blush if spoken to on the tumbril."

August 31.

Use of Harvard College to clear the head of much nonsense that gathers in the inferior colleges.

It shall be a rule in my Rhetoric, — Before you urge a duty, be sure it is one. Try Patriotism, for example.

Edward Taylor came to see us. Dr. Ripley showed him the battle-field. "Why put it on this bank?" he asked. "You must write on the monument, 'Here is the place where the Yankees made the British show the back seam of their stockings.'" He said he had been fishing at Groton and the fishes were as snappish as the people; that he looked to see if the scales were not turned the wrong side, etc.

September 14.

I was married to Lydia Jackson.[1]

1 The marriage took place at the Winslow House, a fine old colonial mansion framed in England, which still stands, though much altered, on North Street in Plymouth. Mrs. Emerson's father and mother had died some years before,

October 2.

The woods are all in a glow.

Charles thinks never was great man quite destitute of imagination.

"The fading virtues of later times were a cause of grief to his father, Archidamus, who again had listened to the same regrets from his own venerable sire," said Agis. PLUTARCH, "Apophthegms," *Lacon*, 17.

Where is the ballad of Tamlane, from which the fine editor of Warton borrows these lines?—

> "Our shape and size we can convert
>   To either large or small;
>   An old nutshell's the same to us
>   As is the lofty hall."

These lines, by the way, I would put into the mouth of the Orators, as parallel to Isocrates' account of eloquence.

October 5.

I like that poetry which, without aiming to be allegorical, is so. Which, sticking close to its subject, and that perhaps trivial, can yet be applied to the life of man and the government of God and be found to hold.

and this house was her home. Mr. Emerson and his bride drove in a chaise to Concord the next day.

"Little was king Laurin, but from many a precious
     gem
   His wondrous strength and power and his bold
     courage came.
   Tall at times his stature grew with spells of gramarye,
   Then to the noblest princes fellow might he be."

I take this to be a picture of a child of nature
who draws his wisdom from the whole world,
and is great only when he has great argument.
(Quoted by Edward Warton from *Little Garden
of Roses*.)

I see this moral in every novel, fable, my-
thology I read. I see it in all Plutarch and
Homer, in Æsop, in the Arabian Nights, in
Ravenswood; in Perceforest and Amadis. . . .

"Never much good comes of black bead
eyes." [AUNT MARY.]

Every man, if he lived long enough, would
make all his books for himself. He would write
his own Universal History, Natural History,
Book of Religion, of Economy, of Taste. For
in every man the facts under these topics are
only so far efficient as they are arranged after
the law of *his* being. But life forbids it, and
therefore he uses Bossuet, Buffon, Westminster

Catechism as better than nothing, at least as memoranda and badges to certify that he belongs to the universe, and not to his own house only, and contents himself with arranging some one department of life after his own way.

Our will never gave the images in our minds the rank they now take there. Anecdotes I read under the bench in the Latin School assume a grandeur in the natural perspective of memory which Roman history and Charles V, etc., have not.

October 10.

This morning Mr. May and Mr. George Thompson breakfasted with me. I bade them defend their cause as a thing too sacred to be polluted with any personal feelings. They should adhere religiously to the fact and the principle, and exclude every adverb that went to colour their mathematical statement. As Josiah Quincy said on the eve of Revolution, "The time for declamation is now over ; here is something too serious for aught but simplest words and acts." So should they say. I said also, what seems true, that if any man's opinion in the country was valuable to them, that opinion would be distinctly known. If Daniel Webster's or Dr. Channing's opinion is not frankly told, it is so much deduction from the moral value of that opinion, and I should say, moreover, that their opinion *is* known by the very concealment. One opinion seeks darkness. We know what opinion that is.[1]

The oak is magnificent from the acorn up. The whortleberry no pruning or training can magnify. Who can believe in the perfectibility of this race of man, or in the potency of Education? Yet compare the English nation with the Esquimaux tribe and who can underestimate the advantages of culture?

Charles thinks there is no Christianity, and has not been for some ages, and esteems Christianity the most wonderful thing in the history of the world. But for that, he can arrange his theory well enough of the history of man. It is, according to him, the first exalting of the bestial nature, the first allaying of clay with the divine fire, which succeeds in a few cases, but in far the greater part the spirit is overlaid and expired. A few, however, under the benevolent aspect of heaven, so coöperate with God as to work off the slough of the beast, and give evidence of arriving

1 Eleven days later, William Lloyd Garrison was mobbed and imprisoned in Boston for his utterances against slavery.

within the precincts of heaven. But the introduction of Christianity seems to be departure from general laws, and interposition. Jesus seems not to be man.

Strange, thinks he, moreover, that so sensible a nation as the English should be content so long to maintain that old withered idolatry of their church; with the history too of its whole manufacture, piece by piece, all written out.

Thompson the abolitionist is inconvertible: what you say, or what might be said, would make no impress on him. He belongs, I fear, to that great class of the Vanity-stricken. An inordinate thirst for notice cannot be gratified until it has found in its gropings what is called a cause that men will bow to; tying himself fast to that, the small man is then at liberty to consider all objections made to him as proofs of folly and the devil in the objector, and, under that screen, if he gets a rotten egg or two, yet his name sounds through the world and he is praised and praised.[1]

The minister should be to us a simple, absolute man; any trick of his face that reminds us

1 Thompson was stoned in some towns.

of his family is so much deduction, unless it should chance that those related lineaments are associated in our mind with genius and virtue. But the minister in these days, — how little he says! Who is the most decorous man? and no longer, who speaks the most truth? Look at the orations of Demosthenes and Burke, and how many irrelevant things, sentences, words, letters, are there? Not one. Go into one of our cool churches, and begin to count the words that might be spared, and in most places the entire sermon will go. One sentence kept another in countenance, but not one by its own weight could have justified the saying of it. 'T is the age of Parenthesis. You might put all we say in brackets and it would not be missed.

Even —— has come to speak in stereotyped phrase and scarcely originates one expression to a speech. I hope the time will come when phrases will be gazetted as no longer current and it will be unpardonable to say, " the times that tried men's souls," or anything about " a cause," and so forth. Now literature is nothing but a sum in the arithmetical rule, permutation and combination.

A man to thrive in literature must trust himself. The voice of society sometimes, and the

writings of great geniuses always, are so noble
and prolific, that it seems justifiable to follow
and imitate. But it is better to be an independent shoemaker than to be an actor and play a
king.[1] . . .

See the noble self-reliance of Ben Jonson.
Shun manufacture, or the introducing an artificial arrangement in your thoughts — it will
surely crack and come to nothing, — but let
alone tinkering, and wait for the natural arrangement of your treasures; that shall be
chemical affinity, and is a new and permanent
substance added to the world, to be recognized as genuine by every knowing person at
sight. . . .

A meek self-reliance I believe to be the law
and constitution of good *writing*. A man is to
treat the world like children who must hear and
obey the spirit in which he speaks, but which
is not his. If he thinks he is to sing to the tune
of the times, is to be the decorous sayer of
smooth things to lull the ear of society, and to
speak of religion as the great traditional *thing*
to be either mutely avoided or kept at a distance by civil bows, he may make a very good

---

1 Here follows the passage on rejected thoughts, "Self-
Reliance," *Essays I*, p. 45, Centenary Edition.

workman for the booksellers, but he must lay aside all hope to wield or so much as to touch the bright thunderbolts of truth which it is given to the true scholar to launch, and whose light flashes through ages without diminution. He must believe that the world proceeds in order from principles. He must not guess, but observe, without intermission, without end; and these puissant elements he shall not pry into who comes in fun, or in haste, or for show. The solemn powers of faith, of love, of fear, of custom, of conscience, are no toys to be shoved aside, but the forces which make and change society. They must be seen and known. You might as well trifle with time. They keep on their eternal way, grinding all resistance to dust. If you will, you may read nothing but song-books and fairy tales, all the year round, but if you would know the literature of any culti-vated nation, you must meet the majestic ideas of God, of Justice, of Freedom, of Necessity, of War, and of Intellectual Beauty, as the sub-ject and spirit of volumes and eras.

What's a book? Everything or nothing. The eye that sees it is all. What is the heaven's majestical roof fretted with golden fire to one man, but a foul and pestilent congregation of vapors? Well, a book is to a Paddy a fair page smutted over with black marks; to a boy, a goodly collection of words he can read; to a half-wise man, it is a lesson which he wholly accepts or wholly rejects; but a sage shall see in it secrets yet unrevealed; shall weigh, as he reads, the author's mind; shall see the predominance of ideas which the writer could not extricate himself from, and oversee. The Belfast Town and County Almanack may be read by a sage; and, wasteful as it would be in me to read Anti-Masonic or Jackson papers, yet whoso pierces through them to the deep Idea they embody, may well read them.

October 13.

Do you see what we preserve of history? a few anecdotes of a moral quality of some momentary act or word, — the word of Canute on the seashore, the speech of the Druid to Edwin, the anecdote of Alfred's learning to read for Judith's gift, the box on the ear by the herdman's wife, the tub of Diogenes, the gold of Crœsus, and Solon, and Cyrus, the emerald of Polycrates; these things, reckoned insignificant at the age of their occurrence, have floated, whilst laws and expeditions and books and kingdoms have sunk and are forgotten. So potent is this simple element of humanity or moral common sense.

My will never gave the images in my mind the rank they now take there. The four college years and the three years' course of Divinity have not yielded me so many grand facts as some idle books under the bench at the Latin School.[1] We form no guess, at the time of receiving a thought, of its comparative value.

Man idealizes every portrait. So are the sentiments of every age unconsciously corrected and pure models upheld in the worst times. The canonizing of a good bishop or monk was a useful preaching to several ages. They who did it would naturally sink the faults and swell the virtues of their friend, and so give to virtuous youth an objective good.

On Party. — The *aliases* of the father of William the Conqueror, who was called Robert the Magnificent, or Robert the Devil, are a good specimen of every man's Janus reputation.

Genius can never supply the want of knowledge, though even its errors may be valuable.

1 This sentence occurs in " Spiritual Laws," *Essays I.*

Madame de Staël tells me, in this fine book of the Influence of Literature, that the English do not admit much imagination into their prose, because, such is the facility of the structure of their blank verse, that every one reserves for poetry all such thoughts. What shall the English, of whom only four or five have ever succeeded in blank verse, say to this? Shakspear, Milton, Young, Thomson, Cowper, Wordsworth.

October 15.

It does seem, in reading the history or the writings of the English in the XI, XII, XIII, XIV centuries, that their eyes were holden that they could not see. They submit to received views of religion and politics that a child would deride nowadays, and exhibit, at the same time, strong common sense in other things. What stuff there is even in Bacon! What a baby-house he builds of diet and domestic rules, — and Montaigne even. The right of civil liberty, how slowly it opens on the mind! Surely they say well who say that God screens men from premature ideas.

A great bump of nonsense in Bacon and in Brown.[1]

1 Probably Sir Thomas Browne is meant.

[Mr. Emerson was preparing the course of ten lectures on " English Literature," which he gave in November and December at the Masonic Temple in Boston, before the Society for the Diffusion of Useful Knowledge. See Cabot's Memoir, vol. ii, Appendix F.]

When we enter upon the domain of LAW, we do indeed come out into light. To him who, by God's grace, has seen that by being a mere tunnel or pipe through which the divine Will flows, he becomes great, and becomes a Man, — the future wears an eternal smile, and the flight of time is no longer dreadful. I assure myself always of needed help, and go to the grave undaunted because I go not to the grave. I am willing also to be as passive to the great forces I acknowledge as is the thermometer or the clock, and quite part with all will as superfluous.

Do not expect to find the books of a country written, as an encyclopædia by a society of *savants*, on system, to supply certain wants and fill up a circle of subjects. In French literature perhaps is something of this order of a garden, where plat corresponds to plat and shrub with shrub. But in the world of living genius all at first seems disorder, and incapable of methodical arrangement. Yet is there a higher harmony whereby 't is set, as in Nature the sea balances the land, the mountain the valley and woods and meadows ; and as the eye possesses the faculty of rounding and integrating the most disagreeable parts into a pleasing whole.

I listened yesterday, as always, to Dr. Ripley's prayer in the mourning house with tenfold the hope, a tenfold chance, of some touch of nature that should melt us, that I should have felt in the rising of one of the Boston preachers of proprieties — the fair house of Seem. These old semi-savages do, from the solitude in which they live and their remoteness from artificial society and their inevitable daily comparing man with beast, village with wilderness, — their inevitable acquaintance with the outward nature of man, and with his strict dependence on sun and rain and wind and frost, — wood, worm, cow and bird, get an education to the Homeric simplicity which all the libraries of the Reviews, and the Commentators in Boston do not countervail.

What a Tantalus cup this life is ! The beauty that shimmers on these yellow afternoons, who

ever could clutch it? Go forth to find it, and it is
gone; 't is only a mirage as you look from the
windows of diligence.

Charles says to read Carlyle in the *North
American Review* is like seeing your brother in
jail; and that Alexander Everett is the sheriff
that put him in.

Far off, no doubt, is the perfectibility; so far
off as to be ridiculous to all but a few. Yet wrote
I once that, God keeping a private door to each
soul, nothing transcends the bounds of reason-
able expectation from a man. Now what imperfect tadpoles we are! an arm or a leg, an eye or
an antenna, is unfolded, — all the rest is yet in
the chrysalis.

Who does not feel in him budding the powers
of a Persuasion that by and by will be irresistible? Already how unequally unfolded in two
men! Here is a man who can only say Yes and
No in very slight variety of forms. But to render a reason or to dissuade you by anything less
coarse than interest, he cannot and attempts not.
But Themistocles goes by and persuades you
that he whom you saw up was down, and he
whom you saw down was up.

The ancients probably saw the moral significance of nature in the objects, without afterthought or effort to separate the object and the expression. They felt no wrong in esteeming the mountain a purple picture whereon Oreads might appear as rightly as moss, and which was the image of stability, and whatever other meaning it yielded to the wandering eye, because they were prepared to look on it as children, and believed the gods built it and were not far off, and so every tree and flower and chip of stone had a religious lustre, and might mean anything. But when science had gained and given the impression of the permanence, even eternity, of nature, and of every substance, and when on the new views which this habit imparted to the learned, wit, wine, derision arose, the mountain became a pile of stones acted on by bare blind laws of chemistry, and the poetic sense of things was driven to the vulgar, and an effort was made to recal the sense by the educated, and so it was faintly uttered by the poet and heard with a smile.

The objective religion of the Middle and after Age is well exemplified in the spite which heightened Luther's piety. "We cannot vex the devil more," said Luther, "than when we teach, preach, sing and speak of Jesus and his humanity. Therefore I like it well when, with loud voices and fine, long and deliberately, we sing in the church, *Et homo factus est : et verbum caro factum est.* The devil cannot endure to hear these words, he flieth away," etc. — *Table Talk.*

October 20.

The hearing man is good. Unhappy is the speaking man. The alternations of speaking and hearing make our education.

October 21.

Last Saturday night came hither Mr. Alcott, and spent the Sabbath with me. A wise man, simple, superior to display, and drops the best things as quietly as the least. Every man, he said, is a Revelation, and ought to write his Record, but few with the pen. His book is his school, in which he writes all his thoughts. The spiritual world should meet men everywhere; and so the government should teach. Our life flows out into our amusements. Need of a drama here; how well to lash the American follies. Every man is a system, an institution. Autobiography the best book. He thinks

Jesus a pure Deist, and says all children are Deists.

Charles remarks upon the nimbleness and buoyancy which the conversation of a spiritualist awakens; the world begins to dislimn.

It is the comfort I have in taking up those new poems of Wordsworth, that I am sure here to find thoughts in harmony with the great frame of Nature, the placid aspect of the Universe. I may find dulness and flatness, but I shall not find meanness and error.

Whence these oaths that make so many words in English books? The sun, the moon, St. Paul, Jesus, and God, are called upon as witness that the speaker speaks truth. I suppose they refer to that conviction suggested by every object that something IS, and signify, *If anything is*, then I did so and so. Yet now they are all obsolete. Except for the court forms, I doubt if ever they would be used. They import something separate from the will of man. " By day and night," " By Jupiter," etc., " By St. Nicholas," etc., i. e., my will, which interferes to color and change all things, interferes not here. This *is*.

October 22.

What can be truer than the popular poetic doctrine of a conjunction of stars? How many things must combine to make a good word or event? Most truly said Mme. de Staël, that 't is tradition more than invention that helps the poet to a good fable.

What can be truer than the doctrine of inspiration? of fortunate hours? Things sail dim and great through my head. Veins of rich ore are in me, could I only get outlet and pipe to draw them out. How unattainable seem to me these wild pleasantries of Shakespeare, yet not less so seem to me passages in old letters of my own.

What platitudes I find in Wordsworth!

> " I, poet, bestow my verse
> On this and this and this."

Scarce has he dropped the smallest piece of an egg, when he fills the barnyard with his cackle.

In the hours of clear vision how slight a thing it is to die. It is so slight that one ought not turn a corner or accept the least disgrace (so much as skulking) to avoid it. The mob may prove as kind and easy a deliverer as a pin or a worm. The mob seems a thing insignificant. It has no character. It is the emblem of unreason; mere muscular and nervous motion, no thought, no spark of spiritual life in it. It is a bad joke to call it a fruit of the love of liberty. It is permitted, like earthquakes and freshets and locusts, and is to be met like a blind mechanical force.

What of these atrocious ancestors of Englishmen, the Briton, Saxon, Northman, Berserkir? Is it not needful to make a strong nation that there should be strong wild will? If a man degenerates in goodness he must be grafted again from the wild stock.

We all know how life is made up; . . . [trifles] eat up the hours. How then is any acquisition, how is any great deed or wise and beautiful work possible? Let it enhance the praise of Milton, Shakspear and Laplace. These oppress and spitefully tyrannize over me because I am an Idealist.

The mob ought to be treated only with contempt. Phocion, even Jesus, cannot otherwise regard it in so far as it is mob. It is mere beast

of them that compose it; their soul is absent
from it. It is to consider it too much, to respect
it too much, to speak of its terror in any other
way than mere animal and mechanical agents.
It has no will; oh no.

Sunday, *October* 25.

Every intellectual acquisition is mainly pros-
pective, and hence the scholar's assurance of
eternity quite aloof from his moral convictions.

Behind us, as we go, all things assume pleasing forms as clouds do far off. Even the corpse
that has lain in our chambers has added a solemn
ornament to the house.[1] In this my new house
no dead body was ever laid. It lacks so much
sympathy with nature.

Mr. Goodwin[2] preached a good sermon this
afternoon and said, "The Almighty never im-
planted in a human breast the right of doing
wrong." As he taught, it seemed pleasant, the
tie of principle that holds as brothers all men,
so that when a stranger comes to me from the
other side the globe, Otaheitan or Chinese, to

1 This sentence occurs in the opening passage of "Spiritual Laws," *Essays I.*

2 Rev. Hersey B. Goodwin, Dr. Ripley's young colleague.

buy or sell with me, he shall have that measure from me as shall fill his mind with pleasant conviction that he has dealt with a fellow man in the deepest and dearest sense.

A talk in the morning concerning eyes and their spiritual and incorruptible testimony. When a man speaks the truth in the spirit of truth, God aids him by giving him an eye as clear as his own heavens. . . . When you think of a friend's character you think of his eye rather than of form or mouth. Weston's story of the boy that was cross-eyed whenever he lied, but the axes of the eyes parallel when he spoke truth.

"In no man's path malignant stood."

Excellent hymn of Cowper concerning "truths which o'er the world rise but never set."

The preacher, thought I in church, must assume that man is the revelation, and that, if he will reflect, he shall find his heart overflowing with a divine light, and the bible shall be a mirror giving back to him the refulgence of his own mind. Let the preacher speak himself in the same faith that we all, his hearers, are urns of the godhead, and will surely know if any word

of our own language is uttered to us, and will
accept it, but that all of us which is divine must
remain forever impassible to anything else. He,
the preacher, let him then acquiesce in being nothing that he may move mountains: let him be
the mere tongue of us all; no individual, but
a universal man, let him leave his nation, his
party, his sect, his town-connexion, even his
vanity and self-love at home, and come hither
to say what were equally fit at Paris, at Canton,
and at Thebes.

There is no wall like an idea.

I used to remark Edward's Greek petulance
disclosed in answers like that of Pyrrhus when
invited to hear one mimic the nightingale: "But
I have heard the nightingale itself." M. M. E.
has made many such speeches. A good one of
this sort — the putting down reverend folly by
childish reason — is Hannibal's answer to Anti-
ochus saying, that "the entrails of the sacrifice
forbade the battle"; "You are for doing what
the flesh of a beast, not what the reason of a
wise man, adviseth." Socrates also.

Webster is in a galvanized state when he makes
the Hayne Speech, and 't is as easy to say gigantic

things, to introduce from God on the world "truths which rise but never set,"[1] as at another hour to talk nonsense. He is caught up in the spirit and made to utter things not his own.

October 28.

The Oriental man: Abraham and Heth, Job, etc. Man stands on the point betwixt the inward spirit and the outward matter. He sees that the one explains, translates, the other: that the world is the mirror of the soul. He is the priest and interpreter of nature thereby.

'Tis a good thing for man that I am obliged to pick my words of low trades with so much care. In England you may say, a sweep, a blacksmith, a scavenger, as synonym for a savage in civil life. But in this country I must look about me. I perhaps speak to persons who occasionally or regularly work at these works and yet do take, as they ought, their place as men in places of manly culture and entertainment.

Wacic the Caliph, who died A. D. 845, ended his life with these words: "O thou, whose kingdom never passes away, pity one whose dignity

1 Cowper's hymn.

is so transient!" TURNER, *Anglo-Saxons*, vol. i, p. 286.

[Here follow quotations from Turner, about Alfred, and from Asser.]

October 30.

It will not do for Sharon Turner, or any man not of Ideas, to make a System. Thus, Mr. Turner has got into his head the notion that the Mosaic history is a good natural history of the world, reconcilable with geology, etc. Very well. You see at once the length and breadth of what you may expect, and lose all appetite to read. But Coleridge sets out to idealize the actual, to make an *epopœa* out of English institutions, and it is replete with life.

November 6.

Burke's imagery is, much of it, got from books, and so is a secondary formation. Webster's is all primary. Let a man make the woods and fields his books; then at the hour of passion his thoughts will invest themselves spontaneously with natural imagery.

Plutarchiana this morn. Verses and words served as hampers and baskets to convey the oracle's answers from place to place. . . . Then was it that History alighted from versifying, as

it were from riding in chariots, and on foot distinguished truth from fable.

He speaks of the lovers of omens, etc., as
preferring rainbows and haloes to the sun and
moon.

Charles says the nap is worn off the world.

[During November Mr. Emerson accepted an
invitation to preach in the church at Lexington
East Village, and continued to do so, not ham-
pered in his manner of conducting the service,
for nearly three years.]

"To know that the sky is everywhere blue,
you need not travel around the world."

November 7.

Advantage of the Spiritual man in the fact of
the identity of human nature. Draw your robe
ever so chastely round you, the surgeon sees
every muscle, every hair, every bone, every
gland; he reads you by your counterpart. So I
read the history of all men in myself. Give me
one single man, and uncover for me his pleasures and pains, let me minutely and in the
timbers and ground-plan study his architecture,

and you may travel all round the world and visit
the Chinese, the Malay, the Esquimaux and the
Arab,— I travel faster than you. In my chim-
ney-corner I see more, and anticipate all your
wonders. Or do you ransack all the histories and
learn what has been done and thought, back in
time, in the XVII Century, in the middle age,
at the time of the consuls, or in the twilight of
history, and I, intent upon the principles of this
one man, will know what you shall say, and will
say that also which shall be made good ages
hence in some far-stretching revolution.

November 14.

Melancholy cleaves to the Saxon mind as
closely as to the tones of an Æolian harp.

When yesterday I read *Antigone*, at some
words a very different image of female loveli-
ness rose out of the clouds of the past and the
actual. That poem is just what Winckelmann
described the Greek beauty to be, — "the tongue
on the balance of expression." It is remarkable
for nothing so much as the extreme temperance,
the abstemiousness which never offends by the
superfluous word or degree too much of emotion. How slender the materials, how few the

incidents! how just the symmetry! Charles
thinks it as great a work of genius as any. Every
word writ in steel. But that other image which it
awakened for me brought with it the perception
how entirely each rational creature is dowried
with all the gifts of God. The universe—nothing less—is totally given to each new being.[1] . . .

But I thought thus yesterday in regard to the
charming beauty which a few years ago shed on
me its tender and immortal light. She needed
not a historical name, nor earthly rank or wealth.
She was complete in her own perfections. She
took up all things into her and in her single self
sufficed the soul.

The way in which Plutarch and the ancients
usually quote the Poets is quite remarkable, as
it indicates a deep and universal reverence for
poetry, indicates a faith in Inspiration. They
quote Pindar, much as a pious Christian does
David or Paul. Where is that reverence now?

Fine walk this afternoon in the woods with
Charles; beautiful Gothic arches, yes, and cathe-

1 Here follows the passage on the hero's being entitled to
a setting of natural beauty to his action, etc. (*Nature*,
"Beauty," pp. 20, 21, Centenary Edition.)

dral windows, as of stained glass, formed by the interlaced branches against the grey and gold of the western sky. We came to a little pond in the bosom of the hills, with echoing shores. Charles thought much of the domesticity and comfort there is in living with one set of men, to wit, your contemporaries; and thought it would be misery to shift them, and hence the sadness of growing old. Now, every newspaper has tidings of "kenned folk."

I projected the discomfort of our playing over again to-night the tragedy of Babes in the Wood. Charles rejoiced in the serenity of Saturday Night. It was calm as the universe. I told him what a fool he was not to write the record of his thoughts. He said it were an impiety. Yet he meant to when he was old. I told him, when Alcibiades turned author, we workies should be out of countenance. Yet I maintained that the *Lycidas* was a copy from the poet's mind printed out in the book, notwithstanding all the mechanical difficulties, as clear and wild as it had shone at first in the sky of his own thought. We came out again into the open world and saw the sunset, as of a divine artist, and I asked if it were only brute light and aqueous vapor and there was no intent in that celestial smile ? Another topic of the talk was, that Lyceums — so that people will let you say what *you* think — are as good a pulpit as any other. But C. thinks that it is only by an effort like a Berserkir a man can work himself up to any interest in any exertion. All active life seems an *amabilis insania*. And when he has done anything of importance he repents of it, repents of virtue as soon as he is alone. Nor can he see any reason why the world should not burn up to-night. The play has been over some time.[1]

Peace and War. "The wounds inflicted by iron are to be healed by iron, and not by words," said the elder Cancellieri, and ordered the hand of Lore to be cut off. MÜLLER, vol. iii.

Magnanimity of Literary men. Argyropulus and Theodore of Gaza. MÜLLER, vol. iii.

[Many quotations from Müller follow.]

In Elizabeth's time the high church was looked upon by intelligent men as "a horse which was still kept always saddled in readiness for the Pope." See Müller.

1 This attitude of mind was probably due to the fact that he was already in consumption, though it was not recognized.

Compensation. Charles V always dissembled and never was believed.

December 7.

Last week Mr. Alcott spent two days here. The wise man who talks with you seems of no particular size, but, like the sun and moon, quite vague and indeterminate. His characterizing of people was very good. Hedge united strangely the old and the new; he had imagination, but his intellect seemed ever to contend with an arid temperament. George Bradford was an impersonation of sincerity, simplicity, and humility without servility.

Carlyle's talent, I think, lies more in his beautiful criticism, in seizing the idea of the man or the time, than in original speculation. He seems to me most limited in this chapter or speculation in which they regard him as most original and profound — I mean in his Religion and immortality from the removal of Time and Space.

He seems merely to work with a foreign thought, not to live in it himself.

In Shakspear I actually shade my eyes as I read for the splendor of the thoughts.

December 12.

I wrote H. Ware, Jr., that his "4th topic, the circumstances which show a tendency toward war's abolition, seemed to me the nearest to mine; for I strongly feel the inhumanity or unmanlike character of war, and should gladly study the outward signs and exponents of that progress which has brought us to this feeling."

The Arts and Sciences are the only Cosmopolites.

AUTHORS OR BOOKS QUOTED OR REFERRED TO
IN JOURNAL FOR 1835

Asser and Alfred the Great, *apud* Sharon Turner's *History of the Anglo-Saxons.*

Richard Hooker; Dunbar of Saltoun, *Golden Targe, apud* Thomas Warton's *History of English Poetry; Robert Wyer, Scole Howse, apud* Warton, also *The Little Garden of Roses* and *Tamlane* in the same collection; Scottish Ballads; Jacob Behmen (or Boehme), *The Aurora or Morning Redness, . . .* i. e., *the Root or Mother of Philosophy, Astrology and Theology from The True Ground,* etc. (Translation, London, 1656).

Dryden; Robert Hooke; Thomas Shepherd,

New England's Lamentation; Edward Bagshaw; Joseph Spence, *Anecdotes*, &c. ; Cowper, *Olney Hymns*; Diderot; Voltaire ;

Jeremy Bentham ; Laplace ; Chatterton ; Sharon Turner, *History of the Anglo-Saxons*; Spurzheim ; Johannes von Müller, *Universal History*; Lyell, *Geology*;

Abner Kneeland ;

Frances Anne Kemble (Butler), *Journal of Residence in America*.

Amos Bronson Alcott, *Record of a School*.

END OF VOLUME III

The Riverside Press
CAMBRIDGE . MASSACHUSETTS
U . S . A